Research Papers For Dummies®

Cheat Sheet

When to Cite Sources

- Provide a citation for all direct quotations from printed, electronic, or human sources.
- Cite the source whenever you employ someone else's ideas, even if you express them in your own words.
- Cite the source when you use a train of logic or an organizational pattern created by someone else.
- Don't cite the source for information that is common knowledge.

What to Include in the Introduction

- Mention the subject and the topic you're discussing.
- If you're writing about a work of art or literature, provide the title and the name of the author or artist.
- If the paper has a thesis — an idea you're proving — state the thesis.
- You may also include the main supporting points or subtopics.

Note Taking Tips

- Keep a master list of all sources, including title, author, date, publishing information, and page numbers.
- Give each source a code number and label each note with the code and page number. If the source doesn't have page numbers, include any other location information.
- If you write the exact words you found in the source, enclose the words in quotation marks.
- If the source credits someone else, write that information in your notes.
- If you highlight information in a book or article, keep a "table of contents" listing the main idea of each highlight and the page on which it appears.

For Dummies: Bestselling Book Series for Beginners

Research Papers For Dummies®

Cheat Sheet

Useful Structures for Organizing Information

- Chronological order
- Comparison and contrast
- Pro-and-con arguments
- Cause and effect
- Groups affected by the event or issue

Grammar Checklist

- Be sure that the subject of the sentence agrees with the verb — singular subject with singular verb, plural subject with plural verb.
- Write about literature in present tense.
- Write about history in past tense. Use the *had* form of the verb to show an action occurring before another action.
- Don't change tenses unnecessarily.
- Be sure that every pronoun replaces one (and only one) noun. Be especially careful with *that, which,* and *this.* Never use these pronouns to refer to a loose collection of ideas.
- Be sure that the meaning of each pronoun is clear. Don't place a pronoun where it may refer to more than one noun.
- Place all descriptions near the word they describe.
- End every sentence with an endmark (period, question mark, exclamation point).

For Dummies: Bestselling Book Series for Beginners

 ™

References for the Rest of Us! ™

BESTSELLING BOOK SERIES

Do you find that traditional reference books are overloaded with technical details and advice you'll never use? Do you postpone important life decisions because you just don't want to deal with them? Then our *For Dummies*® business and general reference book series is for you.

For Dummies business and general reference books are written for those frustrated and hard-working souls who know they aren't dumb, but find that the myriad of personal and business issues and the accompanying horror stories make them feel helpless. *For Dummies* books use a lighthearted approach, a down-to-earth style, and even cartoons and humorous icons to dispel fears and build confidence. Lighthearted but not lightweight, these books are perfect survival guides to solve your everyday personal and business problems.

Already, millions of satisfied readers agree. They have made For Dummies the #1 introductory level computer book series and a best-selling business book series. They have written asking for more. So, if you're looking for the best and easiest way to learn about business and other general reference topics, look to For Dummies to give you a helping hand.

Wiley Publishing, Inc.

Research Papers

FOR

DUMMIES®

Research Papers FOR DUMMIES®

by Geraldine Woods

Hungry Minds™

Best-Selling Books • Digital Downloads • e-Books • Answer Networks • e-Newsletters • Branded Web Sites • e-Learning

New York, NY ◆ Cleveland, OH ◆ Indianapolis, IN

Research Papers For Dummies®

Published by:
Hungry Minds, Inc.
909 Third Avenue
New York, NY 10022
www.hungryminds.com
www.dummies.com

Library of Congress Control Number: 2002106035

ISBN: 0-7645-5426-3

Printed in the United States of America

10 9 8 7 6 5 4 3 2

1B/RY/QW/QS/IN

Distributed in the United States by Hungry Minds, Inc.

Distributed by CDG Books Canada Inc. for Canada; by Transworld Publishers Limited in the United Kingdom; by IDG Norge Books for Norway; by IDG Sweden Books for Sweden; by IDG Books Australia Publishing Corporation Pty. Ltd. for Australia and New Zealand; by TransQuest Publishers Pte Ltd. for Singapore, Malaysia, Thailand, Indonesia, and Hong Kong; by Gotop Information Inc. for Taiwan; by ICG Muse, Inc. for Japan; by Intersoft for South Africa; by Eyrolles for France; by International Thomson Publishing for Germany, Austria and Switzerland; by Distribuidora Cuspide for Argentina; by LR International for Brazil; by Galileo Libros for Chile; by Ediciones ZETA S.C.R. Ltda. for Peru; by WS Computer Publishing Corporation, Inc., for the Philippines; by Contemporanea de Ediciones for Venezuela; by Express Computer Distributors for the Caribbean and West Indies; by Micronesia Media Distributor, Inc. for Micronesia; by Chips Computadoras S.A. de C.V. for Mexico; by Editorial Norma de Panama S.A. for Panama; by American Bookshops for Finland.

For general information on Hungry Minds' products and services please contact our Customer Care department; within the U.S. at 800-762-2974, outside the U.S. at 317-572-3993 or fax 317-572-4002.

For sales inquiries and resellers information, including discounts, premium and bulk quantity sales and foreign language translations please contact our Customer Care department at 800-434-3422, fax 317-572-4002 or write to Hungry Minds, Inc., Attn: Customer Care department, 10475 Crosspoint Boulevard, Indianapolis, IN 46256.

For information on licensing foreign or domestic rights, please contact our Sub-Rights Customer Care department at 212-884-5000.

For information on using Hungry Minds' products and services in the classroom or for ordering examination copies, please contact our Educational Sales department at 800-434-2086 or fax 317-572-4005.

Please contact our Public Relations department at 212-884-5163 for press review copies or 212-884-5000 for author interviews and other publicity information or fax 212-884-5400.

For authorization to photocopy items for corporate, personal, or educational use, please contact Copyright Clearance Center, 222 Rosewood Drive, Danvers, MA 01923, or fax 978-750-4470.

About the Author

Geraldine Woods directs the independent study program at a high school for gifted students. Each year she guides 20 seniors as they select and define a topic, research the material, and write a major paper. She also teaches English and has written 40 books, give or take a few, including *English Grammar For Dummies*. She loves bookstores and libraries, minor-league baseball, Chinese food, and the novels of Jane Austen. The mother of a grown son (Tom, a lawyer), she lives in New York City with Harry (her husband of 30 years) and parakeets Alice and Archie.

Dedication

For my great city, which I love now more than ever; and for the students in the independent study seminar, past and present, whose passion for learning inspires me daily.

Author's Acknowledgments

I offer thanks to the faculty of Horace Mann School, whose love of teaching and passion for learning serve as a model of academic excellence. In particular, I am indebted to Caroline Bartels, Samuel Gellens, Christopher Jones, Janet Kraus, Rudy Reiblein, Deborah Stanford, Joseph Timko, Jeff Weitz, and Don Yates for their valuable suggestions. I also appreciate the careful scrutiny and encyclopedic knowledge of Tom LaFarge and Ginny Nordstrom, the technical editors. I am grateful to my project editor, Linda Brandon, who challenged me with good humor and tact and made this a better book, and to Roxane Cerda, who guided me through the outline and early stages of the project. I also thank my agents, Carolyn Krupp and Lisa Queen, for their support and encouragement.

Publisher's Acknowledgments

We're proud of this book; please send us your comments through our Hungry Minds Online Registration Form located at www.dummies.com.

Some of the people who helped bring this book to market include the following:

Acquisitions, Editorial, and Media Development

Project Editor: Linda Brandon

Acquisitions Editor: Roxane Cerda

Copy Editor: Mike Baker

Technical Editors: Thomas LaFarge, Virginia Nordstrom

Editorial Manager: Christine Beck

Editorial Assistant: Carol Strickland

Cover Photos: © Shoot/photolibrary/ PictureQuest

Production

Project Coordinator: Jennifer Bingham

Layout and Graphics: Stephanie D. Jumper, Jackie Nicholas, Brent Savage, Jacque Schneider, Mary J. Virgin, Erin Zeltner

Proofreaders: Laura Albert, Andy Hollandbeck, Susan Moritz, Carl Pierce, Charles Spencer

Indexer: TECHBOOKS Production Services

Special Help

Michelle Hacker

General and Administrative

Hungry Minds Consumer Reference Group

Business: Kathleen Nebenhaus, Vice President and Publisher; Kevin Thornton, Acquisitions Manager

Cooking/Gardening: Jennifer Feldman, Associate Vice President and Publisher; Anne Ficklen, Executive Editor; Kristi Hart, Managing Editor

Education/Reference: Diane Graves Steele, Vice President and Publisher

Lifestyles: Kathleen Nebenhaus, Vice President and Publisher; Tracy Boggier, Managing Editor

Pets: Kathleen Nebenhaus, Vice President and Publisher; Tracy Boggier, Managing Editor

Travel: Michael Spring, Vice President and Publisher; Brice Gosnell, Publishing Director; Suzanne Jannetta, Editorial Director

Hungry Minds Consumer Editorial Services: Kathleen Nebenhaus, Vice President and Publisher; Kristin A. Cocks, Editorial Director; Cindy Kitchel, Editorial Director

Hungry Minds Consumer Production: Debbie Stailey, Production Director

Contents at a Glance

Cartoons at a Glance

By Rich Tennant

"I know your paper is on infomercials, but I still wouldn't use transitions like, "But wait, that's not all..." and "Act now and I'll include extra information on my topic!" "

page 209

"RESEARCH PAPERS TO AVOID"

Scented Papers

Origami Papers

Frivolous Papers

Confusing Papers

page 7

"I'm searching for a source for my paper "Robin Hood, The Criminal That Stole My Girlfriend." Can you tell me where I can find a pamphlet from the People Against Merry Men organization?"

page 49

"Well, kid, if your paper's as good as your notes, you're getting an 'A' from this gang."

page 111

"Although you have a good thesis statement, it belongs on the first page of the paper — not on page 224."

page 157

"Maybe your keyword search, 'Astronomy, Stars, Signs, Will I be rich someday,' needs to be refined."

page 295

Cartoon Information:
Fax: 978-546-7747
E-Mail: richtennant@the5thwave.com
World Wide Web: www.the5thwave.com

Table of Contents

Introduction

• •

You're sitting at your desk in a classroom or in an airless cubicle, wondering how many minutes are left in the century it's taking the day to be over. Suddenly Ms. Sharkface, your teacher or supervisor, lowers the boom: She wants a research paper. She wants footnotes and a list of sources. She wants originality, accuracy, and good grammar. And — gasp — she wants ten pages! You may be 12 years old or 60 years old, but your reaction is the same — Help! Ms. Sharkface may as well have said, "I want you to run a marathon blindfolded and in sandals!"

Take heart. A research paper may seem daunting, but the project is not impossible. Turning research into writing is actually quite easy as long as you follow a few proven techniques. In this book I show you how to search for information using both traditional printed sources and the electronic treasure troves of the World Wide Web. I explain how to collect the valuable bits and dump the rest, how to make sense of the information you retrieve, and how to write an outline. I give you a step-by-step guide to creating a *thesis statement,* the idea that you argue or prove in the paper, or a *hypothesis,* the "educated guess" that your lab work tests. I show you the easiest writing methods and demystify all the picky stuff, like citations and format.

Much of this book concerns papers written with the help of material that other people have gathered or created — your *sources.* However, those of you who are writing science research papers based on your own lab work will also find useful information in *Research Papers For Dummies.* I don't tell you how to light a Bunsen burner or culture slimy green things, but I do show you how to find studies that relate to your current research, how to incorporate those studies into your paper, and how to cite them. I also explain the conventions of scientific writing. Likewise, I don't ignore those of you who have left your schoolbooks behind and entered the business world. *Research Papers For Dummies* has explanations of business writing style, report format, business-oriented research, and so forth.

How to Use This Book

If you're writing a research paper, chances are you already have a lot of demands on your time. You don't need another huge pile of paper to read. But this book can actually save you time in the long run because it gives you the easiest, fastest, most successful methods for completing your paper.

The best use of this book is to read the sections you need *when you actually need them*, not all at once. You can't learn to ride a bicycle in the abstract; you have to put the rubber on the road. Likewise, you won't remember the information in *Research Papers For Dummies* unless you put it to use. Let this book be a practical part of the paper-writing process, not a theoretical consideration of the task.

Finally, keep a sharp eye out for these three types of examples scattered throughout the text:

- **Source material:** To show you how to take notes and how to deal with sources efficiently (and legally), I provide several excerpts from books and articles that never existed except in my imagination. The source examples are labeled as figures.

- **Sample citations:** When you write a research paper, you have to ensure that the reader knows where you found all the information. The rules for documenting sources are annoyingly complex. To make matters worse, several sets of rules exist, each thicker than the phone book of a medium-sized urban area. I explain these rules, and I also throw in some examples from each set, so that you can see how the finished documentation is supposed to look.

- **Sample sections from research papers:** You can think about writing for hours, but until you actually see a passage — with an explanation of what's correct and what isn't — the theory of good writing remains, well, a theory. Sample sections of research papers, not from real students or employees but from me, show you what to aim for and what to avoid in your writing. I let my imagination roam when I wrote these examples, so be prepared for some really loopy topics, and don't trust any of the information. I made up all the "facts," but the techniques of writing are totally sound.

What You're Not to Read

"Subject-Area Example" icons are scattered throughout the book. These icons indicate that the material is pegged to a particular discipline — literature and language, math and science, history and social science, and the like. Ignore the subject-area examples that are irrelevant to your paper because the format and conventions for one field may differ from those of another. Concentrate on the subject area that your research paper covers. Business-oriented readers should ignore all the subject-area examples and head directly for the material marked with the "Business Alert" icon. Anything not labeled "Subject-Area Example" or "Business Alert" is for everyone.

Foolish Assumptions

In this book, I make a number of assumptions about you, the reader. The wise decision to buy this book tells me (modesty being my best quality) that you're pretty smart. I'm assuming that you purchased *Research Papers For Dummies* because you approach your work seriously. I also assume that you see writing a research paper as a tough job and you want it to go more smoothly. If you're in school, you probably get decent grades. If you're in the working world, you handle your job well. In either case, I assume that you want to do even better.

I am *not* assuming that every reader has a personal computer and Internet connection at home, although I wouldn't be surprised if most do. I am assuming that most readers have an on-ramp to the information superhighway somewhere — at school, at the public library, or at work. Anyone who can't access the Internet will still find plenty of help in *Research Papers For Dummies* because I show you how to research from traditional, nonelectronic sources.

How This Book Is Organized

Research Papers For Dummies is loosely patterned after the process you can use to write your paper. Part I provides an overview of the task, explaining the characteristics of each type of research paper, so you know what you're trying to write. Part II tackles the research process, describing how to find everything about anything. Part III covers note taking, so you know what to do with all that information. Getting ready to write is the subject of Part IV, while Part V describes the best way to create and revise a final draft. The legendary "Part of Tens" of the *For Dummies* series is in Part VI — that's where I tell you the best places to start a search for the process of writing a research paper. The appendix provides a list of proven ideas for the topically challenged reader. Now for more detail.

Part 1: Figuring Out What You Are Writing and How to Write It

What's the assignment, anyway? A term paper, a library paper, or a marketing report? A science research paper? A business plan? Maybe a dissertation? Chapter 1 explains the defining characteristics of each type of research paper, so you know what form your project should take. This chapter also describes the basic ingredients of every paper and outlines the process to follow as you create your masterpiece. (I like to think positive.) Chapter 2 gets you off on the right foot (no offense intended to the lefties out there) by explaining how to keep track of your work. This chapter also shows you how to budget your time and how to adapt to the demands of the particular Authority Figure — the teacher, professor, supervisor, parole officer, extraterrestrial life form, or boss you report to. Chapter 3 reveals how to move from a vague subject to a topic to a thesis. For the lab-coat crowd, Chapter 3 also explains how to state a hypothesis.

Part II: Finding Everything about Anything: Research

In this part, I explain how to find the information you need for your research paper. Chapter 4 takes you on a swift tour of all the research bases, from traditional to electronic to audio-visual. Chapter 4 defines all those terms that Authority Figures love to throw around, such as *primary* and *secondary sources.* This chapter also explains how to evaluate sources. Chapter 5 takes you surfing on the Internet, and Chapter 6 helps you locate and research from more-traditional sources. In Chapter 7 you find out how to get information from actual, breathing human beings, with tips on arranging interviews and getting help from organizations and interest groups.

Part III: Collecting Pearls of Wisdom: How to Take Notes

If you love shoeboxes full of index cards, this part is for you. If you hate shoeboxes full of index cards, this part is for you, too! In Chapters 8 and 9, I describe the easiest, most efficient way to plow through piles of information and the best method of keeping track of what you learn in the process. Tips for the computer-phobic, as well as for the computer-addicted, are also in these chapters. Chapter 10 explains how to avoid *plagiarism* — the crime against intellectual honesty that can get you booted out of school or fired from your job.

Part IV: More Than Sharpening Pencils: Preparing to Write

You've got a binder, a shoebox, a carton, or a tractor-trailer full of facts. Now what do you do? This part takes you through some prewriting steps that make the whole project a breeze. Chapter 11 shows you how to write a thesis statement, the cornerstone of your paper. Chapter 12 helps you choose a structure for the paper that suits your thesis statement. Chapters 13 and 14 reveal how to organize your material and create an outline — the recipe for your paper.

Part V: Turn on the Computer, Fill the Fountain Pen: It's Time to Write

In this part, the big moment arrives, and you actually write the paper. Chapter 15 introduces introductions, showing you where to place your thesis statement and explaining how to avoid sending your reader into a yawning fit. Chapter 16 tackles the body, and Chapter 17 provides the lowdown on conclusions. In Chapter 18, you find out how to cite sources and create a bibliography. I also guide you through the wonderful world of punctuation. Chapter 19 brings you to the finish line, discussing those last, little steps — margins, title pages, and the like — that put your paper over the top. Chapter 20 is a first-aid kit for ailing research papers, just in case you encounter any last-minute difficulties.

Part VI: The Part of Tens

Here I take you to the 20 best places (ten virtual, ten not) to begin your research.

Appendix

If you're having trouble with one of the fundamentals of research-paper writing — choosing a topic — check out the appendix, which provides a list of possible paper topics, plus the "big questions" of each field. The big questions, such as What are the immediate and background causes of a historical event? and Compare early and late works by the same author, are frameworks for zillions of papers. Choose one of the big questions and plug in the ideas most interesting to you, or use one of the topics I supply for each category.

Bonus Web Chapter

For your added reading pleasure, there is a bonus chapter located on the Web. This extra chapter offers great information for writing papers on a variety of different subject areas. "Subject Area Do's and Don'ts" can be found at www.dummies.com/extras.

Icons Used in This Book

Icons are the signposts that flag your attention to certain areas of distinction. Five different ones are used in this book. Here's what each represents:

This icon alerts you to helpful hints, the sort of thing that insiders know and outsiders would love to find out. When you see this icon, just imagine that a seasoned commuter is taking you on a shortcut around five miles of bumper-to-bumper traffic.

This icon alerts you to the potholes on the path to research-paper perfection. When you see this icon, imagine a red flag indicating danger ahead.

This icon marks strategies for the easiest and best way to accomplish a task. Think of it as a playbook for a championship team. (Go Yankees!)

This icon is a signal that the accompanying information targets only one of the following areas: Arts; History and Social Science; Literature and Language; or Science, Mathematics, and Technology.

When you see this icon, you know the information is for those of us who are glued to our desks for far too many hours every day. This icon alerts you to sources for business information, tips on writing in a professional setting, and other stuff that they teach in really expensive business schools.

Where to Go from Here

Before you go any further, take stock of the situation. Look at the assignment. What is the teacher (or boss or coach or drill sergeant) asking for? When is it due? Now look at yourself. What are your strengths and weaknesses? I'm not talking about how you look in a pair of stretch pants or your ability to carry a tune. I'm talking about the way you handle writing tasks and the way you go about gathering information. Figure out, honestly now, which aspect of the process is hardest for you.

Now look at your life. How much time are you willing or able to devote to this project? Be realistic and specific here. "Twenty-six hours a day" is not an acceptable answer. Neither is "Whatever will get me an A" or "Whatever will get me a promotion."

All done? Okay, you're *ready* to turn to Part I for a bird's-eye view of the whole project. Then get out your calendar and make a plan. Chart the steps you need to take, and choose the chapters in this book that help you with each phase of the work. Now you're *set* to write the best-ever research paper. *Go!*

Part I
Figuring Out What You Are Writing and How to Write It

The 5th Wave   By Rich Tennant

In this part . . .

*I*f you've ever made 15 consecutive wrong turns while driving in an unfamiliar city, you've probably wished that you could soar into the air for a glimpse of the route to your destination. (Nice to leave the traffic behind, too.) I can't do much about your car troubles, but in this part, I do give you a bird's-eye view of the process of writing a research paper. Chapter 1 explains what you're writing and why. Chapter 2 outlines the best approaches to a long-term project and explains how to budget your time. In Chapter 2, I also give you some tips on pleasing that all-important Authority Figure, the one who will read and judge your work. Chapter 3 tackles the subject of your paper and shows you how to decide exactly what you're writing about.

Chapter 1

Running a Marathon in Sandals, or Writing a Research Paper

*O*kay, you have a research paper to write and you think your Authority Figure (the one who will ultimately read the research paper that you write) is an Attila-the-Hun-wannabe, intent on ruining your life. Well, I'm here to tell you that the Authority Figure isn't trying to torture you. Forcing you to run a marathon in sandals would be more efficient and cause less pain for your teacher or boss, if cruelty were the intent. Instead, the person assigning the paper may actually want you to learn something. Or, he or she may truly need the information that you dig up. In this chapter, I tell you what you're supposed to gain from the process of writing a research paper. I define the various types of research papers, so you know exactly what you're supposed to be creating. Finally, I give you an overview of the steps involved in all research projects.

Writing Research Papers Is for Your Own Good, Honest

Don't you hate it when Authority Figures tell you that whatever horrible experience they're imposing on you is "for your own good"? That phrase is a pretty good coverup for sadism, but occasionally — as in the case of research papers — it's true.

During some lucky periods in history, people with a small number of learning experiences were able to call themselves educated. A few bookshelves' worth of reading, some music or needlework, a language or two, and bingo — you're set for life. But if you go to a library or a newsstand today, or spend a moment browsing the Web, what do you see? Piles and piles of information! Getting bigger every day! Today, an educated person is not someone who knows a particular set of facts or ideas. Today's educated person is someone who has mastered *the process of learning,* one who knows *how to learn.* You don't have to be a mathematician to see that the next logical step is this equation:

Knowing how to learn = knowing how to research

No matter how much you read, and no matter how smart you are, in the twenty-first century you'll never be able to say, "That's it. I've got all the facts I'll ever need." In the future, at school or work, you'll inevitably be measured not by what you already know but rather by your ability to find the information you need, when you need it. And unless your career plans include a few decades as a hermit, when you find something, you have to communicate it. Therefore, research papers are important to your future success:

Finding information + communicating it = research paper

To be more specific, the process of writing a research paper helps you do the following:

- Identify sources of information
- Evaluate the quality and reliability of the information sources
- Gather information efficiently
- Organize a large amount of information
- Understand the relationship between bits of information from diverse sources
- Analyze the information creatively, perhaps coming to original conclusions
- Communicate the information clearly
- Budget your time so that you complete a long-term assignment before the next ice age

All these skills are career builders, no matter what your immediate purpose for writing a research paper. Whether you want to make it through eighth grade or pick up one more promotion before retirement, this book helps you achieve those goals by taking you through each step in the researching and writing process. And unlike some of the paper-assigners out there, it doesn't torture you. (Yes, I have to admit that a few — a *very* few — sadists do assign papers just to watch you sweat.) This book makes the task of writing a research paper bearable, and maybe even enjoyable. (I can hear you groaning. "Enjoyable" is a long shot, I know, but not impossible.)

Cooking Up a Research Paper: The Basic Ingredients

Writing a research paper? Think sandwich. The filling may be peanut butter or pickled herring, or peanut butter *and* pickled herring (pause to shudder). But no matter what you stuff into a sandwich, the basic design is the same: two slices of some sort of bread, with something else in between. Research papers are like sandwiches:

> **Bread Slice #1:** Introduction
>
> **Filling:** Body
>
> **Bread Slice #2:** Conclusion

The following sections provide a little more detail on the basic ingredients of a research paper.

The introduction

A research paper usually has a *thesis* — an idea you are trying to prove. The introduction states the thesis in a *thesis statement* and outlines the supporting points that you will make to prove the thesis. (See Chapter 11 for how to create a thesis statement.) A science research paper has a *hypothesis* — an idea you're testing. (Scientists never admit that they've proven anything. They won't go further than a statement explaining that their evidence supports a particular conclusion. This habit has something to do with the eternal quest for truth, but I'm not sure what.) Chapter 12 provides information on the hypothesis. If the research paper is simply a *survey,* a collection of ideas about a particular topic, it may not have a thesis statement. Instead, the introduction may contain a *topic sentence,* a statement of the main idea of the paper that alerts the reader to what the paper is about. (Check out Chapter 11 for more on topic sentences.) Regardless of whether the paper contains a thesis statement or a topic sentence, most introductions also include a quotation, an anecdote, or some fact interesting enough to draw the reader into the paper. (See Chapter 15 for the ins and outs of writing an introduction.) Scientific research papers and business reports dump the frills and get right to the point; their introductions are clear and concise and immediately orient the reader to the subject matter.

The body

The body of the paper presents the facts. Here, you organize the research into *subtopics* — logical groupings of information. *Subheads,* or titles for each part of the paper, may introduce the subtopics. With or without subheads, the reader must understand why each subtopic follows the one before it. You create a train of thought that carries your reader from the introduction through to the conclusion. Chapter 16 describes what the body should include.

The conclusion

The conclusion brings home the fact that you have proved your thesis, but it isn't simply a restatement of the introduction. The conclusion gives the reader a wider perspective, explaining the significance of what you've proved. The conclusion answers the *So what?* question (or, as we say in New York City, the *Yeah? So?* question). The conclusion of a science research paper is called a *discussion.* (See Chapter 12.) The discussion explains whether the results support the original hypothesis and considers the implications of the laboratory data. In a paper without a thesis, the conclusion opens the door to related ideas or areas that you haven't covered in the paper. In all papers, the conclusion is the next logical step in the chain of ideas that you've forged in the paper. Go to Chapter 17 for more on conclusions.

Footnotes, endnotes, and parenthetical citations

Sounds like a stuffy law firm, doesn't it? "I just graduated from Harvard Law and joined Footnotes, Endnotes, and Parentheticals!" Stuffy names aside, this part of the paper is crucial. All the information in research papers has to be documented in *citations,* identification tags that allow the reader to retrace your steps and find the information exactly where you found it. The identifying material is contained in (you guessed it) footnotes, endnotes, or parentheses in the text. The rules for documentation are strict (okay, obsessive). You can find more on these picky little guys in Chapter 18.

Title page and front matter

Research papers usually have a title page (see Chapter 19) at the beginning of the paper that states the (guess what) title, your name, and the date. Some research papers also have a table of contents and a table of illustrations. Chapter 19 explains how to create all these finishing touches.

Works cited or bibliography

The paper ends with a *bibliography* (list of books used) or a list of *works cited* — all the sources that you drew upon, including Web sites, articles, and so on. The format of this list follows rules that are just as strict as those for identification within the paper. Chapter 18 shows how to list your sources correctly.

Meeting the Family: Characteristics of Each Type of Research Paper

The research-paper family tree, like most family trees, is a tangle of branches. Each branch has a few qualities common to the whole group (see the previous section, "Cooking Up a Research Paper: The Basic Ingredients"), and each has some special characteristics setting it apart from the others. Like most families (certainly mine), the research-paper tree also has a couple of eccentrics that definitely march to a different drummer. In this section, I describe each type of paper and outline its characteristics and goals.

Report

A *report* — the baby of the family — is the shortest and simplest form of research paper. Young children write reports for homework on such compelling topics as "The Cantaloupe" and "Our Presidents' Middle Names." Overworked cubicle-occupiers get to write reports on stuff like "Sixteen Ways to Regulate Fax Paper Consumption."

Sometimes the word *report* is used for any kind of fact-based writing, as in "Give me a 433-page report on the earnings potential of that lawn furniture conglomerate by 9 a.m. tomorrow." When your personal Authority Figure asks for a report, be sure to ask questions about length, content, and format.

Content
The content of your report should have these characteristics:

- Factual information (such as statistics, dates, names, events, or quotations)
- Opinion that is clearly labeled and limited to the conclusion
- Minimum of two or three sources

Format

Here are some guidelines to format your report:

- ✔ Length from one page to much (much, *much*) longer
- ✔ Title page or heading
- ✔ Formal identification of sources — with footnotes, endnotes, or parenthetical information — or an informal reference to sources in the text of the paper
- ✔ Typed, but occasionally handwritten
- ✔ Generally written without *I* or *we*
- ✔ Serious, formal tone

The *book report,* a time-honored assignment in middle school and high school, describes one text and your reaction to it. Normally you have only one source for a book report — the book that you are reporting on. If you have to write a book report, you may be given a form to fill out. If you don't have a form, provide the following information:

- ✔ Title
- ✔ Author
- ✔ Publishing information — company, date of publication, place of publication
- ✔ Summary of the main points of the book (nonfiction) or plot (fiction)
- ✔ Short description of the important characters (fiction)
- ✔ Evaluation of the quality of the book

Laboratory report

In my high-school chemistry class, my teacher (whose first name was Bernard and whom we dubbed "Bunsen Bernie") created huge purple clouds almost every day, no matter which chemicals he threw into the mix. He called those exercises "experiments," even though we weren't trying to break new ground in science. In fact, all we were trying to do was breathe. At the end of each session, we retired to study hall to write a lab report, a fixture and non-joy of my 16th year.

Lab reports are still around. The research for a lab report is usually collected not from written sources but rather from data that you gather in (surprise!) a laboratory or in the field, if you are observing phenomena outside the lab.

Laboratory research may be reported in a science research paper, which is different from a laboratory report. I discuss science research papers a little later in this chapter.

Content

The content of a laboratory report includes the following:

- Statement of the problem — why the experiment is being performed
- Background — other studies or initial observations that helped form the hypothesis
- Hypothesis — a fancy name for an educated guess about the issue
- Materials and procedure
- Data
- Results — a short summary of the data
- Analysis — whether the data supports the hypothesis, report of any problems in the experiment
- Conclusion — restatement of the hypothesis, generalizations suggested by the experimental results, areas for further research
- Charts, graphs, or illustrations of the data

Format

When you write a laboratory report, keep these formatting points in mind:

- Typed, although handwriting may be acceptable in some cases (check with your Authority Figure)
- Written in past tense, and often in passive voice (*The mixture was cooled,* not *I cooled the mixture*)
- Functional, recipe-like description of what you did and how the experiment turned out (not a narrative)
- Title page optional

Science research paper

When you discover a cure for the common hangnail, perhaps you'll publish your triumph in a scientific journal. Like laboratory reports (see the section "Laboratory report," earlier in the chapter), science research papers report the results of original experiments. You generally hand lab reports to a teacher, but you may submit your science research paper to a journal for review by other scientists and, hopefully, publication. Both lab reports and research papers have some of the same elements, but their styles are quite different.

Lab reports resemble recipes; they get the information across in lists, charts, and short statements. Science research papers read like a story. The sentences are longer and more complex, as are the paragraphs.

Content

Science research papers include these sections:

- ✔ Title — tells what the experiment tested
- ✔ Abstract — the entire paper summarized in 250 words or less
- ✔ Introduction — explains the background, describes previous research by other scientists, and proposes a hypothesis to be tested
- ✔ Methods and materials — how you performed the experiment
- ✔ Results — concise presentation of data, including tables and graphs as appropriate
- ✔ Discussion — whether or not the data supported the hypothesis, comparison of your results to the outcome of other experiments, your interpretation of the implications of the data

Format

Science research papers follow a specific format:

- ✔ Often written in passive voice *(the antibiotic was administered)* instead of active *(I administered the antibiotic)*
- ✔ Experiments are always described in past tense
- ✔ Typed
- ✔ Each journal has little style quirks of its own (check the publication guidelines)
- ✔ Dates in citations emphasized
- ✔ Information is presented in paragraphs, not in lists, and reads like a narrative.

Term (or library) paper

Term papers probably got their name from the fact that they may take one entire term of the school year to write. A term paper isn't necessarily pegged to a particular period of time, though it is usually assigned a month or more before the due date. Term papers, also called library papers, may be on any subject, including literature, history, science, and so on. (A term paper about a scientific subject is not the same as a science research paper, which discusses the results of experiments carried out by the author. To find out more about science research papers, see the section "Science research paper," earlier in the chapter.)

Content

The content of term papers varies as much as the content of a typical library, but term papers do have some common characteristics:

- Usually presents an idea to be proved — the thesis
- Sometimes presents an array of information about one topic
- Comes to a conclusion about the topic
- Often relies on secondary sources — what other people have said about a particular topic
- May analyze primary sources — the actual documents, text, or audio-visual materials that are the subject of the paper
- Includes information from at least three different sources, and often many more (Part II of *Research Papers For Dummies* describes how to find, evaluate, and use primary and secondary sources.)

Format

Keep these points in mind as you format your term paper:

- Typed
- Contains at least 5 pages, and often as many as 10 or 15 pages
- Often has a separate title page
- May include visual aids, such as charts, graphs, or illustrations, but generally text-dominated
- Researched material is credited to the source with a *citation,* an identification tag that explains where the information was originally reported
- Citations presented in footnotes, endnotes, or parentheses in the text
- Includes a *bibliography* (a list of books and articles) or a list of *works cited* (all the sources, including electronic ones) at the end of the paper

Thesis

A *thesis* (plural is *theses*) is a pumped-up term paper. This research paper is usually assigned at the college or postgraduate level, and it may be the only graded work of an entire course. The thesis may also be a graduation requirement, the last hurdle before you're outta there. Because writing a thesis is a major job, you may have a whole year, or even more, to complete the work. Most institutions provide a *thesis advisor* to help with the work, perhaps to ease the feelings of guilt provoked by assigning such a horrible task. The advisor, usually a professor in the field, is assigned by the institution. In the ideal world, the advisor guides you through every step of the process. In the real world, some advisors are great, while others use your submissions to keep coffee stains off their desks.

With annoying but typical economy, English uses the same word — *thesis* — for two different things. Inside a paper, a thesis is the idea you are proving. (For more information on creating a thesis, see Chapter 11.) As noted in the preceding paragraph, a thesis may also be the name of a type of paper, one that contains a thesis. (Academics are so clever!)

Content

The content of a thesis is serious, scholarly stuff:

- ✔ May rely on either primary and secondary sources or some of each
- ✔ Greater number of sources than a term paper — often ten or many more
- ✔ Includes original theories about the topic under consideration and evidence to back up those theories

Format

The format of a thesis is set by the institution, usually according to these guidelines:

- ✔ Generally longer than a term paper (15 to 20 pages is not unusual, and some theses will break your toe if you drop them)
- ✔ Always typed
- ✔ Sources cited and included in a bibliography or list of works cited
- ✔ Separate title page and bibliography or list of works cited
- ✔ May be subject to an unbelievably long and ridiculous set of rules on the type of paper, width of margins, and so on. Check with your Authority Figure.

Dissertation

Now you're on the postgraduate level, the stratosphere of the academic world — but not the financial world. (Serious academics tend to gather pieces of paper with calligraphy on them, not stock portfolios.) If you're going for a doctorate, you're probably writing a dissertation.

How hard is it to write a dissertation? Here's a clue: People who have completed all the requirements for a doctorate *except* a dissertation are called *ABDs* — "all but dissertations." The group is so large that it has its own name! To help you, or to avoid lawsuits charging mental cruelty, the institution gives you an advisor.

Ask your advisor for the dissertation guidelines that are favored by the institution granting your degree. Bring a wheelbarrow.

Content

What's in a dissertation? Read on:

- ✔ Must add to the body of knowledge, not report something that is already known

- ✔ Relies on primary sources, unless the title is something like "The Evolution of Critical Reaction to the Lyrics of the Backstreet Boys," in which case the secondary sources *are* the topic

- ✔ May be based on experimental data or direct observation by the writer

- ✔ Needs a truckload of sources, reported in pages of citations and a bibliography that is as long as the telephone book of some towns

- ✔ Oral defense of the dissertation is probably required, in which the writer spends a few hours answering excruciating questions from experts in the field

Format

The rules for formatting dissertations qualify for an Olympic medal in pickiness:

- ✔ Format varies from university to university

- ✔ Always long, boring, and crucial to success

Even if you have to live on a lentils-only diet while writing your dissertation (graduate assistants make practically nothing), you may want to pay someone to retype and correctly format your dissertation. Just be sure that your employee is good at following ridiculous rules.

Business report

Finished with formal education? Congratulations! But don't heave a sigh of relief at putting research papers behind you. Depending on your field, the boss may ask you for a marketing report, an advertising campaign, an earnings projection, or any number of other business documents, all of which consist of research presented in written form. The only saving grace is that instead of paying truckloads of money to a school for the privilege of writing papers, you now receive a salary to do so.

The content and format of business reports vary enormously, depending on the type of paper, the field, the particular company, and even the preferences of an individual supervisor. When you're told to write a business report, spend some time looking through the company files. Ask co-workers or even the supervisor for specifics: What information are you supposed to include? Does the company have a preferred format? Unless you're working for Attila the Hun, you'll probably get some useful tips.

Business writing should be formal but not stiff in tone. Assume your reader is busy; communicate the information without wasting words. Make the reader understand why he or she should read the report, and then get down to, well, business. Present the relevant facts and your recommendations. Charts, graphs, and other visual aids make a strong impression and present a great deal of information efficiently.

Business plan

When you look in the mirror every morning, do you see the future CEO of the next Microsoft? If so, you need a business plan. A business plan is a formal research paper that an aspiring business owner (or business expander) presents to potential investors. The business plan explains what the new company (or larger company) will offer the public, the projected costs and earnings, an analysis of the competition, and statistics on the business's debt, equity, and requested financing.

Content

Every business plan should have the following content:

- Summary of the main points of the plan
- Examination of the products or services the business provides
- Marketing survey showing how the business's offerings will be received
- Explanation of how the new or expanded company differs from the competition
- Detailed description of the production, distribution, and management segments of the company
- Statement of all the company's assets and debts
- Explanation of the financing that is sought

Format

Presentation (a fancy word for format) matters in the business world:

- Always typed
- Printed on good-quality paper

✔ Wire- or spiral-bound

✔ Often as long as 40 pages

✔ Title page with the name of the business and contact information, as well as the name of the person who will review the report

✔ Contains diagrams, photos, and so on, to illustrate key points

✔ Includes a table of contents

✔ Provides source information for all facts

Climbing the Steps to Successful Research Papers

You can't climb to the top of the Empire State Building with one tremendous stride. Nor can you make the move from "I have to write a paper" to "Here it is; now leave me alone" in one leap. You need steps! (Okay, the metaphor is corny, and I know at least one person out there mentioned "elevator." But give me a break! The basic idea is valid.) Here's the lowdown on the steps in writing most types of research papers — the exception being original scientific research papers and laboratory reports, which are out there in their own separate universe. (For more about how to write science papers, see Chapter 12.)

1. **Decide what to write about.** The Authority Figure may decide for you, but if you are given the opportunity to choose a topic, you need to do some preliminary sniffing around in a library, on the Internet, or in Chapter 3 or the appendix of *Research Papers For Dummies*. You can come up with a subject that interests you (or at least one that won't send you screaming into the night) and then narrow that subject down into a topic.

2. **Conduct a survey of sources.** What's out there? You need to search a bit more thoroughly now, checking libraries and electronic media, until you have a sense of what's available. Then you can narrow your source list from everything ever said about the topic to stuff that looks as if it might be useful and available. Part II gives you the lowdown on a whole range of sources.

3. **Take notes, round one.** Now you actually have the sources in hand (or accessible via computer). You start reading and taking notes, keeping ultracareful records so that you always know what piece of information came from where. Go to Chapter 8 for details on note-taking.

4. **Create a thesis statement or topic sentence.** At some point, the stuff you're writing down should start to make sense. Now, you are ready to create a thesis statement. A thesis statement (see Chapter 11) is the heart of your paper — the idea that you are trying to prove. If the paper is a survey and not trying to prove anything, you can create a topic sentence — the main idea that you are writing about.

5. **Take notes, round two.** Now that you know what you're proving or what you're surveying, your note taking becomes more focused. You may decide to go back to some sources or to reinstate a couple of sources that you initially thought were worthless. You want to gather enough information to prove your thesis.

6. **Prepare to write.** At this stage you construct a battle plan. You reread your notes and sort them into subtopics. You outline the paper. Chapter 14 is available to help you with this task

7. **Write, round one.** Fortified with caffeine and the thought that at some point you may actually finish the project, you create a rough draft of the paper. Part V gives you the skills you need to write the rough draft.

8. **Write, round two.** You go back and marvel at the fluency of your writing and the brilliance of your ideas. Then you get realistic and clean up the grammar, correct the citations, and add the important ideas that you forgot the first time through. You cross out irrelevant information and polish the prose. (Chapter 19 helps you with grammar.)

9. **Place the finishing touches.** You create a title page or heading, a table of contents, and a table of illustrations (if necessary). You add a list of sources. You make a copy for posterity (actually, in case your Authority Figure loses the paper). You staple the whole thing or put it in a binder. You hand it in and, carefree at last, go bowling. (Chapter 19 explains these last few steps.)

Chapter 2

Getting on the Right Track: Tips for Saving Time and Effort

In This Chapter

▶ Choosing techniques suitable for a long paper

▶ Budgeting your time

▶ Finding work methods that complement your personality

▶ Seeking help from the Authority Figure who will judge your work

You're sitting at your desk with your computer booted (or pen filled), outline ready, and notes at hand. You write for a couple of minutes. "Piece of cake," you think. "I'll be typing 'The End' before I know it." A few paragraphs later, you get a great idea. One of the sources you consulted contains a quotation that perfectly supports the point you're trying to make. "It's in here somewhere," you mutter as you begin to skim piles of printouts from the Internet. "Nope. Maybe it was in one of those books?" Now you're on your knees under the desk, flipping desperately through a couple of thick texts.

I've seen lots of people go through the kind of search I just described — people who put considerable time and energy into their work and are brought literally to their knees because they approached a major research project as if it were a short paper. In this chapter I explain the most efficient way to approach projects that span a long period of time. I tackle the issue of time and how to budget it so that you don't end up trying to cram 100 hours of work into the last lunch hour before the paper is due. I also give you an overview of several working methods so that you can pick the one that complements your personality. Finally, I provide some tips on appeasing the Authority Figure who will read and judge your work.

Making a Long Story Short

Most people can write a short paper, one that relies on only a couple of sources, with very little planning. They just read a bunch of stuff, jot down a few notes, and start typing. Maybe not the best method, but one that works fairly well *if* — and this is a big *if* — the work is concentrated. When I say *concentrated,* I mean

- ✔ The paper is only a few pages long.
- ✔ You have only one or two sources.
- ✔ You spend a week or less working on the paper.

Unfortunately, only a small number of research papers fall into this category. Most research papers have more than a few pages, employ a greater number of sources, and take longer to write. Unless you're a rare individual with a photographic memory, you're not going to remember everything you read. Worse yet, you're going to remember *some* of what you read, but not enough to use. Panic time.

Another meltdown may occur because the task of writing a research paper, when viewed as a whole, is overwhelming. How am I going to write ten pages? How am I going to check every single source on this topic? How will I ever get 6,439 facts and quotations into logical order?

These worries are common, but they are also groundless. You don't write ten pages; you write one page, or even one paragraph, and then you write another, and then another, and so on. You aren't going to have a complete picture of the topic, ever, because these days, even experts can't keep up with the sheer volume of information out there. But with care (and some help from *Research Papers For Dummies!*), you can find the most important sources. Furthermore, you never have to put 6,439 facts *anywhere*. You can choose some facts that make your case or illustrate your meaning and put them in the section where they're needed. The rest you can ignore — at least for the moment. And because you have a good record of what's where (see the "Recording your life as a researcher" section in this chapter), you can find the facts you need without mounting a major search-and-rescue operation.

By now the main idea is probably clear: The key to saving time, energy, and hair (you won't pull out as much) is choosing work methods that are appropriate for long term papers. (Notice how the expression *term paper* is cleverly hidden in that phrase.) If you're working on a long research paper, you have to keep good records, and you have to see the project as a series of small steps. This ancient Chinese proverb may be severely overquoted, but it's still true: A journey of a thousand miles begins with a single step.

Recording your life as a researcher

In Part II of *Research Papers For Dummies,* I explain how to find the information you're looking for. In this section I deal with a different aspect of the research process — the secret technique that all top-notch researchers know.

Brace yourself for an exciting moment: To be a successful researcher, you have to keep good records. (Exciting stuff, huh? I'm expecting the tabloids to call at any moment.) No matter what you look up, read, or experience, you must record what you do. If you keep accurate records, you won't lose the material that you went to such pains to find.

Three record-keeping strategies are useful:

✔ **Keep a log of what you do:** Keep track of the Web sites you check, the libraries you visit, the people you call, the television programs you view (the ones that are relevant to your topic — you can skip the soap opera you watched, "just this once," for relaxation). By consulting the log, you won't have to cover the same ground twice.

✔ **Compile a numbered "master list" of all your sources:** When you take notes, label the information with the master-list number. If you keep a master list, you don't have to write the title, author, and other identifying information more than once; you just have to write the master-list number.

✔ **Create a personal index for sources:** Write down a quick summary of what you're likely to need in writing the paper, from that particular source. You can include this information in the master list, or you can keep it separately. Either way, you may find that a personal table of contents saves you a lot of time.

You may also find it useful to keep a "failure list" of Web sites, books, articles, or even libraries that contain nothing of value. With a failure list, you can avoid rechecking something that yields no information.

I got my first computer in 1980 — ancient history in the tech world — and it crashed pretty frequently. I got used to backing up my files early and often during the process of writing. Now my cardinal rule is "back up first, ask questions later." I apply this rule to more than my computer; I stop working frequently to photocopy my lists of sources, notes, and drafts, and I store the backups far away from the originals. I also have backup disks of everything that I store on my computer's hard drive. I'm ready for all the disasters I hope never to see, including fire, flood, and Martian invasion. You should be ready, too. Remember: Back up! Now and forever! (For a complete discussion of record keeping, see Chapter 8.)

Taking the research paper one step at a time

How do you get from New York to West Virginia? Here's a plan:

1. **Get in a car in New York.** Think deeply about where you will park when you get to West Virginia.

2. **Drive south.** If you take a wrong turn, don't backtrack. Just keep going until you get to your destination.

3. **Turn right at Virginia.** Reconsider the look that the traffic cop in New Jersey shot at you when you merged onto the turnpike.

I don't even have to explain why the preceding statements don't belong in my plan; I'm sure that you can see how silly it would be to worry about a parking place hundreds of miles before you need one. Yet some people write a research paper using steps that are just as ridiculous as those I just listed. Their paper plan resembles this one:

1. **Sit down at the computer and start to type.** After a while, decide what your paper is about.

2. **Go on the Internet or to the library and get a bunch of information.** Read everything, whether or not the material relates to your topic.

3. **Take no notes; underline nothing.** Keep the books nearby in case you need something later. If you don't have enough information, too bad.

4. **Hand it in when you've finished writing the whole thing.** What's done is done. Don't try to go over what you've written; you'll only make it worse.

Did you recognize yourself or anyone you know somewhere in the preceding examples? Too many people make their writing lives a lot harder than necessary. Make sure that you're not one of them!

Following a few simple guidelines can remove most of the hassle from writing a research paper, and, as a bonus, improve the final product:

✔ **Take the paper step by step in logical order, focusing only on the current step.** Don't let your mind jump ahead. When you are choosing a topic, for example, don't worry about how to format the bibliography.

✔ **Keep your ideas in an "idea file."** No one can control exactly when a good idea will arrive. If something comes to you, such as a good introduction or an idea for the conclusion, write it down and place it in your idea file (on the computer or on paper). Before you move on to a new step, check the idea file.

✔ **Keep a to-do list and let it hold your anxiety, as well as your duties.** For example, if you are worried about *citations* (identification labels for sources), write "find out how to cite sources — Chapter 18 of *Research Papers For Dummies*" on your to-do list. Then stop worrying. When you get to the rough draft, check out Chapter 18 and cite the sources correctly. End of worry! And you didn't let that anxiety sabotage your work on other aspects of the paper.

> ✔ **Don't skip any of the steps.** For example, don't tell yourself that note taking is a waste of time and go directly to the "writing the rough draft" step. You may end up trying to take notes directly into your rough draft. Neither the notes nor the rough draft will turn out well because you didn't give your complete attention to either.

> ✔ **Don't be afraid to backtrack if you make a mistake.** If you are writing the rough draft and discover that you need more information on a certain aspect of your paper, put the draft aside and do more research. Then return to the rough draft.

Timing Is Everything

I live in the real world, and I know that real people may have a tough time thinking about work that is not due for a month or so. (Actually, I know that real people may have a tough time thinking about work at all. Life offers so many possibilities for fun!) Nevertheless, you should take a stab at creating a plan. In this section I give you guidelines for long (ten-week), medium (five-week), and short (two-week) assignments. I also tackle a delicate question: What should you do when the paper is due tomorrow and you haven't even started yet?

Don't assume that all weeks are created equal. Before you make a paper-writing plan, consider everything else that you have going on, including events that have no relation to the research paper you're writing. Read this section with a calendar or day-planner in hand — one that has events like "sister's wedding," "voyage to the North Pole," and "math final" listed.

Now write start and end dates for each step in your research paper. Schedule a lot of work for weeks that look relatively free, and give yourself a free pass (or light duty) during busy times.

Work habits are as individual as fingerprints. In this section I provide some general guidelines, but you should adapt them to your own strengths and weaknesses. For example, in the ten-week plan I allot three weeks for research and three-plus weeks for writing. But if you are a jaguar when it comes to reading and a tortoise when it comes to writing, change the distribution to two weeks for research and four-plus weeks for writing.

If you're reporting on the results of your own scientific experiments, figure out how much time you need to do the actual lab work and add that time to the schedule below. Because I'm not the white-coat and microscope type, *Research Papers For Dummies* focuses on the book/article/Web research and the actual writing, not on the test-tube and lab-rat stuff.

I've got all the time in the world: The ten-week plan

No, you don't have all the time in the world. Ten weeks will become a memory faster than a survivor who's been kicked off the island. Get started right away so that you have time to polish that paper into perfection. Here's a solid plan:

- ✔ Selecting a topic (includes preliminary reading) — two weeks
- ✔ Conducting research (finding and evaluating sources, note taking) — three weeks
- ✔ Creating a thesis statement, writing a topic sentence, or formulating a hypothesis — three days
- ✔ Designing the paper (choosing a structure, identifying subtopics, outlining) — four days
- ✔ Writing first draft — three weeks
- ✔ Writing final draft — four days
- ✔ Making finishing touches (title page, bibliography, and so on) — three days

The *thesis statement* is a declaration that you will prove in your paper. Don't confuse a thesis statement with a *thesis,* which is a type of research paper. (For more on what a thesis is, see Chapter 1. For information on creating a thesis statement, see Chapter 11.)

Notice that I allot more time for the first draft (three weeks) than for the final draft (one week, including the finishing touches). You will do better if you put most of your energy into a great rough draft, leaving the final draft for polishing your prose, checking details, and so on. Don't skimp on the rough draft! It's important. But don't skip the final draft, either. You'll be surprised by how much you can improve your paper if you give it two drafts.

I can take my time: The five-week plan

Depending on the length of the paper and the number of sources you plan to use, you may not be able to take your time at all. Here's a suggested budget:

- ✔ Selecting a topic (includes preliminary reading) — one week
- ✔ Conducting research (finding and evaluating sources, note taking) — ten days
- ✔ Creating a thesis statement, writing a topic sentence or formulating a hypothesis — one day

✔ Designing the paper (choosing a structure, identifying subtopics, outlining) — two days

✔ Writing first draft — ten days

✔ Writing final draft — four days

✔ Making finishing touches (title page, bibliography, and so on) — one day

One day for finishing touches assumes that you have kept very good records and will not have to spend a lot of time worrying about the format of your citations (footnote, endnote, or parenthetical identification of sources). You should take care of those issues when you write the rough draft.

I'm in a hurry but not in a panic: The two-week plan

A two-week plan is called for because of one of two situations:

Situation #1: The Paper Assigner gave you only two weeks because he or she wants only a limited number of sources and a fairly short piece of writing.

Situation #2: The Paper Assigner gave you three months, and you spent the first two-and-a-half chasing the perfect wave on your surfboard.

If Situation #2 applies to you, ask (actually, beg) the Paper Assigner for more time. If the answer is no, you're going to have to compress a lot of work into a short period. (Also, you're going to have to put the surfboard — and everything else that is fun — away for the duration.)

Here's the timetable for either situation:

✔ Selecting a topic (includes preliminary reading) — two days

✔ Conducting research (finding and evaluating sources, note taking) — four days

✔ Creating a thesis statement, writing a topic sentence or formulating a hypothesis — one-half day

✔ Designing the paper (choosing a structure, identifying subtopics, outlining) — one-half day

✔ Writing first draft — four days

✔ Writing final draft — two days

✔ Making finishing touches (title page, bibliography, and so on) — one day

Somewhere out there, a mathematician is reading this book with a calculator in hand, trying to catch me in an error of scale. ("Gotcha! You allotted 30 percent of the time to research in the ten-week plan and only. . . ." You get the idea.) I admit it: I am not a mathematician. But even if I were, I wouldn't try for a consistent scale. Some things (like one day for finishing touches) can't be adjusted without becoming unrealistic. ("Allow .567 days for finishing touches. . . .")

It's due tomorrow!

Okay, you're in big trouble. I see two possible situations here:

> **Situation #1:** Your Authority Figure took part in the Spanish Inquisition and is keeping the old torture skills sharp by assigning impossible amounts of work in ridiculous amounts of time.

> **Situation #2:** You went surfing (see Situation #2 in the preceding two-week plan) and left the work until the last minute.

Your only remedy is to come clean, confess that you can't do the job, and hope for mercy. If the answer is no, find out the penalty for late papers and work as quickly as you can. Load up on the major food groups — salt, grease, caffeine, and sugar — and unplug the phone. Turn off the instant messaging function on your computer, too. Pick a minimum number of sources (Internet or traditional) and read as fast as you can. You'll probably be able to create only one draft, but try (really, really, really try) to allow time — even an hour — to revise this draft. Your paper will be better in the long run. Also, after you hand the paper in, but before you go to sleep, take a moment to record your New Year's Resolutions:

> **Resolution #1** (for Situation #1) — I won't take any more courses from professors who have trained in dungeons, *or* I will read the want ads every day until I find a new job.

> **Resolution #2** (for Situation #2) — I will plan my time better so that I can avoid feeling as if my eyelids were glued to my forehead when the next paper assignment comes around.

No matter what the temptation, don't fool around with artificial stimulants (other than a couple of cups of coffee or a few sodas). Little pills guaranteed to disrupt the usual human need for sleep are not worth the risk to your health. Take the rap — the lower grade or the boss's wrath — and do better the next time. Stay on the safe side so at least you know that there will *be* a next time.

Finding a Method That Suits Your Madness

As I type this paragraph, I am sprawled on my living-room sofa with my laptop propped on my thighs and my favorite CD humming along in the background. I have a glass of mint tea on the end table, notes arrayed nearby on the floor, and an outline propped against the arm of the sofa. The living room is a mess, but I'm happy. I'm in writing mode, working in a situation that suits me.

You probably have some favorite writing habits also, and they may be totally different from mine. Where do you put your outline, your notes, and your knees? Chances are, you have a whole set of preferences for location, music (or silence), refreshment, and ambience. I doubt that you decided these preferences consciously; you probably just gravitated towards habits that felt right for you.

The methods that you use to write your research paper should also feel comfortable. How do you find comfortable writing methods? Choose those that mesh well with your personality. If you achieve a good fit, you get more work done in less time, and your product is better.

The following sections may help you select the writing methods that are best for you.

Choosing a topic

Do you like to have everything set from the very beginning, with no uncertainty and nothing left to chance? If so, choose a topic from the appendix or ask your Authority Figure for an assigned topic.

Does a bit of mystery appeal to you? Are you the type of person who wants to see what develops? Avoid the suggestions in the appendix and allow a little extra time for preliminary reading when you budget your time for the project. Let yourself — for a while, not forever — see what shakes out, before you settle on a focus for your research and writing.

Taking notes

Do you enjoy the feeling of a pen in your hand? Do you have good memories of September trips to the stationery store for new school supplies? Do you love opening a fresh notebook or a pristine pack of index cards? If you answered yes to the previous questions, you may want to take notes by hand. (See Chapter 8 for hints on how to take notes efficiently.)

Do you hate signing your name because you're only comfortable in front of a keyboard? Do you think that handwriting is "so-o-o over"? Has anyone ever asked you if the computer was surgically attached to your body? If so, computer note taking may be for you. (Chapter 8 also tackles this method.)

Writing

Does your best writing flow from one long, intense session of work? Do you hate to get up when you're in the groove, even for a bathroom break? Do you understand why famous beat writer Jack Kerouac wanted to write on a continuous roll of paper to avoid stopping every few minutes to insert a new sheet of paper into his typewriter? If you identify with this group of questions, you may want to find one or two days in your calendar that are clear of any other obligations. (For an extremely long paper, a dissertation perhaps, you may want to schedule a clear month or more — or if that's not possible, at least an open day or two every week.)

Do you think best when you've had a break to refresh your spirit? Do you like frequent but short work sessions? After an hour of writing, does your brain begin to resemble a giant bowl of oatmeal? If so, block out about an hour (you have to allow for setup and takedown of notes, the outline, and so on) from every day's schedule. Don't let anything short of bubonic plague interfere with that time slot, but enjoy yourself during the rest of the day. For a complete discussion of the writing process, turn to Part V.

Discovering a Method That Suits Your Authority Figure's Madness

I'm going to take a wild guess here: You're probably not writing a research paper for your own pleasure or to fill the void created when you outgrew that turtle-racing hobby. You're probably writing a research paper for other people — people who can order you around and who have the power to judge your work (also known as Authority Figures).

When *you're* the Authority Figure, you'll have the complete freedom to tell your underlings what to do, and you'll be able to make every little decision about the research paper yourself. Until that happy day, you have to find out exactly what your paper-assigner wants, and then follow those wishes as if they were commands. Come to think of it, they *are* commands.

Some Authority Figures are very clear about their desires. They give you a written memo describing exactly what you are supposed to do. For example:

FROM: Professor Swampthing

TO: Menial Students Taking Robotics 101

RE: TERM PAPER THAT WILL MAKE OR BREAK YOUR ENTIRE CAREER

Your course grade (as well as everything that ever happens in the rest of your life) depends on a term paper that I will grade as if you were all professional writers who have won Nobel prizes. The paper will be 160,000 pages long. It will refer to no fewer than 802 sources and no more than 804 sources. At least 45.3 percent of your sources must be journal articles, with 5.98 percent coming from the journal that has the good taste to publish my own work.

Your paper will begin with a short introduction (approximately 16.9 lines long) that will include . . .

It's too painful to go on, but you get the idea. Professor Swampthing has given you no freedom at all. The length, topic, format, and so on are all decided for you.

Professor Swampthing's opposite, Mr. Groovy, passes you in the hall and casually mentions, "I want a paper on something that moves you. Begin when you are ready to mold your inner self to the universe's heart, and stop writing when the spirit has left you. Include sources."

Mr. Groovy may be more fun to hang out with, but his paper assignment is just as bad as Professor Swampthing's. Now you have too much freedom. You don't know what Mr. Groovy is expecting or how he will evaluate your work. But rest assured, Mr. Groovy knows what he is expecting; he just hasn't explained it. And if he doesn't receive a paper that matches the one that he sees with his inner eye, you're in trouble.

Professor Swampthing and Mr. Groovy are obviously exaggerations, but most paper-assigners lean towards one extreme or the other. If you're stuck with a project that is similar to the one assigned by Professor Swampthing, don't put even a toe over the line without asking permission. Follow the directions that you've been given and ask about anything that is unclear. If a Mr. Groovy-type project has landed on your desk, you also need to ask questions. First, formulate a plan. Then ask whether the plan is acceptable. Be specific. Don't say, "Should the paper be short, medium, or long?" Instead say, "I was planning to write ten pages. Is that length okay with you?" You should check your plans early and often with both Professor Swampthing and Mr. Groovy.

Asking the right questions

Check out the following questions to gain some useful tips on what you should be finding out from your Authority Figure.

Before you do anything, ask your Authority Figure the following:

- Is there a particular topic that I should write about? An approved list?
- How long should the finished paper be?
- When is the paper due?
- Do you want to see any of the intermediate stages?
- How many sources of information should I use?
- Do you accept Internet sources? What type of sources may I include? Do you expect a mix of sources, or may all the sources be of one type (all books, all Web sites, and so on)?
- What kind of documentation do you want? Do you have a preferred manual of style?

Manuals of style are books of rules. Each manual of style tells you how to indent, capitalize, and so forth. A large chunk of every manual is devoted to documentation — the way you identify sources. The rules in one manual of style do not always match the rules in another. Find out which one you are supposed to follow and then buy or borrow a copy. (Chapter 18 describes several popular manuals of style.)

When you begin your research, ask your Authority Figure the following:

- Can you suggest any sources that might be useful?
- Are any of my sources out-of-date or unreliable?
- Am I missing anything that is crucial?
- I'm leaning toward this thesis — what do you think?
- How many supporting points do you expect?

As you write, ask your Authority Figure the following:

- Do you expect a particular format for the introduction?
- Should a subhead introduce each of the subtopics?
- I'm making this point in my conclusion. Am I on the right track?
- I found a piece of evidence that doesn't seem to fit well. Can you help me work it into my argument?
- Do you expect a particular number of quotations?
- Should I include visual aids?
- My paper is turning out longer (or shorter) than I anticipated. Is that a problem?

As you hit the home stretch, ask your Authority Figure the following:

- Should I include a title page? What should be on it? Is a heading preferable?
- Do I need a table of contents?
- Do I need a table of illustrations?
- Do you care where I place the page numbers?
- I read the manual of style, but I don't know how to cite this particular article. Is this correct?
- I read the manual of style, but I am not sure about the format for the bibliography. Will you check it?

Using realism as a tactic

If you are able to get answers to each of the questions in the previous section and can tailor your work to the response, your paper will probably turn out to be one of the all-time greatest hits of your field. However, be realistic. Any person who assigns research papers probably receives a lot of them. Reading the finished products can take a weekend, if not a month, of the Authority Figure's "free time." (Some of the emotion I feel as an overworked teacher may be leaking onto the page right now.) Answering a thousand questions from each writer eats up a huge number of hours. So if you ask all the questions, you may turn into one of the all-time pests of your field. And Paper Evaluators, however much they try to be fair, are human. They may be tempted to downgrade the work of someone who interrupted their Super Bowl party to check on a footnote. (This actually happened to me.) So here's the cardinal rule: Be reasonable. Choose the most important issues — the ones you're really sweating over. Take an educated guess on the rest.

Chapter 3

What Am I Writing About?

The average kitchen in a Manhattan apartment is the size of a bath mat, so we New Yorkers have a lot of experience with menus for both take-out and eat-in establishments. (Some people in my apartment building order in so frequently that their concept of kitchen renovation is installing a new phone.) New York City also offers unparalleled opportunities for people watching, so I've come to some conclusions about how human beings relate to menus. If the menu is very short, diners decide slowly and reluctantly. The general feeling seems to be that the decision is all-important; one of those choices leads to a luxury car and a vacation in Hawaii and the other to a moldy tennis ball. If the menu is very long, diners decide very quickly. Then they "undecide," choose again, re-choose, and gradually work their way into a state of paralysis.

When selecting a subject and later a topic for your research paper, you may resemble the diners I've just described. If the Authority Figure assigning the paper (your teacher, unit supervisor, game warden) limits the choices sharply, you may place too much importance on your decision. And if the menu of choices facing you is too wide, you may be lost in indecision.

Not to worry. In this chapter I tell you how to deal with both extremes and everything in between when deciding what to write about. I also explain how to whittle a subject down to a topic and how to begin the move from a topic to a thesis.

Defining Terms: Subject, Topic, and Thesis

What are you writing about? A subject, a topic, or a thesis? Actually, all three. So before I go any further, here's a short tour of a minor province of the wonderful world of research-paper vocabulary.

Subject

The *subject* of your paper is what you are writing about, in a general sense. You can state the subject in extremely broad terms (science, social issues, history) or in narrower terms (pollution, teen pregnancy, World War I). The very broad terms are about as useful as a shopping list that tells you to buy "stuff." So when I speak of subjects, I refer to the narrower terms.

Topic

The *topic* of your paper is a small slice of the subject. Here are a few subjects, carved into manageable portions:

Subject	*Possible Topics*
pollution	arsenic in drinking water, carbon dioxide emissions, toxic waste, the Clean Air Act, oil spills, alligator waste in NYC sewer systems
teen pregnancy	attitudes of the mother toward her baby, pregnancy prevention strategies, welfare policies, support by teen fathers, exploitation of the problem by politicians running for re-election
World War I	trench warfare, shell shock, introduction of airplanes for reconnaissance, pacifist movement, effect on the roles of women, helmet designs as a fashion influence

The line between subject and topic is blurry. In the preceding list, the topics may themselves be narrowed down. For example, "the Clean Air Act" may be divided into "politics," "underlying science," "public attitudes," and so forth. Don't worry about terminology. Just be sure that you end up with a clear, focused idea to write about.

Notice that the subject, like the trunk of a tree, may give rise to any number of branches (the topics).

When you write a research paper about a scientific subject, you choose a topic and a thesis as I describe in this chapter. If you're writing a science research paper based on your own laboratory research, the process of writing is different. Check out Chapter 12 for all the details.

Thesis

Most research papers have a definite point of view. (The exceptions are simple surveys of information, which I describe in "Surveying the Territory" later in this chapter, and those based on original laboratory research, which I discuss in Chapter 12.) The paper you're writing probably argues a case, presenting the position you decide to take after a gazillion hours of research on the topic. This position is the *thesis* of your paper — the idea that you have formulated about the topic.

The thesis is the idea you formulate at the end (or nearly the end) of the research process. However, you state the thesis in a *thesis statement* at the *beginning* of the paper because it is the beginning of the argument you are going to make in the paper itself. (To learn how to create a thesis statement, see Chapter 11.)

Just to give you an idea of what a thesis statement looks like, here are a few:

> Arsenic levels currently permitted in drinking water should be lowered.
>
> Arsenic levels currently permitted in drinking water are safe.
>
> Teen mothers often see their babies as burdens.
>
> Teen mothers may believe that their babies will offer them the affection that is missing in the mother's life.
>
> Many casualties of World War I resulted from unsanitary conditions in the trenches.
>
> The military leaders of World War I did not know how to conduct an air war effectively.

Notice that the thesis statements about arsenic contradict each other. (Reminds me of an old joke: Do you have trouble making decisions? Well, yes and no.) When you write your research paper, you choose a position and present evidence that supports your view. The cliché about "two sides to every story" applies here; the same information can probably be interpreted in several different ways depending upon the beliefs and life experiences of person who is interpreting it. Never fear: Research papers usually fall into the no-right-answer category. If you make a good case and present it well, you're probably okay no matter which position you take. The best papers generally flow from the personal beliefs of the writer, so follow your heart (as long as you have evidence to back up your ideas).

In the preceding paragraph I said that making a good case for your thesis and presenting it well are generally more important to the success of the paper than the position you take in the thesis statement. Unfortunately, those of you who write research papers for business will probably be held to a different standard, because your thesis statements will resemble the following:

> Hysterium Industries is a good investment.
>
> Marketing New Blue Margarine through the Internet will increase sales by at least 50 percent.
>
> The company will easily absorb the extra workload created by downsizing the Department of Bureaucratic Mix-ups.

In the paycheck world, in contrast to the theoretical academic world, the correctness of your thesis becomes apparent quickly. If Hysterium Industries tanks, so may your job. The sales figures for New Blue Margarine will prove or disprove your marketing projection. And employees disgruntled by the overtime they have to put in after the company downsizes may force you to barricade yourself in the lavatory. So cubicle-dwellers beware: Formulate your thesis with extra care.

Even though you argue a specific point of view in your paper, you should also acknowledge and answer the opposing arguments. See Chapter 16 for how to write a "concession and reply" paragraph.

Selecting a Subject for Your Paper: The Subject of Your Affection

According to a famous story that may even be true, Henry Ford said that buyers of his Model T could have any color they wanted, so long as it was black. Your subject choices may be equally limited, or you may be faced with a world of possibilities. In this section I explain how to select a subject when you have a choice and how to deal when you don't.

When the choice is yours

When you write a research paper, you're going to be stuck with the subject for a very long time. You may as well choose something that you find bearable or even (in a perfect world) fascinating.

The best subjects for papers arise from the subjects that inspire your passion. (Shame on you! I'm talking about research papers here, not *that*.) When it's time to choose the subject of your paper, spend a few minutes making an inventory of your own personal turn-ons and turn-offs. What do you get in trouble for doing when you're supposed to be working? What do you avoid at all costs?

Now consider whether you can connect your passion to the paper you are supposed to write. Here's a story to illustrate what I mean. I was once the advisor of a young man who was absolutely nuts about football. In eighth grade he wrote a report on the history of the National Football League. When he took economics in high school, he wrote a paper on tax revenues generated by professional football teams. When he studied Modern American History, he wrote about the effect of Title IX (the law that prohibits sex discrimination in institutions receiving money from the federal government) on college football programs. I don't think he worked the subject of football into his class on Medieval Poetry, but not because he didn't try. By the way, he did *not* get a job with the NFL when he finished college. He now works in sports broadcasting, specializing in — you guessed it — football.

If you can't write about something that's close to your heart, at least look for a subject that you find mildly interesting. Imagine that you are putting together a dinner party. You can invite anyone in the world, living or dead. Who's at the table? What are their areas of interest? If you're inviting them, you must have at least some curiosity about the subjects they would bring up at the dinner table. So now you've got some possible subjects.

If you have access to the Internet, you've got access to online help in selecting a subject. Several major search engines, such as Yahoo! (www.yahoo.com) and AltaVista (www.altavista.com), have subject catalogues on their home pages. Browse through the subject headings until something grabs your attention.

If you don't have access to the Internet, you can go to a local or school library or a bookstore and check out the subject headings on the shelves. Which shelves look interesting? Those are possible subjects for your paper. Or, look at the reference section of the library. You'll probably find some general encyclopedias. Flip through some pages; something may catch your eye. After you choose a general subject, check the reference shelves for subject-area encyclopedias or specialized dictionaries (*The Encyclopedia of Boy Bands, The Dictionary of Radish Agriculture*). Skim those pages for ideas.

Don't have time for the Internet or the library? Not a problem. *Research Papers For Dummies* is the answer to your prayer. Check out the appendix, which lists subjects and topics that appeal to even the pickiest writer.

Having too many subjects to choose from may be daunting. If you find yourself overwhelmed with possibilities, don't despair. Choose a subject and be done with it. Resign yourself to the fact that you are not going to be able to learn about everything that interests you in one paper. Tell yourself that the subjects you haven't gotten to are not lost; you can always use them for future papers.

After you choose a subject, move on to "Attending to the Topic of Topics" later in this chapter. Even if you have two or three possible subjects, it's still time to move on. During the process of narrowing the subject into a topic, one of the subjects will emerge as the right one for you.

When you've got no choice

The Authority Figure who assigned the research paper may take all the guess-work out of the issue by assigning a subject, and maybe even a topic. ("Write a paper on the global economy. . .urban planning. . .the poetry of heavy metal lyrics.") If you're writing a paper for a course in school, the subject of the course (*Rock Lyrics of the Baby Boomers, Developing Economies of the Third World, Arithmetic and You!*) often defines the subject of your paper.

Another limit you may face is structure. Instead of giving you a subject or a topic, the Paper Assigner may decree that your paper follow a particular pattern or structure — a comparison of two different playwrights, an analysis of the viewpoints of all the interested parties in a particular event, a pro-con discussion of a major issue, and so on. If the structure is assigned, you may still have some leeway in choosing a subject.

The appendix of *Research Papers For Dummies* contains some of the most common writing structures (I call them "big questions") with suggestions for applying them to each subject. The appendix also suggests topics for each "big question."

Even if your Authority Figure assigns a subject, you haven't lost every aspect of free will.

Remember that subjects are general in nature. Check the assigned subject for wiggle room. Can you focus it a little on something more appealing (or less repulsive) to you? For example, suppose you're a poet at heart, stuck in a physics course so boring that you have to staple your eyelids open. The teacher is expecting a paper on (drum roll) *physics*. Okay, how about time? Physics drips with all these wonderful theories about the nature of time. And poets also spend a lot of time thinking about time. Maybe one of those theories will inspire an ode.

If the assigned subject is completely horrible and you have no breathing space at all, don't despair. Later, when you choose a topic, you'll probably have another chance to connect to something you like.

Another consideration in choosing a subject is the difficulty of finding the research material. You may not be particularly enthralled with politics, but if your cousin is a senator, chances are you have access to a lot of great information. And who knows, you may even be drawn into the subject and run for office yourself!

Attending to the Topic of Topics

After you've nailed down a subject, turn your attention to the choice of a topic. The standards I describe in the preceding section on subjects hold true for topics as well:

- Choose something you like, assuming you have any choice at all.
- If you're dealing with a list of assigned topics, see if the Authority Figure will allow you to focus on an aspect of the topic (a "subtopic") that interests you.
- Consider any personal connections or special access to information that may give you an advantage in one particular topic.

But topics are a little more complicated than subjects. Many more topics than subjects are floating around out there, so you have more to choose from and more standards to apply. In this section I explain how to evaluate potential topics beyond the three considerations just listed.

What information is available?

You can probably find *some* information on anything, but you probably can't find *a lot of* information on every topic. Before you commit to a topic, be sure that you'll have enough material to work with. For example, suppose you're interested in global warming (the subject). Your focus may be on any of these topics:

- Carbon dioxide emissions
- The ozone layer
- The Kyoto treaty on limiting fossil fuels
- Greenpeace's stand on the issue
- The relationship between global warming and the cement plant in your town

You don't have to be a librarian to know that information on the first four topics is easy to find. Lots and lots of articles have been written on all of them. Books too. But the last topic presents a problem. You probably won't find your local cement plant described on the Internet, and it's likely that no one has written a book about it either. Do you have to give up on the topic? Not necessarily. You just have to get creative. For example, you can check out what sort of emissions have been linked to global warming. Find out what scientists, environmental activists, and the government have to say about the problem. Read statements on the issue from all viewpoints. Then take a trip to the cement plant. Interview the manager. What comes out of the plant's smokestacks? Is it an emission you've read about? If the answer isn't familiar, look it up. Ask the manager what environmental measures are in place at the plant. Do any of those measures resemble something you've read about? With a little original research and a lot of digging from standard research sources, you'll probably have enough for a paper. (And if you've done a good job and no one else has written about it, you may even find someone to publish it. Then you'll be a source for someone else's research paper.)

Original research can be rewarding, but sometimes it's difficult. Interviewing real live people (see Chapter 7 for tips) is time-consuming and unpredictable, and you may not dig up enough information no matter where you look or how hard you try. Approach original topics with care and allow enough time for a change of course in case you come up dry.

What structure will I use?

As explained in the section entitled "Selecting a Subject for Your Paper: The Subject of Your Affection" earlier in this chapter, the person who assigns the paper often specifies a particular structure. If you're creative enough, you can make almost any topic fit into any structure. However, some topics slide more easily into the slot you've been stuck with. For example, if your English teacher wants a comparison-and-contrast paper, you may choose

> Two authors living in two different time periods writing about the same situation (for example, Jane Austen and Virginia Woolf on meeting one's marriage partner)

> Two works by the same author written at different times in the author's career (say, a poem by Langston Hughes from the 1920s and one from the 1960s)

> Works from two different genres, such as poetry and prose, dealing with the same theme (views of male-female relationships in Gregory Corso's poem "Marriage" and Virginia Woolf's novel *Mrs. Dalloway*)

See the appendix for a vast number (okay, maybe not a *vast* number, but a lot) of suggested topics suitable for all types of structures.

Is there anything left to write?

Someone once told me that an overeager researcher trying to find something new to say about Shakespeare actually X-rayed the roof of the Bard's house in Stratford. I don't know if the researcher found anything new (or even if the story is true). I do know that this type of activity falls under the heading "Desperate Behavior." With all the topics in all the subjects in the world, why would you want to walk into one that's pretty much used up?

Calm down. I'm not saying that you can never write about Shakespeare (although as an English teacher I have to say that a ten-year moratorium on reinterpretation of the Bard has a certain appeal). I am saying that scholars have written more on some subjects than on others. If your Authority Figure stresses originality and clearly wants you to come up with something new, you may find it easier to tackle a writer whose possessions have not been CAT scanned.

Here you walk a fine line. If you select something that is too obscure, you really have to hunt for information. If you choose something covered by whole libraries, you run the risk of repeating someone else's research. The middle ground is probably safer, although if you wear a doublet and speak in iambic pentameter, you may as well settle in with old Will and be happy. Likewise, if you're really into the newest, hippest writer, follow your heart. You may not find much information, but you'll probably find enough to get you through.

Moving from a Topic to a Thesis

What are you trying to prove? In some situations those are fighting words, but I'm asking about your thesis, not picking a fight with you. A thesis is an idea that grows in your brain as you research your topic. You express it in the paper as a thesis statement, and then you prove it with the evidence in your paper. In this section, I draw a basic roadmap for moving from a topic to a thesis to a thesis statement. For a complete guide to that journey, see Chapter 11.

Getting an idea

The seed of the thesis may sprout fairly early in the process. A few nanoseconds into the topic, the Spanish explorers' treatment of the Aztecs may inspire such thoughts as "unfair treatment of American Indians" and "murderous explorers." Neither of these ideas is a fully developed thesis, but you're on the road.

The thesis may remain a complete mystery until quite late in the research process. After collecting tons of notes, you may still have no idea what you want to say about the topic. Don't panic. Reread the notes and go for a walk. Let a few ideas percolate through your consciousness. Return to your desk and pull out a sheet of blank paper. Jot down some ideas in random order. Eventually something — or the faintest hint of something — will turn up.

Developing the idea

After you have a general idea of your thesis, you need to develop it. Think of the process of developing a photo (when you do it yourself, not when you send it to the local photo shop). The image emerges gradually. Your thesis takes shape gradually, too. As you continue your research, zero in on the aspect that you've identified as a possible thesis. Check to see whether you have enough information — or a good chance of finding more — about the ideas you're considering. Each possible thesis should be an assertion that you can prove with supporting facts, quotations, and experts' views. Don't stop until you've got a couple of possibilities.

Creating the thesis statement

After you've come up with some candidates for the starring role, take the final steps. Look through your notes, checking for information on each possible thesis. If you can't make a case for one, scrap it. Now take whatever's left and turn it into a statement — one sentence that proclaims an idea that your paper will prove. Choose the sentence that appeals to you the most. If they all appeal to you, blindfold yourself and stick a pin in the paper (taking care not to spear any body parts along the way). Now you have it: your thesis statement.

Some thesis statements are too broad, and some are too narrow. Other pitfalls include thesis statements that are too vague or those that are too obvious. Chapter 11 tells you how to create an appropriate thesis statement.

Science research papers have a hypothesis instead of a thesis. Chapter 12 explains how to create a hypothesis.

Surveying the Territory: When Your Paper Doesn't Need a Thesis

Are you inhaling chalk dust while sitting on a rather small piece of furniture waiting for the lunch bell to ring? (In other words, are you in middle school or high school?) If so, you may not need to create a thesis for your research paper. Many teachers of teens assign "reports" or survey papers that rely on library research. The teacher expects you to (no shock here) survey the information available and write a general paper on what you've found.

Assignments that fall into the "survey" category may look like this:

- ✔ A report on Uruguay
- ✔ A composition on the United Nations
- ✔ A paper on Unidentified Flying Objects

You don't need a thesis in this type of paper; you need a *topic sentence.* A topic sentence tells the reader what to expect, what you're writing about. It doesn't always state a position, and the paper doesn't always argue a case. You may simply present the material ("Just the facts, Ma'am," as Sergeant Friday used to say on that television oldie-but-goodie *Dragnet*). Examples of this type of topic sentence include

- ✔ One of the most fascinating countries in South America is Uruguay.

- ✔ The United Nations, founded in 1945, is an association of sovereign states from all over the globe.

- ✔ Unidentified Flying Objects or UFOs have been drawing attention ever since human beings first looked at the night sky.

For more information on writing topic sentences, see Chapter 11.

Notice that the assignments I just listed are quite general. If you've struggled through this entire chapter, you know that the assignments name subjects, not topics, of papers. Don't blindly assume that the teacher wants a general survey of information when he or she assigns a subject. The teacher may expect you to narrow the subjects into a topic and then create a thesis statement. So before you begin work, find out what the teacher expects. After all, you're going to discover that information anyway when the teacher returns the graded report. The top of your paper will say one of the following:

> Marvelous survey of the land and people of Uruguay! Thoroughly researched and brilliantly written! A+++

or

> All you did was present some general information about Unidentified Flying Objects. This report needs greater focus and a point of view. What do *you* believe about UFO's? D——

Bottom line: Ask first. Then write.

You don't have to be in middle school to receive a survey assignment. Suppose your boss asks you for a report on the investment income of the company's major competitors. You'll do the research and present the information without taking a position on the results. Any judgment about the material will come from the boss, whose astronomical salary requires such deep thoughts.

Part II
Finding Everything about Anything: Research

The 5th Wave   By Rich Tennant

"I'm searching for a source for my paper 'Robin Hood, The Criminal That Stole My Girlfriend.' Can you tell me where I can find a pamphlet from the People Against Merry Men organization?"

In this part . . .

These days everyone's talking about highways and webs of information. But I prefer to think of research material — books, articles, Web sites, interviews, and so forth — as an ocean. You can wade in at almost any point and find something of interest, but you have to take care that a tidal wave of facts doesn't swamp you.

In this part I show you how to navigate the Information Ocean. I give you an overview of what's out there — all the traditional as well as the new electronic resources that may provide material for your paper — and discuss how to use each source efficiently.

Chapter 4

Casting a Wide Net: Choosing Sources for Your Paper

- -

In This Chapter

▶ Deciding how many sources you need

▶ Surveying traditional and modern sources

▶ Evaluating the reliability of sources

- -

So you have the assignment — ten pages on the element marshmellown-ium and its effect on the peanut-butter sandwich. Now what do you do? No, the answer is not to rip up the assignment pad and head for the mall. The answer is to look for sources of information. But how many and what kind of sources do you need? And how do you choose the most reliable?

In this chapter I provide a field guide to stalking the wild source. I cover every type of source from the oldest (books) to the newest (electronic media). I also explain how to evaluate the accuracy of the information you're gathering.

Sourcing Your Paper: How Many and What Kinds Do You Need?

Your topic is how a hamburger-flipping robot affects the fast-food market. You're ready to rumble. All you need is information. But how much informa-tion? To rephrase the question, how many sources do you need? The answer depends upon a number of factors:

✔ **The length of your paper.** A 4-page report may need only two sources; 20-page paper may need a dozen sources.

✔ **The depth of your paper.** If you are studying the basics of a particular subject, two or three sources may be all that is required. If you are the district manager for a fast-food chain and have spent 20 years in the business, more-in-depth analysis is your goal, and that may require 10 or 20 sources.

✔ **The expectations of the Authority Figure for whom you are writing.** A high-school teacher may ask for three or four sources about hamburger flipping. The Director of Labor Operations for O'Burger's Best Beef may expect 20 sources, analyzing everything from the robot's maintenance schedule to fire-code compliance.

When in doubt, ask. Even when not in doubt (you *think* you know, but you haven't actually checked), ask. The Authority Figure should provide guidelines on the number and type of sources required.

Next issue: What kind of sources should you tap? The source world is divided into two giant families: primary and secondary. *Primary sources* rely on material that has not been filtered, interpreted, or reshaped by another writer. (*Primary* means "first," and primary sources are firsthand accounts.) Examples of primary sources include:

✔ A transcript of Franklin Roosevelt's speech on Pearl Harbor

✔ The text of the law prohibiting spitballs

✔ Lines from the poem "Ode to Information" by U. Foundit

✔ Survivors' descriptions of the sinking of the *Titanic*

✔ An oral history of immigrants from Antarctica

✔ Records of fog from the lighthouse keeper's log

Secondary sources report someone else's reaction to a primary source. When you read a history book on the *Titanic,* you're reading a secondary source.

The distinction between primary and secondary sources depends somewhat on the subject of your paper. Suppose you read a review of *Rocky XV.* That source would be secondary if your topic is the *Rocky* series of movies, because the reviewer is interpreting the movie for you, the reader. (The movie itself would be a primary source for a paper about the *Rocky* series.) But if you are studying the way critics have reacted to Sylvester Stallone's acting, the review becomes a primary source, because your topic *is* the review.

Examples of secondary sources include:

✔ A history textbook entitled *Why the World Is a Mess and How It Got That Way*

✔ An essay of literary criticism, "Blood on the Tracks — An Analysis of the Influence of Bob Dylan on the Literature of Railroads"

✔ Reference books such as *The Encyclopedia of Vampires*

✔ A tape of the January 14 episode of *Panel of Experts,* a bottom-ranked show on mushroom gathering

Should you rely on primary or on secondary sources, or some of each? In deciding, consider the nature of your topic, what sources are available, what you are likely to understand, and what your Authority Figure wants. For example, if you are writing about Icelandic epics, you may want to look at the literature itself (in translation, assuming you don't speak Icelandic). Even in translation, you're dealing with a primary source. You may also want to read some interpretations of the literature by scholars who specialize in Icelandic literature. Those interpretations are secondary sources. If you have a great eyewitness account of a performance of one of the epic Icelandic poems, you may not be able to use it if the account has never been translated. That primary source will have to remain untapped, as you turn to an English-language book, *Iceland, My Iceland: A Study of Poetic Performance,* a secondary source. As usual, the best course is to ask the Paper Assigner what he or she expects and then let reality be your guide.

Unless you are very young, you should probably not rely solely on huge reference books (such as general-interest encyclopedias and almanacs) that cover millions of topics very lightly. Likewise, a couple of printouts from the Web's most general sites on your topic will probably not impress the person who is evaluating your project. Tell the Authority Figure what sources you are planning to use, while you have enough time before the deadline to change the plan, just in case the Authority Figure breaks into hysterical laughter and says, "That's all you've got? Don't buy any nonrefundable airline tickets for the summer — you'll be repeating this course."

Stalking the Wild Source: A Field Guide

In almost all the sci-fi television shows that I watch (and I watch a lot of them), the characters seek information from little plastic tablets or by saying, "Computer, calculate the number of seconds before we escape the gravitational pull of that orange-striped planet." And they get an answer! Life should be so easy for you. Instead, you have to trudge to the library (or let some Internet electrons do the trudging for you). Just so you know what to look for, this section gives a brief survey of some of the sources you may consider for your paper.

Books

No, they're not obsolete (after all, you're reading one right now). Yes, they're still useful, even now in the Golden Age of Webdom. Some books, like this one, trace their roots to Gutenberg (the movable-type guy) and to the ancient Chinese (inventors of paper). Others, like e-books and online reference works, have entered the electronic age. In either form, books may provide

✔ An in-depth view and/or overview of your topic

✔ The considered thoughts of an expert in the field (the author or some-one the author quotes)

✔ A quick statistical snapshot (in almanacs, yearbooks, and other such ref-erence books, many of which are now also available online)

I love books, but then again I am an English teacher. Even so, I have to admit that they have their limitations:

✔ Print-on-paper books take a long time to publish, so the latest, up-to-the-minute story is not going to appear in a book between two covers.

✔ Books may be expensive.

✔ They go out of print fairly quickly, and then they're harder (but not impossible) to find.

✔ They make your backpack feel like you're carrying chunks of rock.

You're more likely to find books that suit your research needs if your topic is literary or historical, or if you're looking for a summary or basic explanation of a scientific topic (not the latest discovery). Books also help with topics that require the kind of analysis that can be completed only over a long period of time — the ups and downs of the business cycle, the reaction of the stock market in times of national crisis, and so on.

Books may be useful even if your topic is a current event or issue. The seeds of the present may have roots in the past, and if so, somebody probably wrote about your topic and published it as a book. You may find yourself reading books for background material and then turning to other sources for the latest developments.

Regardless of your age, for a rapid overview of your topic, check out a chil-dren's or young-adult book on the subject. A few minutes of reading provides a quick summary of the most important ideas. General encyclopedias (the ones that are printed on paper or their electronic cousins on CD or the Web) also take you for a quick tour through the subject you're researching. Even subject-area encyclopedias (*The Encyclopedia of Root Vegetables*) may pro-vide an overview of that particular area of interest, though of course they go into greater depth than the all-purpose reference books. (For more informa-tion on locating books for your research paper, see Chapter 6.)

Magazine and journal articles

What's the difference between a magazine and a journal? "A couple of hun-dred bucks a year in subscription fees" is the simple but frequently true answer. The more complicated answer is that magazines are intended for the general public and journals are written by and for experts, or at least readers who have mastered the basics of the subject. A magazine may have a general interest article on the census entitled, "Why We Count," but a journal covers the census with articles like "Multi-Variable Analysis of a Random Sampling of Census Data, 1830-2000."

Magazines and journals may be very useful sources of information because of the following factors:

- Since they come out relatively frequently and fairly soon after the articles were written, the information is more up-to-date.

- They may publish a greater variety of writers, not just the esteemed elders of the field.

- They may be cheaper than books (but see note on journal prices at the beginning of this section).

Of course, I also have to point out the downside:

- Magazines and journals fold faster than a pleated skirt, and back issues disappear with equal speed. You may find out *about* the perfect article, but not necessarily find the article itself.

- Libraries' budgets are limited, so your local library may not have *The Journal of Dreams*, or whatever is the journal of your dreams.

- Not all magazines employ fact checkers, and many employ freelance writers of varying degrees of expertise. The information may be unreliable.

Beleaguered researcher, take heart: Libraries often have back issues of magazines and journals, either on paper or on *microfilm* or *microfiche* (photos of the articles that may be read on special machines). Chapter 6 explains how to locate back issues in libraries. More and more magazine and journal articles are also available online, and some of them are free. Also, many libraries that subscribe to large databases of articles and provide the service to library patrons for free or for a small fee. Check out "Electronic sources" in this section for a quick rundown of what's available. Chapter 5 shows you how to find magazine and journal articles on the Web.

Newspapers

Once, a journalist speaking to my class described the hectic atmosphere in his newsroom and the steps involved in publishing a daily paper. "I don't know how it ever comes out," he said. "It is a miracle that so much information can be printed every day." Miracle or not, newspapers provide the researcher with insights not available anywhere else:

- Most newspapers are daily publications, and some major papers, like my hometown rag, *The New York Times,* have a couple of editions every day. When you read an article, you're probably getting the undigested, you-are-there stuff. For history papers, this perspective is invaluable.

- ✔ Needless to say, you can turn to newspapers for the latest statistics, current policies, and most recent events.

- ✔ Newspapers provide a glimpse of the total reality of a particular time and place.

- ✔ Newspapers are cheap! (However, reprints of old articles are not always cheap.)

Newspapers have disadvantages too:

- ✔ If you're writing about stem-cell research, you may end up plowing through five months' worth of daily articles before you get to the one you want: President George W. Bush's decision to limit federal funding in this field. If your topic is the decision itself, all those articles may be helpful because you can follow the process, track the influence of interest groups, and so forth. But if all you want to know is what he decided, 99 percent of what you read is a waste of time. Newspapers seldom summarize; they report what happened that day . . . and the next day . . . and the next.

- ✔ Many smaller papers aren't online; you have to visit the newspaper's headquarters (if the paper still exists) or a very large library and page through yellowing piles of paper (or squint at dimly lit microfilm). Plus, the really old stuff may not exist at all.

- ✔ Reporters write and editors edit at lightning speed because the paper has to come out today! If an error creeps in — and errors do — it won't be corrected until the next day or even later, if at all. If you are reading an article from May 30, you may miss the one from June 15 explaining that Governor Flutterblub did not in fact veto the spending bill as the paper had previously reported.

If you don't have access to the Internet at home, investigate the public library. Many libraries have electronic databases of major newspapers that let you read full-text articles at a computer terminal.

Pamphlets and newsletters

The article your chess club writes today, "Smart Moves by Chess Players Lead to State Championship," may be a source tomorrow for someone writing a paper entitled, "Chess-Team Membership as a Predictor of Future Success." Especially now that desktop publishing has made the process so easy, every organization under the sun, from the Anteater Association to Zookeepers of Zimbabwe, publishes a newsletter and maybe a couple of pamphlets. Lots of libraries keep files of these materials, usually stuffed into manila folders in a very dusty corner. The organizations themselves are often willing to supply copies of their publications for free or for a small charge.

How many tons of information do you want?

Be careful what you ask for — you may actually get it. Years ago when I was writing a book on the pros and cons of gun control, I wrote to a number of organizations asking for books and pamphlets on the subject. A week later, a large brown truck pulled up to my building and unloaded a couple of cartons of material. The following week another truck pulled up . . . and then another. You get the picture. At the time I was one of three people living in a fifth-floor walk-up apartment with only one closet. I had to carry all those cartons of material up five flights of stairs and figure out where to stow them. Then I had to read it all! Not to mention all the stuff that arrived after the book was already in print. In fact, to this day an envelope still shows up from time to time! Moral of the story: When you ask for information, be as specific as possible and provide a date for the end of the project. With luck, the organization will winnow the information for you and stop after the paper is complete.

Pamphlets and newsletters offer several advantages to the researcher:

- ✔ The material is usually free or cheap.
- ✔ The information comes from people who are directly involved in the subject.
- ✔ Most pamphlets and newsletters are current, with up-to-date facts.

Now for the downside:

- ✔ Quality control is an issue. The organization probably has a point of view, and the material may reflect that bias.
- ✔ Dedicated volunteers write much of this sort of literature. You have no way of knowing whether the editor has the heart to reject an article lovingly crafted by a co-worker just because the piece is inaccurate.
- ✔ Few periodical indexes list pamphlets and newsletters. The International Baked Goods Appreciation Society may send you three breadboxes full of information, but you have to read every last issue of their newsletter to find the one entitled, "Scones, Not Just for Scots Anymore."

The age of the electronic pamphlet and newsletter has arrived. (Be still my beating heart!) Lots of organizations pour the energy that used to go into newsletters and pamphlets into Web sites. Check out the "Electronic sources" section later in this chapter to get an idea what's out there. Chapter 5 explains exactly how to find the Web sites you need for your paper.

Published research papers

Yes! You too could see your work on file someday, a source for the doctoral dissertation candidate who is also studying "Sediments of the Cretaceous." Research papers written on the postgraduate level are often published online or collected in bound volumes in university libraries. For information about the online versions, see Chapter 5. Chapter 6 explains how to track down the printed, bound papers.

Electronic sources

Accessing an on-ramp to the most popular road ever constructed (the information superhighway) provides you with a wealth of material for all sorts of research projects. But the home computer isn't the only path to electronic sources; many local and school libraries maintain electronic, full-text collections of magazine and newspaper articles and pay-per-use, online databases. (Sometimes they're free to library-card holders, even when working at home.) Even without a library card, if you're willing to open your wallet, you can access these pay-databases through your own home computer.

The amount of information available through electronic resources can be overwhelming. Not to worry: In Chapter 5 I tell you how to find what you need without drowning in sources.

The advantages of electronic sources include:

✔ Source material may be posted instantly. For the absolute latest data, check an electronic source.

✔ Anyone with a computer and access to the Internet can post information on the World Wide Web, so experts on things like antique lace from Provence, who may be unprofitable for mainstream publishers because the market for their work is too small, have a chance to show what they know.

✔ You can walk around without looking like the Hunchback of Notre Dame. Just select the information from the source that you need, click "copy," and then "paste" (another click) the material to a file on your computer. You're done! No heavy book bags to lug around the campus. (Be sure to credit the original source. For tips on avoiding plagiarism, see Chapter 10.)

Nothing's perfect, including the electronic media. Here's the bad news:

✔ Anyone (and I do mean anyone) can post something on the Web. Much of the material you find on the Web has not been checked for accuracy. Let your motto be *Downloader beware.*

✔ Books that haven't been taken out of the library since the wheel was invented *look* old. Besides, you can always check the copyright date in a book. But everything on the Web looks new and shiny, even outdated material. Once again, the rule is *Downloader beware*.

✔ Not everything on the Internet is free; some sites charge entrance fees ranging from practically nothing to if-you-have-to-ask-you-can't-afford-it. Some of the best online databases cost a bundle.

✔ Are you a Webaholic, depending on your computer for everything? Okay, most of the time this addiction is harmless — until the Internet service provider starts thanking you "for your patience" while it deals with "an interruption in service." If you get one of these messages and you've left all your research until the last minute (which always seems to be a minute after the traditional library closes), you're in trouble.

✔ The Web contains *so much* information that you may assume that it contains *all* the information on your topic. Not so. Traditional ink-and-paper sources may be better for some research.

Now that you know the pros and cons of electronic sources, here's a brief guide to the major players. (A more in-depth discussion on researching with electronic sources is in Chapter 5.)

The Internet

These days the World Wide Web, which I discuss in the next section, has overshadowed the Internet in the public's mind (if the public has a mind — every election season I start to wonder). But the Internet is still around, underlying and supporting the Web. Whenever one computer communicates with another — sending or receiving data — the Internet makes the transmission possible. If you access one of the pay-for-use databases like Dialog (discussed a little later in this section), send or receive a file, or communicate by e-mail, you're using the Internet.

You'll probably research via the Internet if you

✔ Send or receive e-mail about your topic

✔ Need specialized information, especially from technical or scholarly journals, via electronic databases

✔ Check online library catalogues via Telnet (a text-only form of access)

The World Wide Web

Colorful pictures and clickable links tell you that you're navigating the World Wide Web. In the virtual online world, the Web is a subsection of the Internet and has a similar structure. (Picture a net and a web; they both have a power-sharing pattern, not a top-down hierarchy.) Each stop on the Web is a *site,* or *Web site*. Who posts Web sites? The government, organizations, educational institutions, companies, publications, and private individuals. In other words, anyone with a computer and a desire to publish (and publicize).

Web sites have a *home page,* the first page you see when you arrive at a site. Most sites have many other pages, which you access by way of mouse clicks. But Web sites generally aren't constructed in a linear way (they don't go from page 1, to page 2, to page 3, and so on). Computer users browse through the pages that are interesting or helpful, clicking new pages or links to other sites in whatever order strikes their fancy.

This lack of order means that getting lost on the Web is unbelievably easy. See Chapter 8 for tips on keeping track of your Web searches.

What type of research can you do on the Web? You can

- ✔ Read material posted by organizations, publications, and experts in the field
- ✔ See topic-related photos, maps, artwork, film clips, and other visuals
- ✔ Listen to relevant audio material, such as speeches, music, and newscasts
- ✔ Copy and paste notes directly from a Web site into a word-processing file

Newsgroups

Imagine 450 people who are all passionately interested in your research paper topic, "The Pinhole Camera as an Artistic Medium." Some of them know a lot, and some of them know very little (all of it wrong). Now, imagine that those 450 people are in the same room, talking about pinhole cameras. Would you like to listen in? You can. The Web is home to thousands and thousands of such focused conversations, which are called *newsgroups.* You can search for a newsgroup on your topic (pinhole cameras, for example) and then search for one part, or *thread,* of the conversation (portraiture, perhaps), or you can read at random. With this type of research you can

- ✔ Find out what real people think about your topic. Some of those real people may even be the recognized authorities on the subject
- ✔ Ask questions and get a ton of answers, some of which may be right
- ✔ Put forth your pet theories, to be validated or shot down

Many newsgroups (but not all) have coordinators who try to impose some sort of quality control, but they face an uphill battle. Newsgroups are open 24/7, and many coordinators have other jobs and an occasional hour of private life outside the newsgroup. Also, the coordinator of a newsgroup may screen out something that you're interested in. The moral again: *Downloader beware.* Don't accept everything you read on the screen as gospel truth without double-checking the information, and don't assume that you have the whole story.

Mailing lists

Mailing lists, sometimes called *listservs* because of a software program that tracks them, are similar to newsgroups. Fans of a particular subject converse via e-mail with each other. You must subscribe to a mailing list, and once you have, you receive new messages as they are posted. The advantages and disadvantages of mailing lists are about the same as for newsgroups, but mailing lists are generally more controlled. Moderators attempt to screen out the crazies, but you have no protection from postings that are simply wrong. Also, depending upon how active the group is, you may receive a flood of e-mails that you never have time to read.

Online newspapers

Want to read what *The New York Times* or *The Washington Post* has to say about yesterday's poll, the one you want to include in your paper on "Polls: Who Asks the Dumbest Questions"? Check out their Web sites and then dig a little deeper. What position has *The Navajo Times* taken on polling? How about *El Heraldo de Aragon* from Spain? Or papers from Portugal, Indonesia, and South Africa? Read them on the Web.

Most of these sites allow access to recent news stories for free. Some newspaper sites maintain archives going back a few months or even a few years (though depth is rare), but you may be charged for your work in the archives. Some sites allow you to search by keyword; in others you have to browse until you find something useful. Chapter 5 guides the way to the best newspaper sites and explains how to search them.

Check newspaper Web sites in order to

✔ Read papers that are not sold in your neighborhood (or country)

✔ Search for articles pertaining to your topic

✔ Read the news-behind-the-news — stories that the print version of the paper didn't have room for (Not all sites provide this background information, but many do.)

✔ Send a question via e-mail to a reporter

Online magazines, zines, and journals

Like newspapers, many popular magazines have established a presence on the Web. Some publications — *zines* — appear only in electronic form. And electronic publishing has been a boon to low-budget, scholarly (Did you ever notice that those two words seem to be synonyms?) publications. You can read some for free, but others charge a fee. Either way, you can find more journals on the Web than in most major libraries. And you don't have to be quiet while you read them.

Check these Web sites in order to

- ✔ Access publications not available in your local library
- ✔ Search for current, in-depth, and advanced information by experts in the field
- ✔ Save money (maybe) in subscription and photocopy charges

Chapter 5 tells you how to find the journal or magazine (or zine) that fits your topic.

Digital libraries

The cave people who carved the first publications into handy rocks didn't worry much about preserving their work, perhaps because they were more worried about preserving their own skins. But modern librarians must consider the lifespan of the material in their charge. Paper crumbles, books come unglued, and photos fade. One solution? Digital libraries. Only a fraction of the millions of words written throughout history have been placed on the Web, but more appear every year. If you are writing about a classic work of literature, you may find an electronic version of the full text. Also, many libraries with rare photo collections and artifacts now display highlights of their collections on the Web. Digital libraries help you with your research paper by allowing you to

- ✔ Read books you do not own and cannot buy
- ✔ Check for a certain word or phrase in a book without an index, allowing you to zero in quickly on the relevant section
- ✔ View images relating to your topic
- ✔ Block off sections that you want to quote so that you can "copy" and "paste" them into a word-processing note file or into the finished paper ("Copy" and "paste" are two computer commands.)

Online library catalogues

About a million years ago when I was young, I had to walk all over New York City, visiting public and university libraries, to complete my research. In each library I'd check the little index cards filed in oak cabinets, the library catalogue. Now, all I have to do is check the libraries' online catalogues. No oak cabinet, no index cards, and no sore feet at the end of the day! Many major research institutions and even some smaller organizations have electronic catalogues on the Internet. You can check their listings to see whether a particular book is available; sometimes you can borrow the book via interlibrary loan. (More on interlibrary loans appears in Chapter 6.) Online catalogues will be helpful to you, if you

- ✔ Don't know which books were written on your topic
- ✔ Need an out-of-print book

✔ Want to check information for a bibliography or footnote

✔ Want to identify the experts in the field

✔ Want to learn whether any of the libraries in the area own the book you need

Real people

Researchers always have their noses in a book, right? Wrong. Some of the best information comes from actual, breathing human beings. You'll find them in newsgroups or on mailing lists (see the "Electronic sources" section earlier in this chapter). You may also find them by contacting organizations that have an interest in your topic. When I was writing about the use of animals in laboratories, for example, I wrote to the Humane Society, to People for the Ethical Treatment of Animals, and to the Center for Alternative Testing, among other groups. I asked for the name of an expert who was willing to sit for an interview. Sixteen hours of tape and one day-long visit to a research laboratory later, I had reams of information for my project. Interviews in person, over the phone, and by e-mail will be useful to you if you want to

✔ Hear about firsthand experiences

✔ Gather an expert's opinion of some aspect of your topic

✔ Include original quotations in your paper

Interviews also present problems:

✔ An expert may agree to sit for an interview on May 5, close to your deadline of May 20, but not impossible. Then, on May 5, you may get an e-mail saying that June 10 is more convenient.

✔ Interviews are very time-consuming. You have to find knowledgeable people, set up appointments, prepare intelligent questions, conduct the interview, and review the tape or notes. And then you sometimes find that you have gathered no new insights into the topic.

✔ Just because someone is willing to talk with you doesn't mean that everything he or she says is accurate. Human memory may change or fade over time. Even with an eyewitness, you have to check facts.

I include a step-by-step guide to interviews — how to find the interview subjects, how to formulate questions, and how to take notes — in Chapter 7. Chapter 16 explains how to punctuate the interview quotations that you weave into your text.

Audio-visual sources

Are you researching the ancient South American civilizations? Would it help to visit a Mayan ruin or an Aztec altar? You bet. You may not be able to afford the plane fare, not to mention the time away from home, but you can view these far-off places anyway thanks to a thoughtful filmmaker and the video library that carries her work. Similarly, most public and school libraries have audio collections. If you are studying the modern civil rights movement, you'll understand the emotions of the era better if you listen to the historic "I Have a Dream" speech given by Dr. Martin Luther King, Jr. Audio-visual sources add to your paper by:

✔ Showing three-dimensional views of places, procedures, and art works

✔ Giving you the sights and/or sounds of important people or historic events

✔ Allowing you to listen to experts talk about their subjects

Now for the downside:

✔ Audiovisual material does not normally come with a table of contents. You may have to watch 15 hours of a series on Op Art to find the 15-second clip on the painter you're writing about. CDs and audiotapes, of course, are often divided into tracks. Even so, you won't be able to locate the portion of the track that you want without listening to the whole thing. Fortunately, as technology develops, more "searchable" audiovisual material is becoming available. But these hi-tech items are still the exception, not the rule.

✔ When you do find a useful audio-visual clip, you may have to translate what you're seeing and hearing into words on the page. Some paper-assigners may accept hypertext documents (with clickable links to audio-visual material), but others want plain old ink and paper. Photocopies of art works or stills from a tape or movie may be inserted into your paper, but something is lost in the process.

Firsthand collection of data

If you are writing a laboratory report or a science research paper about an experiment you conducted, you've spent some time measuring, watching, sniffing, questioning, and recording. The data that you gathered becomes part of the research material in your report or paper. You may also have data from other researchers, reported in a survey of relevant experiments at the beginning of your paper.

See Chapter 1 for a description of laboratory reports and science research papers. Also, check out Chapter 12 for more detail on how to write a science research paper.

You may also have firsthand data if you've sat in on a focus group for an advertising campaign, conducted a poll for a politician, or watched an expert in action in his or her field. Your observations are raw material for your research paper that explains how the product should be pitched (soap powder or congressional candidate), how the flamethrower functioned, and how the lion tamer dealt with an unruly animal. Firsthand observations add

✔ Proof for your scientific hypothesis or thesis

✔ Interesting anecdotes to liven up your writing

✔ Immediacy to your arguments

What could be bad about experimental data? Plenty:

✔ Your material is only as good as the observational powers of the experimenter. If you go out for coffee during a crucial moment, your paper may reflect the wrong conclusion because the data is flawed.

✔ You may misinterpret the data because the design of the experiment is faulty. Once, for a test of children's intelligence, children were left alone in a room with a tasty chunk of chocolate that was just out of reach. The experiment measured how quickly the kids figured out how to get the candy. One child never reached the candy at all and was graded poorly. What the experimenters did not know was that the child was allergic to chocolate!

✔ Gathering firsthand data may be expensive and time-consuming.

Distrusting What You Find: A Guide to Evaluating Sources

A few years ago, I was working on a writing project that called for a particular statistic: the number of babies born addicted to crack/cocaine. The first source I checked had the answer: 350,000. So did the second source: 35,000. Sigh. The life of a researcher is never easy. If you do enough research, I guarantee that something like my differing-answer dilemma will happen to you. And if you do any research at all, you have to be concerned with the quality of your sources. (How many babies were born addicted to crack/cocaine? I have no idea. I solved the problem by explaining that estimates ranged from 35,000 to 350,000, giving the source for each number.)

Whether you are reading a book, scanning an article, or clicking on a Web site, you have to evaluate the source. The following sections offer a handy guide explaining how to find out what's good and what's not.

Check the publisher

Who's putting the information out there? For printed material, is the publisher someone you recognize? If not, check what else the company publishes. Also investigate what the reviewers say about the company.

On the Web, check who maintains the site. Is it an individual or an organization? A governmental department? A company? A school or university? You've got no guarantees that material from any of those groups is reliable. But in general, if the institution maintaining the site is reputable, the site should be also.

In Chapter 5, I list some of the more reliable starting points for Web research.

Online databases (see "Stalking the Wild Source: A Field Guide" earlier in this chapter for more information) and subject catalogues (see Chapter 5) generally screen the content for you. Nothing's foolproof, but you can probably rely on the material that you get from them.

Check the date

Printed material has a copyright date and/or an issue date. If you're studying the myths of ancient Greece, recent dates may not matter (although with a later date, you get the benefit of the latest scholarly thought on your subject). But if you're researching the market share of major clothing retailers, you definitely need the most recent material.

A Web site may tell you when a particular item was posted, but not when the item was written. Don't assume that material that *looks* current *is* current, unless you know for sure.

Check the author

Do you know anything about the author? The jacket blurb will tell you some things; reference sources such as *Contemporary Authors, Current Biography,* and reviews will tell you more. You can also check the author's list of publications in one of the online bookstores. If you know nothing about the author, don't automatically assume the worst. One of the best facets of the Internet is its democratic approach: People that the publishing establishment may have overlooked have a chance to strut their stuff on the Web. But if you don't know anything at all about the author and you've getting some really weird information from his or her writing, you should probably not put it in your paper until you have confirmation from a second source. (Even that's no guarantee: The second source may simply be quoting the first one! Check a couple of other sources, and review the author's credentials as described previously.)

Check the organization

If the author is anonymous, but you know which organization published the material, consider the organization's mission. If the Society to Outlaw Wool Gathering (SOWG) writes that the average sheep cries for ten minutes after being sheared, you have to wonder whether the organization is being completely objective in its report. Try to find out something about the organization from an independent source.

Don't assume that the name of an organization or a Web site tells you the beliefs of the group or of the author. Some hate groups have cleverly concealed their viewpoints with names that seem to suggest an opposing idea.

Always cite your sources. If the source is wrong, you may get in trouble for relying on poor screening skills, but at least you won't be penalized for mistaken information. The original source takes the blame.

Check the language

Are you pro-choice? Pro-life? Anti-abortion? Anti-choice? Pro-abortion? The terms you choose indicate something of your ideas. (For the record, people who believe that abortion is wrong generally call themselves "pro-life" and refer to the opposing group as "pro-abortion." People who support legalized abortion refer to the other side as "anti-choice" and call themselves "pro-choice.") You shouldn't discount a source simply because it expresses a point of view, but you should consider that point of view when you evaluate the information the source is presenting.

The more sources you check, the more likely you are to spot biases and mistaken information. Chances are someone has rebutted the arguments you've read in one magazine, assuming a basis exists for a challenge to the information. Similarly, if you are reading a posting in a newsgroup or from a mailing list (see the section, "Stalking the Wild Source: A Field Guide," earlier in this chapter for definitions), read *all* the postings in the thread. Someone claiming that the earth was created in 1965 will probably be challenged by a couple of readers. If you follow the whole thread, you see the original information *and* the correction.

You don't have to read the whole thing

At some point during your 15th straight hour of research, you may find a 583-page book, *Macramé in History,* that looks perfect for your project on the history of macramé. Before you tote it home from the library, and before you read all 583 pages, read something much shorter: the table of contents. Also glance through the index. You may find that the book really *is* perfect, or you may find that the title is misleading. For example, *Macramé in History* may cover the reaction of art critics to macramé, not the changes in technique that interest you. The table of contents should guide you to the, well, contents. Similarly, if you look up "weaving techniques" in the index and find nothing, you may decide not to be the very first person ever to take *Macramé in History* out of the library.

Chapter 5

Surfing Safari: Researching Online

I spent an hour in Kenya and then dallied in the American Southwest, specifically in the Navajo Nation. I glanced at Harlem in the 1920s before roaming through a Gothic cathedral. When the phone interrupted me, I was taking in the big picture — and I mean The Big Picture — viewing our planet from a satellite in space.

Before the Internet and the World Wide Web, such a range of experience would be beyond the reach of any one person. Now, surfing the globe from the comfort of your home or office is commonplace. And while the information superhighway is a great way to tour the wonders of the world, this path is an even better way to research your paper. But be warned: You can get lost in the virtual research world and easily drown in too much information.

In this chapter I tackle the specifics of electronic research: how to define a search that retrieves relevant information. I explain how to use search engines and subject catalogues to find what you need. I also describe some of the best online databases and give you the antidote to information overload.

Creating an Effective Search

Random travel — guessing at a site address and typing it in — is fun, but the results depend partly on luck. You may spend a lot of time hunting and still come up empty. A much better tactic is to look for information with a planned search. But, as we say in New York, there are searches and then there are *searches*. How happy you are with the results depends upon how well you define the *search terms* — the words you ask the computer to look for.

In this section I explain how to create an effective search. (In later sections of this chapter, "Taking You Where You Want to Go: Search Engines and Subject Catalogues" and "Searching Online Databases," I tell you where to use the searches that you create.)

In general you've got two basic options for searches — simple and advanced.

Simple searches

Suppose you're researching the plays of the seventeenth-century French dramatist Molière. If you type "play" in the search box for AltaVista (a general search engine described in the next section, "Taking You Where You Want to Go: Search Engines and Subject Catalogues"), you get 1,288,080 hits, including many that have nothing to do with Molière:

- Children's *play*
- How to *play* music on your new electric harmonica (somebody posted an instruction manual)
- The odds of winning when you *play* lotto
- Animated basketball *plays*
- Current Broadway *plays* (including reviews and how you can't get tickets unless you know someone famous and/or own a bank)
- Every amateur theatrical in the world

Somewhere in the list are references to Molière's plays, but where? A dart thrown in a dark library is more likely to hit a Molière play than your mouse is at this point.

Your next tactic may be to search for "Molière." Now the list is better — only 33,500 hits — but it still includes

- The life of Molière
- Descriptions of 7,605 college courses that include works by Molière
- An offer to find missing relatives and draw "your Molière family tree"
- References to dozens of online bookstores that sell Molière's works
- Announcements of every amateur theatrical in the world that ever presented a Molière play, including a second-grade production of *The School for Wives*
- Reviews of all those amateur theatricals, including the second-grade production of *The School for Wives*

✔ The complete text of Molière's plays in various languages

✔ General surveys of French literature and history that mention Molière at least once

✔ Critical works on Molière

This last category — critical works — is the one that interests you. But by the time you find it, your hair will be gray, if it wasn't already. (Adding to the fun of searching, your result list is *not* sorted into categories — the second-grade play is next to a link to a bookseller, which is next to a link to a college course entitled "Post-Molière French Literature," and so on).

Now suppose that you start a new search by typing in *"Molière's plays"* — both words, plus the quotation marks. You may lose the life of Molière and surveys of French history, but you still end up with all the others, including the second-grade play. Furthermore, you may lose sites that talk about "the plays of Molière."

Some search engines, faced with a search request like *Molière's plays,* search for sites that include references to either "Molière" or "plays" or both. You get a gazillion hits. If you place quotation marks around the words, the search engines goes after the entire phrase. Typing *"Molière's plays"* (quotation marks included) gives you sites that include those two words in exactly that order. Other search engines assume that you intend to search for the phrase even when you don't place quotation marks. Click the "help" icon on the search home page for a ruling on quotation marks.

You could try other phrases enclosed in quotation marks, such as:

✔ "plays of Molière"

✔ "criticism of Molière"

✔ "criticism of Molière's plays"

But there's a better way. Time for an advanced search.

Advanced searches

You can activate an advanced search by clicking on a little button labeled (surprise) "advanced search," "custom search," or some similar term. When you click on the advanced-search button, you get a little form to fill out. Depending upon the search engine, the form allows you to specify which words must be included, which must not be included, which exact phrase must appear, and so forth. In this section I explain how to design the most effective advanced search.

Advanced searches rely on what mathematicians call Boolean logic, which in turn is based on three little words — "and," "or," and "not." In an advanced search for the plays of Molière, I fill in the blank asking for "All of these words" with

    All of these words: Molière play

The computer searches for sites that include both words — "Molière" and "play." (Notice the Boolean word "and.") Now I don't have to worry about sites that tell me how to *play* lotto, unless somebody named Molière is a star gambler. I also lose the French history sites, unless they include places where a play is performed. I can put as many words in the "all of these words" blank as I wish:

    All of these words: Molière play criticism

My result list should include only sites that mention all three words. Here I lose the sites carrying the text of Molière's plays as well as the second-grade production of *The School for Wives,* unless the second grade was the target of criticism for its overemotional acting. I'm probably still picking up sites that allow me to buy books of criticism of Molière's plays. That's fine if I'm in the market for old-fashioned print sources, but if I want online information only, those sites clutter up the list. The solution? The blank that asks for "none of these words" — the Boolean term "not." Take a look at this search:

    All of these words: Molière play criticism

    None of these words: price

The computer looks for sites that mention "Molière," "play," and "criticism," but it rules out sites that mention "price." Down go the booksellers.

Another useful blank is "exact phrase." The computer searches for all the words I type in this blank in the same order they're written. In other words, the blank acts like a set of quotation marks. If I type

    criticism of Molière's plays

the computer looks for sites that include that phrase. However, it doesn't look for sites that include phrases like "criticism of the plays of Molière." So use this blank only when you're sure you want pinpoint accuracy.

So far I haven't mentioned the Boolean term "or," which appears as a blank labeled "any of these words." Suppose I'm looking for good old Molière, and I'm interested in criticism or biography. Now I may formulate my search this way:

    All of these words: Molière play

    Any of these words: criticism biography

My results include only sites that mention "Molière" and "play" and either "biography" or "criticism."

Some search engines (computer programs that actually carry out the search you've designed) want you to type the words "and," "not," and "or." Some use math symbols: + for "and," – for "not." In this system I'd type

Molière + play + criticism – price

to get results that include these three words: "Molière," "play," and "criticism" — but not the word "price." Click the "help" section of the search engine's home page for instructions.

If you're not sure what you're looking for, a general search may give you a few ideas. But don't waste too much time on general searches. Before you sit down at the computer, ask yourself a couple of questions. What exactly do you want to find out? What will your ideal site include? Then define your search as precisely as possible.

Once you find something worthwhile, don't let it get away! Most *browsers* — the computer programs that take you through the Web — include a command to bookmark a site. The "bookmark" command in your browser may be called "add to favorites." When you "bookmark" a site or "add [the site] to favorites," your computer saves the address of the site in a file. Then, you can always click on the saved address and go right back to the corresponding site. Don't assume that you'll remember where the site is or the series of clicks that got you there without a bookmark. The Web has millions of pages and no roadmap. (For more information on record keeping, see Chapter 8.)

Little things mean a lot, especially in searches

A couple of tricks can shave minutes (or even hours) from each online search and yield better results:

- If one search term doesn't give you what you need, try a synonym or a related word. For example, suppose you are writing a paper about illegal drugs (that's *about*, not *on* illegal drugs). In addition to typing "illegal drugs," try "drug abuse" and "overdose."

- A little star — an asterisk — may also help you. For a paper on automobiles, you can

search separately for "automobiles," "automotive," "automaker," and so on. If you type "autom*" the computer searches for all the words beginning with those five letters, regardless of the ending.

Put the more unusual terms first when you search. For example, the search engine will hunt more quickly for "Navajo Indians" than for "Indians Navajo."

Taking You Where You Want to Go: Search Engines and Subject Catalogues

Once you define the search, you have to find a way to carry it out. Not a problem! Lots of Web sites are ready and waiting to do your bidding. These sites are called *search engines* or *subject catalogues.* Searches engines and subject catalogues used to be located in separate Web sites, but now the distinction between the two is blurring. Search engines are programs that scoot all over the Web, indexing what they find. When you enter search terms, the search engine checks its index for matches and lists the positive results, or *hits.* Subject catalogues do pretty much the same thing, but instead of comparing your search terms to an index of everything on the Web, they check only the particular category or subject area you clicked (literature, science, business, and so on). Plus, most subject catalogues include only sites that have been screened by experts. If you use a search engine to check "Charles Dickens" for an English research paper, your list of hits will be almost endless. Mixed in with scholarly papers will be sites that say things like "Hi! I'm *Charles* Xanful and I've worked like the *dickens* to set up the best-darned Web site in the world. Click here to see my collection of prechewed bubble gum." If you search the "Literature" or "Humanities" category of a subject catalogue, your list will be shorter and perhaps more reliable.

When you go to any search site on the Web, you see a lot of ads (after all, they've got to pay the bills), category names (that's the subject catalogue), and a small, blank box next to a "search now" or "go" button. The blank box revs up the search engine. (The label on the button varies.) If you enter your topic in the blank box, the search engine gives you the results from anywhere on the Web. If you click a subject heading and then enter your search topic, only results from that category will be listed.

Some of the most popular and effective search engines/subject catalogues include the following:

- ✔ AltaVista (www.altavista.com)
- ✔ Google (www.google.com)
- ✔ Excite (www.excite.com)
- ✔ Yahoo (www.yahoo.com)
- ✔ Northern Light (www.northernlight.com)

Northern Light indexes the Web, but it also checks your topic in its "special collection" of articles that are not available to other search engines. Northern Light searches for free, but to see some of the documents it turns up, you have to pay a fee. The cost of each document is small — a few dollars for most of the articles. But if you're looking through a lot of material, the bill may rise quickly.

E-mail plus research

If you are one of the millions of people who send e-mail via America Online (AOL), Microsoft Network (MSN), or CompuServe, you have easy access to online searching. These Web sites are very user-friendly, and for beginning researchers, they're a godsend. On AOL, enter the keyword (a general subject or topic) and see where you end up. Or tune in to one of AOL's "channels," the company's word for subject catalogues. In MSN, look for the "search" blank on the home page or click on one of the subject categories. Then enter your search terms. If you're a CompuServe customer, check out the IQuest function, which takes you to some good research databases (including some that charge a fee).

Every search engine likes to bill itself as the "most complete" or "most comprehensive" tool for research. However, no search engine covers every single site on the Web. Checking everything on the Web is an impossible task, in my opinion, because the Web changes faster than Superman in a phone booth. Also, some sites are *gated* — not open to the general public. The search engine's checkers, which are called *spiders* because they crawl around the Web, can't get into most gated sites, so the content inside is not listed in search results. The best tactic, if you really need to know what's out there, is to run your search through more than one search engine. (Some super-sized search engines do this for you. See the "Traveling Express: Metasearch Engines" section later in this chapter.) If the free search doesn't turn up the answer to your prayer — well, to your question — you may consider prying open some of those gates with a little bit of cash. (For more on searching gated sites, see the section "Searching Online Databases" later in this chapter.)

Traveling Express: Metasearch Engines

Instead of typing the same topic in the search box of several different search engines, you can hit a *metasearch engine* and save wear and tear on your finger muscles. Metasearch engines run your question through a bunch of other search engines. However, the metas don't have some of the advanced search features of the regular search engines. (In the "Creating an Effective Search" section earlier in this chapter, I explain why hitting the "advanced search" button saves you time and annoyance by providing you with a more focused list of hits.) Still, for simple queries metasearch engines can be helpful. Here are a few of the best.

- ✔ Ask Jeeves (www.askjeeves.com)
- ✔ CNET Search.com (www.search.com)
- ✔ Ixquick Metasearch (www.ixquick.com)

Searching Online Databases

The Web gets the most publicity, but it's not the only game in town when it comes to online research. Before the Web was woven, databases of articles from newspapers, magazines, and journals were created. You can access these databases from any computer with an Internet connection. The catch is that you have to pay to use them. Some charge a fee per article; others require a subscription. The subscription databases are probably beyond the range of the average user (unless you're in the Bill Gates league of multimillionaires). However, many school, public, and company libraries subscribe to one or more databases, and those institutions may allow you to sign on for free. For descriptions, possible uses, and advantages of online databases, see Chapter 4.

If you're paying for each article you retrieve, designing an efficient search is crucial. You don't want to waste money on irrelevant hits! See the section "Creating an Effective Search" earlier in this chapter, for search tips that may save you time and money.

The following sections cover the major players in the online database world.

LexisNexis and Westlaw

These are the two big databases for legal information. LexisNexis (www.lexis-nexis.com) has two halves. The "lexis" part includes everything about law — the laws themselves, cases, law reviews, journals, and so forth. The "nexis" half has news, statistics, economics, and other items of interest to business. Westlaw (www.westlaw.com) sticks with the law. If you've ever hired a lawyer, you know that they charge a lot more than the rest of us mortals for every second of their time. Guess what? So do these legal databases. You can pay for each search or sign a contract for a lot of searches. (What? You need a lawyer to negotiate the contract? Now we're talking Really Big Bucks.) Some school or public libraries provide free access to these databases.

Dialog

Dialog (www.dialog.com) has a world-class database of scholarly, technical, and business-oriented material. Dialog also has its own strange language resembling cryptic notes from Transylvanian spies. Go to Dialog's home page and click on "library" for a list of Dialog's databases — about 600 in all — and instructions for using them. If they look relevant to your project, you may want to subscribe. In the old days you had to learn Dialog-ese — the

Transylvanian-spy language — as well as the special quirks of each individual database to conduct a Dialog search. Now, I'm happy to say, you can hunt in plain English with a "guided search" option. My advice is to take the guided search option!

Dow Jones Interactive

The Dow Jones Industrial Average is a fixture of the nightly business report on my television, and that fact gives you a clue to the nature of this site. If you're in business or if you're gambling the family jewels by investing in the stock market, you'll like Dow Jones Interactive (www.djinteractive.com), but you'll pay for the privilege. Dow Jones Interactive gives you business-related news from newspapers all across the United States and from foreign news services. It provides market research reports (so you can find out whether that semiconductor plant is a good place to invest your retirement fund), articles from all the major business journals, and statistics on a huge number of companies and industries.

OCLC FirstSearch

OCLC provides access to a broad range of databases on a variety of topics. Among its offerings are full-text articles, document ordering, electronic journals, World Wide Web links, and the holdings of many large libraries. If your library or company subscribes, ask the librarian or research department how to access OCLC FirstSearch.

ProQuest, EBSCO, and InfoTrak

ProQuest, EBSCO, and InfoTrak are the premier players in the database world. You need megabucks to subscribe, but fortunately many libraries subscribe to at least one. (Ask the librarian how to achieve access.) These databases provide articles (often in full text) from major newspapers and a spectrum of periodicals from general interest magazines to more scholarly journals.

Other helpful online databases

Here are a few smaller online databases, all providing the full text of articles:

- ✔ Columbia Granger's World of Poetry: Locates poems in anthologies and includes full text of and commentaries on the most frequently anthologized poems.

✔ Ethnic NewsWatch: A collection of articles from periodicals, including newspapers, that concentrate on issues of race and ethnicity.

✔ GenderWatch: Covers women's issues, stereotypes and gender roles, and the like.

✔ Gale Group Reference Databases: Particularly strong in the areas of biography, health, history, and literature.

✔ H. W. Wilson Web Databases: Access to general information as well as the gamut of information in all major subject disciplines.

✔ SIRS Knowledge Source: Full-text articles from these areas: social science, applied science (medicine, technology, engineering, and so on), physical science, arts and humanities, and current events.

Finding the Best of the Internet: Good Spots to Begin Your Research

In case all the search engines and subject catalogues I discuss earlier in this chapter aren't enough, in this section I provide a few more. Check the following headings to see what matches your project. The sites I describe in this section usually have a small blank box for search terms. Keep in mind that with those boxes you're sometimes searching the site itself and sometimes the entire Web. (Look for buttons labeled "help," "about us," or something similar for details.)

General reference sites

These sites provide names and numbers, facts and figures. If you're looking for the meaning of *polyglot,* a map of Turkey, the year Neil Armstrong first stepped on the moon, the author of *To the Lighthouse,* or about a zillion other things, general reference sites will help. These sites also offer other research possibilities (like articles or Web sites devoted to a particular topic) in many fields:

✔ The Internet Public Library: When you go to the Internet Public Library (www.ipl.org/ref), you see a drawing of a cute, little room with shelves labeled "reference"; "education"; "law, government, and political science"; "sciences and technology"; "arts and humanities"; and so on. Click on one of the labels and you're in a public library with a huge number of high-quality resources.

✔ The Virtual Public Library: No cute little room, but a valuable subject catalogue. In the Virtual Public Library (http://virtualpubliclibrary. com) experts in the field maintain each catalogue of Web pages and screen the sites for quality. Subject areas include everything from "agriculture" to "engineering" to "international affairs" to "science" and "humanities."

✔ FAQ Archives: Many Web sites devote a page to *FAQs* — Frequently Asked Questions. The FAQs provide a wealth of information — if you can find them. The FAQ Archives (www.faqs.org) help you search by topic or author. But keep in mind that FAQs are only as reliable as the people who write them. Downloader beware! Double-check the source for quality before accepting it as true. (For more information on evaluating sources, see Chapter 4.)

✔ Argus Clearinghouse: Argus (www.clearinghouse.net) maintains links to subject catalogues best suited for scholarly research. If you need the advanced stuff — the articles that interest experts in each field — Argus is a good place to begin your search. Click on the subject and then click on the subject catalogue that matches your topic.

Government sites

If you're a working U.S. resident, you pay for these sites with your taxes, so you may as well use them. (If you're not, welcome! Enjoy the free stuff.) The government of the United States (as well as the governments of states, cities, towns, and for all I know clusters of sheds) posts Web sites to hand out information.

✔ The Federal Government — FedWorld (www.fedworld.gov)

✔ U.S. Census Bureau (www.census.gov)

Literature and language

Ah, an area close to my heart. If you're writing about literature or linguistics, these sites are for you:

✔ Project Gutenberg (www.gutenberg.net)

✔ Bibliomania (www.bibliomania.com)

✔ Medieval and Classical Works (http://sunsite.berkeley.edu/OMACL)

These sites contain the full text of hundreds of classic works of literature. If you have more printer paper than sense, you can download *Pride and Prejudice, The Canterbury Tales,* and other works and read them for free. I doubt you'll choose that option, but these full-text sites are handy for quoting or for checking a section of a book without going to the library. Another good site,

Literary Resources on the Net (www.andromeda.rutgers.edu/~jlynch/Lit) leads you to literary information, including author biographies, of scholarly quality.

Science and math

Is your paper about the bubonic plague? Are you trying to understand chaos theory? Do you need to know the properties of a radioactive element or how a fuel cell functions? Try these sites.

The National Library of Medicine

At the National Library of Medicine (www.nlm.nih.gov) site you can click on "PubMed" to search for journal articles from the mid-1960's to the present, some of which are available as full-text. The same site leads you to "MedlinePlus," which contains medical information more suited to the non-MDs among us.

Science sites

Here are two sites that lead you to every branch of the sciences, from life sciences to technology to engineering and more:

- ✔ SciCentral (www.scicentral.com)
- ✔ The Scout Report (www.scout.cs.wisc.edu/report/sci-eng/current/index.html)

Math Research

You number people thought I forgot you, didn't you? Never fear. Go to www.scientific-search-engines.com (which is really a metasearch engine for all sorts of subjects) and head for the math categories. You can find every type of math you can imagine, and a few you can't.

Geography, history, politics, and social science

The general reference, government, and current events sites I describe elsewhere in this section may be good starting points for your research in these disciplines. Here are a couple of other likely spots:

- ✔ The Library of Congress (www.lcweb.loc.gov)
- ✔ The World Factbook (www.odci.gov/cia/publications/factbook/index.html)

Business and economics

Dow Jones Interactive, described elsewhere in this chapter, has terrific business information, but you do have to pay a fee. Here are additional business sites — some free, some not:

- Hoover's Online: This site (www.hoovers.com) gives you background information on companies in the United States and elsewhere. Some information is available for free, but not all.

- Dun and Bradstreet: You pay to use this site (www.dnb.com), but if you're serious about investing, Dun and Bradstreet can help. This site provides in-depth reports on companies and industries.

- Bizjournals.com: More than 40 local business journals are collected online at this site (http://bizjournals.bcentral.com).

Arts

Are you interested in a virtual tour of a Frank Lloyd Wright building? Would you like to see a Tang dynasty painting? Are you writing about dance or theater? Check out these sites:

- The Smithsonian (www.si.edu)
- Web Gallery (www.kfki.hu/arthp)
- Artcyclopedia (www.artcyclopedia.com)

Current events

Are you writing a paper about a current issue or recent event? Do you need to know how the media get information and report it? These sites will help:

- American Journalism Review (http://ajr.org)
- NewsLink Associates (http://newslink.org)

Note: The American Journalism Review and NewsLinks Associates maintain these sites for professional journalists, but you don't need a press pass to get in. You have to pay for some of the information, but free stuff is also available. At these sites you can search for a particular topic and read articles from all the major and some of the minor newspapers in the United States. These sites also include some magazines and international publications as well as broadcast media (television and radio stations).

Drowning in Information? How to Swim to Shore

Ten seconds into a Web search one dominant thought may cross your mind: "Help! I've got too much stuff! I'll never get through it all." No, you won't. But before your tears short out the computer, read these tips for coping with information overload:

- Resign yourself to the fact that no human being can read everything on the Web. You will find and read some things, but not all.

- Set a predetermined time limit for your search. When you reach that limit, stop. Look at the sites you've found and check out the most promising. If you have enough information for your paper, stop searching.

- Don't run your query through 15 search engines or 3 metasearch engines. One or two regular search engines or just one metasearch engine is plenty. You don't need to read everything, and you can't anyway.

- No matter how much research you do, someone will come along two minutes after you hand the paper in and say, "You mean you didn't check www.perfectpaper.com? Uh oh." Put earplugs in your ears and smile. The perfect Web site is like the horizon; you will glimpse it in the distance but *never* reach it.

Chapter 6

Working from Traditional Sources

These days the line between "traditional" and "high tech" has blurred. Internet/World Wide Web research, which I describe in Chapter 5, often sends me to a printed source. And when I visit my local public library, I may check its catalogue at a library computer or locate an article using one of the library's online databases.

My house has been connected to the Internet since people were still deciding whether to say "period com" or "dot com." ("Dot com," of course, won.) But in addition to the high-tech stuff, I have always found worthwhile research material in more traditional ways: by going to a library or bookstore and walking home with a pile of printed material.

The librarian is your friend

According to a popular stereotype, the average librarian is 162.2 years of age and has either no hair or a tightly wound gray bun. While frowning severely, the librarian spends most of the day stamping "Overdue! Penalty: Five Years in Prison!" on people's foreheads.

Not true! (Okay, some librarians *may* be balding or bunned, but hairstyle is *not* part of the job description.) A more accurate portrait of the average librarian includes these traits: highly educated, skilled at finding information on every possible topic, interested in helping researchers locate material, and hip to the latest trends in information technology. In other words, the librarian is a secret weapon just waiting to make your research paper a resounding success. Moral of the story: Make the librarian's desk an early stop when you visit the library to research your paper.

In this chapter I describe time-tested research materials — books, magazine and newspaper articles, pamphlets, papers, and so on. I tell you how to locate the material *without* the benefit of a connection to the Internet. (However, I point out when you're likely to find online versions of the same sources.) I also include some tips on locating photos and audio-visual resources.

Researching from Library Books

Somewhere on the bookshelves of the world is the volume that will solve all your research problems. But where? In one of three places: on the real shelves of the library or a bookstore, or on the virtual shelves of the Internet. Yes, the Internet. In this section I concentrate on one of the bricks-and-mortar spots, the library. In the "Finding Books in Bookstores" section also in this chapter, I tell you about one of my favorite pastimes, spending money on books. Check out Chapter 5 for information about online, full-text works of literature.

You probably have access to a couple of libraries: in your school or at your job site and in your community. Once you get to the library, it's likely that the Dewey Decimal System will help you find what you're looking for. Invented in the late nineteenth century by the not-too-modest Melvil Dewey, the Dewey Decimal System is used in most libraries to keep track of nonfiction books. (Fiction is usually off in its own little corner, filed alphabetically according to the author's last name.) The Dewey Decimal System divides books by subject. Don't bother learning the numbers of each subject area unless, of course, you want to be a librarian. You can always look up what you need, when you need it.

The Dewey Decimal System assigns numbers (in libraryspeak, *call numbers*) to all nonfiction books. The number is usually on the spine of the book and inside the front or back cover. The books are filed in numerical order. Libraries that don't use the Dewey Decimal System still assign call numbers to their holdings; the numbers just look different. When you're prowling through the shelves for a particular book, you need to know its call number.

A few libraries store the books away from the public. In those libraries you fill out a book request form — still with the call number — and hand the form in. A little while later your book surfaces, usually from the kind of dusty underground stacks haunted by the book-loving ghost in *Ghostbusters*.

Checking the catalogue

The best strategy for locating books is to check the *catalogue,* the list of the library's holdings. In the old days the catalogue was generally a lovely piece of wooden furniture with small drawers filled with *catalogue cards.* The cards listed the title, author, subject(s), and call number of each book. Some libraries still use catalogue cards (although a librarian told me recently that the catalogue card is "officially dead"). More and more libraries have computerized their catalogues. Instead of a little piece of cardboard, you check a listing on the screen. Regardless of the format, the information is the same for each book.

The computerized catalogues have a number of nifty features. In some you can click on one of the subject headings assigned to a book and find all the other books with the same subject headings. The computerized catalogue may also tell you whether the book is checked out and, if so, when it is due to be returned to the library.

Some libraries have computerized part but not all of their catalogues. The newer purchases may be in a computer database and the older material in those wooden drawers. With such a system, you have to check two separate places to find out what the library owns. Also, some libraries maintain two separate listings (on computer or on cards): one for the author or title and the other for the subject. Ask the librarian to explain the system in your library.

To search for material in the catalogue, look for any of these items, listed here with examples:

- **The author's last name:** Griswold, Aethelbert T.
- **The title of the book:** *A Tale of Two Noses*
- **The subjects:** Allergies, Plastic Surgery, Olfactory Sense

When you look up a title, look for the first word, but ignore *a, an,* and *the.*

Although each catalogue card contains all the data listed previously — author's name, book title, subject(s) — the data is listed differently depending on how you look up the information. If you know the author's name, look for the *author card* since it lists the author's name first. Figure 6-1 shows an author card (she said humbly) for one of my books, retrieved when I searched under the author's (my) name. On the *title card* in the catalogue, the title appears first, followed by the author's name and other information. You can also locate this book by its *subject cards.* The sample card, shown in Figure 6-1, tells you that *Science in Ancient Egypt* is listed under three subjects: "Science," "Egypt," and "Technology." Two of those subjects are subdivided: "Science" includes a "History" category, and "Egypt" includes a category devoted to history, which also has a subdivision for the ancient era. Within each division and subdivision, alphabetical order usually takes you right to the target. If the subdivision is a time period, chronological order gets you where you want to go.

Here are all the paths to this book:

- **Author:** Look up "Woods, Geraldine."
- **Title:** Look up "Science in Ancient Egypt."

✔ **Subject:** Look up "Science," and within that category, look under the letter "H" for "History."

✔ **Subject:** Look up "Egypt," and within that category, look under the letter "H" for "History." Within the "History of Egypt" category, look for "Ancient." (Try time order for this category — "Ancient" is probably the first subdivision, with later eras arranged after it.)

✔ **Subject:** Look up "Technology."

509.32 Woods, Geraldine
Science in Ancient Egypt.
New York: Watts, 1988.
Discusses the achievements of ancient
Egyptian science.
Science - History; Egypt - History - Ancient; Technology.
Includes Index

Figure 6-1:
An example
of an
author card.

No matter where you start, the book has the same call number, 509.32, which appears on the card or in the computer listing and on the book itself.

Many researchers who question the accuracy of online sources automatically place their trust in books. Bad idea! Don't assume that everything you find in a book is true, just because someone went to the trouble of printing it. Remember, the theory that space aliens constructed the pyramids was published in a book. One way to evaluate books is to read the reviews. Many libraries carry *Book Review Digest,* a multivolume work organized by date of publication and then by the author's name.

Brother, can you spare a book?

You've discovered the perfect book, the one that will answer every question you ever had about your topic. The only problem is that your library doesn't own the book, and you can't get it at the local bookstore because it's out of print. What's a deprived researcher to do? Ask about interlibrary loan. Many libraries have formed partnerships with others in the area — university or state libraries, perhaps, with many more resources than a small local institution can afford. With interlibrary loan, you fill out a form in your own library, and the staff forwards the request to a library that owns the work. A few days later the book arrives, usually by mail. When you're finished, you return the book to the local branch. One warning: Don't expect interlibrary loan to yield instant results. You have to wait for the local library to process the request, for the distant library to fill it, and for the postal service to deliver. Also, you may be charged a small fee.

Gathering search terms

If you know exactly which book is Mr. or Ms. Right for you, the search is simple. Just look for the title or the author. But if you don't know what's been written on your topic, you need to dig a little. Think of all the possible subject headings (also known as *keywords*) for your topic. If you're writing about teen acne, check "Acne" and "Teenager," as well as "Adolescence," "Teenage Years," "Skin Diseases," "Childhood Diseases," and "Dermatology." Some of these keywords may be arranged as subdivisions of a larger subject. For example, you may find "Childhood Diseases" and "Skin Diseases" as subdivisions of "Disease." Sometimes you can find great information in one chapter of a book that covers a larger field — perhaps a family medical guide, as in this example.

All research roads will not necessarily lead to the best source material, but *many roads will.* For the best results, approach the topic from several different directions with several different search terms.

Once you get a hit from your catalogue search, look at the subject headings that appear below the title and the author. Check all of these subject headings (keywords) for additional sources. For example, suppose your paper is about childhood in Victorian England. A friend gave you a book entitled *Victorian England: A Mother and Child Case Study.* (This isn't a real book, so don't try to find it in the catalogue.) The book looks great, chock full of relevant information. You check the library catalogue by looking up the title, and you find the catalogue card shown in Figure 6-2.

941.08 Victorian England: A Mother and Child
    Case Study.
               Displiou, Regina P.
               London: Batherqick Press. 1999.

Examines the lives of a typical mother and child in
    Victorian England.
Great Britain - History - Victorian Era; Child Psychology -
    Historical Studies; Motherhood

Figure 6-2:
An example
of a
title card.

Now you know that you should look under "Great Britain," subdivision "Victorian Era," for more books. You should also search "Psychology," subdivision "Historical Studies," and "Motherhood."

Some online catalogues allow you to look at a master list of subject headings. I've seen master lists of subject headings on paper as well, though these are less common. Scan the list of subject headings for possible search terms.

If you find a valuable book, flip through the last few pages. The author may have included a bibliography or a list of works cited. You may find some good books on that list. Also, some books are nothing *but* bibliographies — lists of all the works on a particular topic. Finding one of those volumes is the research equivalent of discovering a cure for baldness. You've got it made! For example, the *American Historical Association's Guide to Historical Literature* (Ed. Mary Beth Norton. 3rd ed. New York: Oxford UP, 1995) lists and briefly describes all the books that these historians think are worth your attention. The books are grouped by subject. A research gem! To search for bibliographies on the reference shelves, check the Dewey Decimal number 016. Or, look in the catalogue under the subject that interests you, and then check the subtopic "bibliography."

Locating the best reference books

Most libraries have a spot in the corner devoted to reference books. You can't take these volumes home (and you probably wouldn't want to since most of them weigh a ton), but you can read them in the library and photocopy the exciting parts. (See Chapter 10 for directions on how to keep your photocopying legal.) In this section I discuss a few types of reference works you may find helpful.

If I listed *all* the great reference books out there, *Research Papers For Dummies* would arrive by truck — one copy per vehicle. Think of this list as a sampling. Look through the reference section of your own library — and talk with your own librarian — for other suggestions.

Dictionaries

You've probably got at least a pocket dictionary in your house somewhere, but your library may own the mother-of-all-dictionaries, the giant-sized *Oxford English Dictionary,* which takes up an entire shelf. A smaller, abridged version has microscopic print and comes with its own magnifying glass. (You can also access an online version through a library or some online, pay databases. See Chapter 5 for more information about online databases.) The *OED,* as it is affectionately known, traces the history of a word, from its first use (explained with an example) through all the changes in the word's meaning, ending with the present day. Most libraries also own foreign language dictionaries, for those of you who *hablan* or *sprechen* other languages. (Those words mean *speak* in case you didn't take — or slept through — Spanish and German classes.)

The library also may own specialized, subject-area dictionaries. These volumes tell you more than you ever wanted to know about the terminology favored by the insiders of a particular field. Here's a sampling:

✔ **Arts**

- *The Harvard Concise Dictionary of Music and Musicians.* Ed. Don M. Randel. Boston: Harvard University Press, 1999.

- *The Oxford Dictionary of Art.* Ed. Ian Chilvers and Harold Osborne et al. 2nd ed., rev. New York: Oxford UP, 1997.

✔ **History and social science**

- *Dictionary of American History: From 1763 to the Present.* Peter Thompson. New York: Facts on File, 2000.

- *Dictionary of Race and Ethnic Relations.* Ed. Ellis Cashmore, et al. 4th ed. New York: Routledge, 1996.

✔ **Literature and language**

- *A Dictionary of Literary Terms and Literary Theory.* J.A. Cuddon. Revised by C.E. Preston. 4th ed. Malden, MA: Blackwell, 1998.

- *The Oxford Classical Dictionary.* Ed. Simon Hornblower and Antony Spawforth. 3rd ed. Oxford: Oxford UP, 1996.

✔ **Science, mathematics, and technology**

- *Dictionary of Computer Science.* Ed. Valerie Illingworth and John Dainteth. 4th ed. New York: Facts on File, 2000.

- *Concise Dictionary of Scientific Biography.* Ed. American Council of Learned Societies. 2nd ed. New York: Scribner's, 2000. (Includes mathematicians.)

✔ **Business**

- *Concise Dictionary of Business Management.* David A. Statt. 2nd ed. New York: Routledge, 1999.

Encyclopedias

Encyclopedias cover a lot of ground quickly; the general encyclopedias include short entries on everything from *abacus* to *zither.* You probably shouldn't write a paper based solely on information from a general encyclopedia, because this sort of reference work doesn't have the space to go into depth on any one topic. But for a fast introduction, encyclopedias can't be beat. Many companies publish fine general encyclopedias; the *Encyclopaedia Britannica* and the *Encyclopedia Americana* are two of the best. Younger researchers often find the *World Book* extremely user-friendly. Most of the major encyclopedias also have online versions, updated more frequently than the print editions and providing links to current events covered in magazines and newspapers.

Subject-area encyclopedias narrow the focus to one branch of learning. Since these works aim at a more limited target, subject-area encyclopedias provide more information about each item they discuss. (Just to confuse you, some subject-area encyclopedias call themselves "dictionaries.") Here's a tiny sampling of encyclopedias and encyclopedia-like dictionaries, just to show you what these books may cover:

✔ **Arts**

- *The Dictionary of Art.* New York: Grove, 1996. (also online)

- *The New Grove Dictionary of Music and Musicians.* Ed. Stanley Sadie. 2nd ed. New York: Grove's Dictionaries, 2001. (also online)

✔ **History and social science**

- The *American Heritage Encyclopedia of American History.* Ed. John Mack Faragher. New York: Henry Holt, 1998.

- *Worldmark Encyclopedia of Cultures and Daily Life.* Ed. Timothy L. Gall. Detroit: Gale, 1997.

✔ **Literature and language**

- *The New Princeton Encyclopedia of Poetry and Poetics.* Ed. Alex Preminger and T.V.F. Brogan. Princeton: Princeton UP, 1993.

✔ **Science, mathematics, and technology**

- *Companion Encyclopedia of the History and Philosophy of the Mathematical Sciences.* Ed. Ivor Grattan-Guinness. New York: Routledge, 1993.

- *McGraw-Hill Encyclopedia of Science and Technology.* Ed. Sybil Parker. 9th ed. New York: McGraw-Hill, 2002. (Also available online as *Access Science*)

✔ **Business**

- *McGraw-Hill Encyclopedia of Economics.* Ed. Douglas Greenwald. 2nd ed. New York: McGraw, 1994.

Almanacs

Almanacs are published once a year and are good for up-to-date facts and fig-ures: the gross national product of a country, statistics on AIDS, the names of national leaders, and so forth. *The World Almanac and Book of Facts* (New York: World Almanac Books) and *Canadian Almanac and Directory* (Detroit: Gale) are good general almanacs. Some almanacs concentrate on a single topic, such as *The Facts on File World Political Almanac: The Facts and Figures of Governments and Leaders, Political Parties and Constitutions, Wars and Treaties* (New York: Facts on File), which covers world governments and their leaders.

Atlases

Atlases are map books — miles and miles of maps of all types. Proving once and for all that I am a total nerd, I confess that I love to spend an hour or so with a good atlas, imagining the real places drawn on those flat pages. Some atlases display the current world, with today's boundaries, roads, and so forth. Other atlases deal with history, natural features, human population, and endangered species. A good general atlas is the *Hammond Atlas of the World* (5th ed. Maplewood, NJ: Hammond, 1998).

Because atlases tend to be large, they often don't fit on the regular library shelves. Look for a special area or piece of furniture.

Other reference books

The reference shelf groans under the weight of lots of other types of books — guides, chronologies (time lines with explanations), handbooks, and others that don't have a particular name. To find the best books, browse through the shelves of the reference area devoted to your subject. (The librarian will help you figure out where to look.) In the meantime, here's a tiny taste of the feast that's available to you:

✔ **Arts**

- *The Wilson Chronology of the Arts: A Record of Human Creativity from Ancient Times to the Present.* George Ochoa and Melinda Corey. New York: Wilson, 1998. Timelines and explanations of art from over 40,000 years ago through the late twentieth century.

✔ **History and social science**

- *Reader's Guide to Women's Studies.* Ed. Eleanor B. Amico. Chicago: Fitzroy Dearborn, 1998. A bibliography of works by and about women and women's issues.

✔ **Literature and language**

- *Granger's Index to Poetry.* 11th ed. rev. New York: Columbia University Press, 1997. In this book, you can look up the first line and find out the name of the poem, the author, and the books in which the poem appears. (Also online.)

✔ **Science, mathematics, and technology**

- *CRC Handbook of Chemistry and Physics.* Ed. David R. Lide. New York: CRC Press, 2001. This reference work lists the qualities of elements and chemical compounds and information about the properties of solid materials.

Writing a business paper? Check out *Hoover's Handbooks* (Austen, TX: Hoover's) come out every year or so and provide information on individual businesses, including privately held and government-owned companies and nonprofits.

Finding Books in Bookstores

If you think that owning books beats borrowing them, get used to shelling out some cold, hard cash. (Does anyone know why the cliché says that cash is "cold and hard"? The pitifully few bills in my wallet seem rather soft and warm.) Anyway, here are a couple of ways to part from your dough:

- ✔ A reference work available in most libraries and bookstores as well as online, *Books in Print* tells you which books are available, who publishes them, and everything else you need to know in order to locate a particular title.

- ✔ Check your local independent bookstore or a branch of the megachains. If they don't carry the title you're looking for, they'll probably order it for you.

- ✔ University bookstores or specialized bookstores (devoted to dog books, mysteries, astronomy, lentils, whatever) may carry some of the weirder titles on your list. The business telephone directory may help; look for "Books — Sales" and then subtopics.

- ✔ Out-of-print books are tougher to locate, but not impossible. The book review of the Sunday paper may carry advertisements from local companies that specialize in locating rare or out-of-print material.

Order books online at these sites:

- ✔ www.Amazon.com — all types of books, including an out-of-print service

- ✔ www.bn.com — the site for Barnes and Noble

- ✔ www.alibris.com — specializes in out-of-print books

Locating Newspaper and Magazine Articles

Early on in my career as a researcher (shortly after the Big Bang), I needed an article from a little-known newspaper from the 1930s. I found it in a mysterious division of the library called the annex — the kind of dusty old building in which television's private eyes always get shot. I filled out a form, waited three hours, and finally received the article. The paper was brittle and yellow, and I sneezed for two straight days.

I tell you this story not because I want you to feel sorry for me. Instead, I want you to understand that newspaper research is not always easy, even today. Neither is magazine research. Libraries that can't afford to go online face storage problems. They often solve those problems by chucking the older issues or by stashing them in an out-of-the-way spot. Sometimes the issues are filed in a box, and sometimes they're bound into a hardcover book.

Making do with microform

To save space, many libraries buy *microform* versions of printed material. Microform is not that wiggly thing you were supposed to culture in biology lab; it's a name for very small versions of newspapers, magazines, and other writing. Members of the microform family include *microfilm* and *microfiche*. Microfilm is (surprise!) film in a roll, and microfiche is a little plastic sheet that looks like a slide picture without the cardboard border. You read microform versions of newspaper and magazine articles on special machines, which in my experience always break or burn out a bulb the minute I sit down at them. (I'm not even going to tell you about the time the film whipped off the reel and spun out all over the reading room.) If the machines do work, you may still get a headache from staring at the screen. I do. Some of the machines allow you to print a copy of the article, usually for a fee. If you read an article from a nonprinting machine, you have to take notes.

Sorting through CDs

A far better space-saving (but more expensive) storage medium for articles is CD or CD-ROM discs. You still have to read the material on a special machine, but the process is simpler, at least for me. You insert the disc into the machine, press enter, and wait a moment until the contents pop up on the screen. Many of these machines are attached to a printer, so you can take home a paper copy of the article that interests you.

If you or your public library has an Internet connection, you can skip the sneezes and the headaches and forget about feeding discs into a machine. Chapter 5 tells you how to find online versions of newspaper and magazine articles.

Investigating indexes

Despite the annoyance of researching from periodicals, you still need them from time to time because they provide information you can't easily get anywhere else. But before you can read that fantastic article on alien abduction, you have to locate it. Where? In an index.

Articles in databases of newspapers and magazines are accessed through keyword searching or a controlled vocabulary, that is, subject headings established for a particular database (see Chapter 5). The major popular magazines are indexed in *The Reader's Guide to Periodical Literature,* a set of extremely thick books with small print. You can look up articles under the author's last name or under the subject. Two respected newspapers, *The New York Times* and *The London Times,* are also indexed in large books with very small print. Check the reporter's last name or subject. These indexes usually cover one year in each volume, so to locate everything printed in the last ten years for your biology paper you'll have to look up "protoplasm" in ten separate places. The indexes provide the date of the periodical, the page where the article may be found, the title, the author, and sometimes a short summary. However, to read the article itself you have to go to bound volumes or microform, if your library has them.

Happily, your library may have a CD or CD-ROM version of *The Reader's Guide* or the *New York Times* index, or other indexes of articles. The discs tell you everything that the printed indexes do — date, page, title, author, and so on. But they include the full text of some articles as well. Also, they allow you to search many years' publications at one time.

The Reader's Guide to Periodical Literature is also available online, with the full text of recent articles. Indexes and some full-text articles of *The New York Times* and *The London Times* are also online.

See the "Gathering search terms" section earlier in this chapter for help in defining the search terms for your hunt through newspaper and magazines indexes.

Searching online databases and bibliographies

If you're looking for a scholarly article or a dissertation, an online database is your best bet. (See Chapter 5 for all you need to know about online databases.) If you can't get online, you may have some luck checking book-length bibliographies. (See the section entitled "Locating the best reference books" in this chapter for more information.) Also, check books on your subject. They may include a bibliography listing scholarly articles. If you're looking for a dissertation published before 1997, check *Dissertation Abstracts,* an index listing the title, author, institution, date, and main idea of the dissertation. For dissertations written after that date, you have to check online.

Panning for Gold in the Pamphlet File

The Forty-Niners who rushed to California in the mid-nineteenth century to pan for gold met with mixed results. Some spent months sorting through worthless chunks of wet rock. Others found a nugget or two of the real thing — enough to make the trip spectacularly worthwhile. Researching in the pamphlet file, which librarians for their own mysterious reasons call the *vertical file,* has a similar success ratio. You may thumb through a ton of material and find nothing, or you may score big time. Here's the deal. Your library may have a file cabinet, a room, or floor full of file cabinets, all stuffed with pamphlets, flyers, pictures, and similar items. The material is organized according to subject, and you generally need permission from the librarian to look through it. The stuff comes from the government and private organizations, not from traditional book or magazine publishers.

You may find treasure in a pamphlet file, but researcher beware. Quality and accuracy may be an issue. Before you accept the source, check the following:

✔ Who wrote, printed, and distributed the material? If it's the government or a well-known organization, the material is probably reliable. If it is a group you've never heard of, you may want to look a little further, verifying the facts with another source. If no author, printer, or distributor is identified, you *definitely* need to verify the information before using it.

✔ When was the material printed? Depending upon your topic, the pamphlet may be outdated. A brochure on the monasteries of Medieval Europe is not likely to be date-sensitive, but a booklet on immigration statistics may be. If no date is given, researcher beware.

If you find something good, note the name and address of the agency or organization responsible. Call or write and ask for additional material. Also, if you find an outdated pamphlet, call or write and ask for the newest edition. (See the "Associating with Experts" section in this chapter for more information on contacting organizations.)

Finding Audio-Visual Sources: You Oughta Be in Pictures

To the dismay of many traditionalists (the kind of people who carry around yellow pads and sneer at computers and even typewriters), many libraries also carry audio-visual material such as videotapes, DVD discs, audiotapes, CDs, and CD-ROMs. (They used to have records, too, but I think records, like the dodo bird and docs who make house calls, are pretty much extinct.) Even if you're a traditionalist, you may find audio-visual material — music, dramatic performances, speeches, and a ton of other stuff — helpful.

If the library has a computerized catalogue, you may enter a search term and specify the medium you want (a book or a tape, for example). A list of material pops up. If the library's catalogue is on little cards, the audio-visual material may be in a separate drawer or cabinet. Ask the librarian for help. Either way, check the "Gathering search terms" section earlier in this chapter for help in defining an effective search.

If the library doesn't own the movie or audiotape you need and your bank balance isn't written in invisible ink, try these two catalogues for purchasing information:

> ✔ *Bowker's Complete Video Directory.* New Providence, NJ: Reed Elsevier, 2001.

> ✔ *Bowker's Words on Cassette.* New Providence, NJ: Reed Elsevier, 2001.

Associating with Experts

One of the handiest books in the library, in my humble opinion, is the *Encyclopedia of Associations,* which is also available online. There's one for the United States, as well as an international edition. In the *Encyclopedia of Associations* you can find zillions of special-interest groups. When they aren't busy paying off (sorry, contributing to) politicians, special-interest groups often publish books, pamphlets, and periodicals with tons of information on (surprise!) their special interest. Some even produce films and tapes. If *your* special interest — your paper topic — matches *their* special interest, bingo!

Here's how to use the *Encyclopedia of Associations:*

1. **Look for your topic in the volume that lists keywords.** Try all possible terms that relate to your search. (The "Gathering search terms" section in this chapter tells you how to find keywords.)

2. **Jot down the number or numbers that follow each keyword.** Each number represents one organization.

3. **Look up the organization in the other two volumes where the organizations are listed in numerical order.** Each entry tells you the name of the organization, the address, phone number, e-mail or Web address (if there is one), and the organization's activities and interests. Publications and prices may also be listed.

4. **Write or call an organization that matches your interests.** Ask for any free material and a price list or catalogue.

5. **Request to interview someone with expert knowledge of your topic, if you wish.** (Chapter 7 gives you the lowdown on researching with help from human experts.)

Take care not to leave your search of the *Encyclopedia of Associations* until the last minute, because you may have to wait quite a while for a reply. But if you're lucky, this research tactic will really pay off.

Be cautious when contacting strangers. Don't give out too much personal information unless you're sure that the person you're dealing with is reliable. If you arrange a personal interview, take a friend with you and meet in a public place, such as your school or office.

Also, keep in mind that the research material you receive from a special-interest organization may reflect only that group's point of view. Unless you're familiar with the group, verify the accuracy of the information with another source.

Examining George Washington's Letters: Researching from Special Collections

Jack Kerouac's original manuscripts, the blueprints for the Empire State Building, and John F. Kennedy's appointment calendar. Where are they? In special collections. *Special collection* is a catchall term for a bunch of real stuff that once belonged to someone famous or that played an important role — or what the collector sees as an important role — at one point in history. Special collections also include rare books or very complete holdings of books on the particular interest of the collection. Special collections are located in libraries, in museums, in universities, and in other spots.

If your research takes you to a special collection, you gather more than information. You pick up the thrill of dealing with something real. You may also gain insight that's simply not available anywhere else. For example, I once spent dozens of hours reading transcripts of the Salem witch-trial proceedings. I thought I knew a lot about the mindset of the Puritans, both judges and victims. And I did! But until I viewed the handwritten documents from the trials — the indictments, the death sentences, the confessions — I couldn't fully appreciate the horror. The yellowed paper, the cramped writing, the cross-outs, and the little tears on the documents made the event more real to me.

For good, comprehensive listings of special collections, check

> ✔ *The New York Public Library Guide Book of How and Where to Look It Up.* Ed. Sherwood Harris. New York: Prentice-Hall, 1991.

> ✔ *Directory of Special Libraries.* 2nd ed. Detroit: Gale, annual publication.

Working in a special collection means following the rules of the collector. You won't be able to take materials home, and you may have to leave your belongings in a locker, wear gloves, and work under supervision. Don't sweat the small stuff! The experience is more than worth the trouble.

Chapter 7

Real Live People: Interviewing Techniques

*P*aper and ink and the Internet may be all you need to construct the world's greatest set of research sources. But sometimes a real live human being comes in handy. Imagine how much a personal interview with an expert in the field, an eyewitness, or a passionate critic (or fan) can add to your paper! And if a personal meeting is impractical because, for example, you're interviewing a business executive who's based on another continent, an e-mail exchange or phone conversation may still provide unique information for your report.

In this chapter I tell you how to find interview subjects and how to prepare for your meeting with them. I explain how to get the most out of the time you spend with the interview subject. I also discuss how to turn spoken words into written quotations.

Finding Interview Subjects: Where the People Are

You're writing about whales and their environment, and you've gathered a lot of information. But part of what you've read is confusing. Also, you want to know what working with these amazing mammals is like. In other words, you need an interview. How can you find a whale expert? In a few ways:

✔ Check the list of all your research sources for names. Chances are your list contains the name of a scientist so knowledgeable that she could be an honorary aquatic mammal. (When she sees a fin, she says things like "That's L549! She just calved, mother and baby doing fine! Hi, L549!") If time permits, write to the author of the book or article that mentions Ms. Whale Expert, asking the author to forward your interview request. (If Ms. Whale Expert *is* the author, make your request to her directly.) Send the letter in care of the book's publisher or the magazine's editor. Include your address, phone number, and (if you have one) e-mail address.

To find the address of a book publisher, look on the back of the title page, where the copyright date is printed. Or, check *Books in Print,* a reference book found in most libraries and online. To find the address of the magazine's central office, check the *masthead,* a section usually found near the beginning of a magazine where all the editors' names are listed.

✔ Contact professional organizations that deal with whales, the environment, or both. Send an interview request to the organization's address or via the organization's Web site. Ask to speak with a specific individual, if you know who may be an appropriate interview subject, or simply explain what you need and let the organization suggest someone.

Most libraries own a print copy of the *Encyclopedia of Associations* — a multivolume work that lists every organization you can imagine (and some you could *never* imagine). The listings are grouped according to the association's main interest or cause. So any group that concerns itself with whales — from marine biologists to whale harpooners — is listed under the keyword "whales." The listings include addresses, telephone numbers, and contact information for each organization. Online information services such as Dialog and LexisNexis carry an electronic version of the *Encyclopedia of Associations,* though you have to pay to use it. (Check out Chapter 5 for more information on these online information services.) If your budget is limited, check the local library. Some libraries subscribe to the electronic version and allow patrons of the library free access.

✔ Make like Sherlock Holmes and figure out where whale experts hang out. For example, try calling the nearest aquarium. Ask to speak to the director of education or public relations. Present yourself as a humble seeker of knowledge who is looking for advice. (That's what you are, right?) The aquarium people may not know a whale expert personally, but they may know someone who knows someone who knows someone. . . . You may be surprised how helpful people can be!

✔ Search the Internet. Newsgroups and listservs (mailing lists) on whales, the environment, or both may provide you with the names of experts. (Chapter 5 gives you the lowdown on newsgroups and listservs.)

The Internet allows people to reinvent themselves, so not every "expert" in a newsgroup or listserv knows what he or she pretends to know. You may unknowingly correspond with a 12-year-old who has never even seen a whale — the same 12-year-old who cheerfully responds, "Yes, I'm a marine mammal expert. How may I help you?" Downloader beware. If possible, check the credentials of potential interview subjects. Look for publications or membership in responsible organizations.

✔ Look to AltaVista and other search engines (see Chapter 5 for more information) that allow you to conduct a "people search." After you have the name of a likely interview candidate, check for his or her e-mail address and send a note.

Be careful when you contact strangers via the Internet. Never set up a face-to-face meeting with someone you don't know, unless you're meeting in a safe place with lots of backup (your school or office, for example). Phone interviews are a good bet too, for safety reasons. If you have any doubts, go for written responses via e-mail or regular mail.

Getting the Interview

After you've found the perfect interview subject, how do you convince him or her to talk with you? Grovel and beg. (Kidding — sort of. A little groveling does help.) Here's a plan:

1. **Make the first contact in writing (e-mail or letter), if possible, and follow up with a phone call.** Cold calling — a phone call with no prior contact — surprises and annoys people. If you've written first, you can say, "I'm following up my note about an interview for my research paper on whales."

2. **Explain who you are, what you are writing, and why you want the interview.** Be accurate and clear. Don't promise anything that you can't deliver (such as publication, money, or Nobel prizes).

3. **Pull out your etiquette manual and follow it closely; good manners score points.**

4. **Be sure to acknowledge that the interview subject's time is valuable.** Explain how much time you'll probably need and offer to cut that amount if necessary. (The section entitled "Conducting the Interview" later in this chapter explains how to deal with time limits.)

5. **Offer the interviewee a chance to read and correct a draft of the paper before you hand it in.** (However, be sure that the subject understands that he or she is not to edit quotations from other people. Believe it or not, I've seen people try this!) A subject who worries about being misquoted or misrepresented may turn you down.

6. **Do research from other sources, or line up a couple of potential interview subjects.** If one interview subject says no, go to Plan B. (Never put yourself in a situation where there *is* no Plan B.) As my grandma used to say, "Honesty is the best policy, but insurance never hurts either."

> ## Never underestimate the power of a kid
>
> If you are a young person (I'm letting you define that term), you may have an advantage in obtaining interviews. Lots of older people like to talk (you may have noticed), especially to an admiring beginner. One of my students actually spoke with a reclusive writer who had not granted an interview in years. I'm not sure whether her blue hair and nose ring had anything to do with his decision to talk; I suspect it was her firm belief, passionately expressed,
>
> that he is the best writer who ever walked the planet. In asking for an interview, you may want to state how old you are, if you think the low number will impress the potential subject. One warning: Interview subjects who spend a lot of time with kids or who have a lot of young admirers are less likely to be swayed by the age factor. On the other hand, if you're 98, you may have an edge with that sort of interview subject.

Preparing for the Interview

Quick! Come up with an answer to these questions:

What is your philosophy of life?

So what's the deal with your career?

Can you explain your main interest in life?

Like, what can you tell me?

Dead silence, right? You can't answer these questions — and neither can your interview subject — because they're not questions. They're an unsuccessful attempt to conceal the fact that you haven't a clue what to ask. How do you get a clue? You do research. You find out about the individual and his/her area of expertise. You identify the holes in your own knowledge about your chosen topic and figure out which holes you can plug yourself and which you can't. Then you formulate specific, answerable questions.

Time for a little more detail on interview preparation. The imaginary Ms. Whale Expert illustrates what I mean.

✔ Do general background reading on your topic. Your questions should show that you have prepared for the interview. For example:

Good question: What factors influence the survival of the humpback?

Bad question: What's a whale?

✔ Choose questions that call for detailed answers, not a simple yes or no:

Bad question: Is it fun to work with whales?

Why it's a bad question: The answer will probably be yes, followed by two minutes of silence.

Good Question: Tell me about the best day you ever spent with a whale.

Why it's a good question: It leads to a story, not to a syllable.

✔ If you absolutely must ask a short-answer question, prepare a follow-up. *Why* and *how* are especially good words. Most valuable words: *Tell me more about that.*

✔ Read other interviews with the subject, if they exist, to find out something about Ms. Whale Expert's life and career.

✔ After reading other interviews with Ms. Whale Expert, you know which stories she's told a million times. Can you come up with new questions that she's never heard before? If so, you have a chance to hear something original.

Conducting the Interview

Turn on the television and watch an interview. Looks smooth, doesn't it? One question leads logically to another. No one stumbles, drops the tape recorder, or stares speechlessly into the night. Ah, the power of editing! If only you had the opportunity to edit reality! In real life, experiences that I've had during interviews include a broken tape recorder, an inaccessible electrical outlet, and a subject who did a great impression of a mute sleepwalker. I'm not even going to mention the pigeon that swooped down and "soiled" my questions ten minutes before the interview.

Keeping the interview running smoothly

You can't protect yourself totally from interview disasters, but a little preparation goes a long way. Here are some suggestions for successful interviews:

✔ Arrive a few minutes early for the interview and be prepared to wait. When you interview someone, you're in an unequal power situation, with the scale tipping away from you. Better that you wait for Ms. Whale Expert than have her wait for you.

✔ For phone interviews, call as close to the agreed-upon time as possible.

✔ Write your questions on index cards (or, cut out typed or word-processed questions and tape them to cards). Put the questions in the order of their importance to you. In other words, put the question you most need an answer to *first*, and the question that you care the least about *last*. If you run out of time, you leave knowing that you got the most crucial information.

✔ Another helpful tactic when time is an issue: Organize your questions into subtopics. Some super organized interviewers color-code their subtopics (the smaller divisions of the topic) with markers or with multicolored index cards. Before the interview, decide how long you want to spend on each subtopic. Keep your watch in full view during the meeting, and switch to the next subtopic (the next pack of cards) at the appropriate time, even if you've got a few leftover questions from the previous subtopic. Be sure to arrange the questions in each subtopic in order of importance.

✔ *Listen* to the answers. If you ask Ms. Whale Expert about conservation and she explains that she favors a ban on hunting, ignore the index card that says "How do you feel about hunting?" even if that's the next question in the pack.

✔ React to the answers you receive. If Ms. Whale Expert suddenly starts talking about her belief that whales speak grammatically, follow up with a question about the language of whales, even if you had nothing prepared on the subject. (However, if you have absolutely no interest in the language of whales and need to know only about environmental conditions and whale survival, nod politely in response to her comment on whale grammar and move on.)

✔ Remember that an interview is not a conversation. Keep your mouth shut as much as possible. Your job is to get the other guy to talk, not to explain your own undoubtedly fascinating views on the topic.

✔ Resist the urge to be a prosecuting attorney. If you disagree with something the subject says, explain your disagreement in the paper. Don't try to "nail" the interview subject with comments like "Oh yeah? Then how do you explain this tape from a hidden camera?" Legitimate challenges are fine, but be courteous in making them.

✔ Don't editorialize in your question. Here's what I mean:

Bad question: Given that whales are beautiful, incredibly intelligent creatures, how do you feel about hunting them down and slaughtering them?

Why it's a bad question: You haven't exactly concealed your feelings about whale hunting. Your interview subject knows that as far as you are concerned, only one answer is correct. So why are you asking the question? To embarrass someone who disagrees with you or to confirm your own views? Either way, you're wasting Ms. Whale Expert's time.

Good question: What are your views on whale hunting?

Why it's a good question: The neutral wording places the focus on what the interview subject thinks, not on your own ideas.

✔ When the interview is over, thank the subject. Follow up with a note expressing gratitude and explaining how the interviewee helped you. If he or she requests a copy of the finished paper, provide it. Do these things because (a) you should always practice good manners and (b) you may need further help from the interview subject.

All this interview advice boils down to one main point: Do everything you can to get the interview subject to speak freely about the topic. If you keep that goal in mind and use common sense, you'll be fine.

Saving it for posterity: Tape or notepad?

In some movies reporters run around taking notes on cocktail napkins with pencil stubs. Then they call the paper and say things like "Stop the presses" and "Gimme the city desk." In other movies, reporters secretly record every twitch and syllable with cameras and microphones as small as tooth fillings. Then they post the interview on the Internet.

You're not likely to resemble either type of interviewer. Instead, you should probably choose between a regular notebook and a normal-sized tape recorder. Which one is better? Neither, really. Researchers have had triumphs and disasters with both. As the cliché states, each method has advantages and disadvantages.

Using a tape recorder

If you tape the interview, you never have to worry about getting the quotation right because you can check and recheck the subject's actual words. During the interview you're free to focus your full attention on what the subject is saying. And you don't have to speed write to keep up.

However, some interview subjects get "mike fright" when faced with a tape recorder, and you have to coax them into speaking freely. With a taped interview you also have to worry about sound level, batteries or electrical outlets, and mechanical failure.

 Do an equipment check before the interview and a sound check when the interview subject arrives. Ask the subject to say "Testing one, two, three" or "I am a Martian." Play the tape and adjust the microphone position if necessary.

The real hassle with taped interviews comes when you attempt to extract information and quotations for the paper. In Chapter 8, I tell you the easiest ways to select and transcribe the parts of the interview that you need.

Interviewing by telephone? You don't need an expensive setup. You can get an inexpensive taping device, a wire with a plug on one end and a suction cup on the other, at stores that sell telephone accessories. Stick the suction cup on the outside of the phone's earpiece, push the plug into the recorder, and speak normally. The sound quality is usually quite good. Also, some answering machines function as tape recorders. Check your manual. Be sure to tell the interviewee that you're taping the conversation.

Working with a notebook

If you're working with a notebook, you don't have to worry about equipment failure, unless of course your pencil point breaks. (Bring a spare.) And if you're a good note taker, the transcription is a cinch. Just run your eyeballs down the notes and extract the quotation or fact you need.

The problem with taking notes is accuracy. Speaking is faster than writing, and you can't get every word onto the paper. You have to make a lot of quick decisions, leaving out small words that you can probably fill in later. Furthermore, in a notebook interview you split your attention in half. One part listens to what the subject is saying and plans the next question, and the other part writes what the subject just said. Not an easy task, but not an impossible one either.

Number your questions, which of course you have written out in advance. As you take notes, write the number of the question next to the response.

- ✔ What the question is: Question #2: How many whales have you met personally?

- ✔ What you can write down: #2: 5409.

- ✔ What you don't have to write: I have met 5409 whales personally.

- ✔ What you've saved: five words.

If you're taking notes by hand, ask the subject for a couple of extra minutes at the end of the interview. Read back the quotations that you are likely to use in the final paper. The interview subject then has a chance to correct any inaccuracies. Or, ask the interview subject if he or she is willing to read and correct a rough draft of the paper. Highlight the relevant parts of the rough draft for the subject's convenience.

If you send a rough draft to an interview subject, be sure to indicate a deadline for the response. Insert a sentence saying, "If I don't hear from you by November 20, I'll assume everything is fine." Allow a reasonable amount of time, and enclose a stamped, self-addressed envelope for a reply.

In Chapter 8 I explain how to index information in a notebook or on a tape. Chapter 16 goes over the rules for punctuating quotations.

You've got interview: The e-mail connection

Tape recorders and notepads may soon follow rotary telephones and record players, not to mention typewriters, into the Discarded Technology Hall of Fame. If you have an account, the easiest way to interview your subject may be via e-mail. Ms. Whale Expert, for example, probably has e-mail and probably doesn't have a great deal of time. (Becoming an expert at anything just eats up those hours!) She may say no to a personal meeting fearing that she'll be stuck at the office (boat? tank?) until midnight, finishing the work that an interview with you will make her miss. But e-mail is a different story. She can answer e-mail whenever she has a free moment.

If you conduct an e-mail interview, strategy is important. As with a personal interview, create questions that lead to stories or explanations, not to one-word answers. (See the "Preparing for the Interview" section earlier in this chapter for more tips on creating effective interview questions.) List your questions in the order of their importance *to you*. Number the questions and, in a note preceding the list, explain which questions are crucial to your paper and which ones you can live without if the expert is pressed for time.

If you found the interview subject through a Web site, read everything on the Web site before writing your interview questions. Pay special attention to the FAQ page, if the site has one. A *FAQ* is a list of *Frequently Asked Questions*. Happily, the FAQ page includes answers, too, making it a FAQAA — Frequently Asked Questions and Answers. Duplicating questions from a FAQ is bad manners. Your interview subject will know immediately that you're not prepared. Also, the interviewee probably wrote the answers to the FAQ, and he or she will not be pleased with anyone who ignores it. You can, however, ask the interview subject to clarify or expand a point in the FAQ.

Because e-mail zips around the universe so quickly, you may be tempted to turn the interview into a long conversation. Hitting "reply" and following up every answer from the interviewee with another question is just too easy. Try to restrain yourself. If you overdo it, your interview subject may grow tired of your communications and "block sender," stopping your e-mail from reaching her desk. Then where will you be if you sit down to write the paper and discover that you really, really, really need one more thing?

TIP

Also on the subject of manners, a thank-you note — brief but specific — goes a long way towards establishing good will. You should send the note for all the right reasons (you truly are grateful) and for a wrong reason too. (You don't want to annoy the interviewee and end up with "block sender" status. If you have just one more question, you want it to get through.)

Cleaning Up: Changing Real Speech into Readable Quotations

that's um I'm glad you asked about the blue whale I went a couple of years ago I went to my boss have you met Mr. Orca he's great to say that I thought we should study the blue whale's teeth to see whether cavities were a problem and he he er he told me not to bother because blue whales don't have teeth the great white shark well that might be I might study them the blue whale is huge did you know like a subway train

No, Ms. Whale Expert is not illiterate, tongue-tied, or verbally challenged. She's just human, and the above passage, written as if it were taken directly from a tape recording, illustrates how human beings really speak. They begin, interrupt themselves, backstitch over a sentence they've already covered, veer off into new topics, wind back, and generally reach the target in the end. But if you read a word-for-word account — a literal transcription — they sound like idiots.

How do you, an honest paper writer, quote from the transcript above? You don't. First you clean it up, and *then* you quote. Here's a step-by-step guide:

1. **Remove instances of *um, er,* and *you know,* unless you are trying to illustrate the speaker's personality.** (Even then, don't overdo it. You can leave in a few *you know's,* but don't bore the reader with too many.)

2. **Place punctuation appropriately.** Human beings don't speak with punctuation marks. People do pause briefly, and sometimes they pause for a longer period of time. They also ask questions. When you write a quotation, the brief pause will probably translate into a comma, and the longer pause will probably become a period. The questions end with question marks. However, some pauses occur because the person speaking needs a moment to think, and some sentences sound like questions, but aren't. Don't place commas and periods in those spots. Instead, follow grammar rules. Turn the subject's words into complete sentences, and place the commas where they should appear in formal, correct English. Put question marks next to sentences that truly express a question.

3. **Take out the digressions or the parts of the quotation that you simply don't need.** If any important words have been omitted, place three dots. (For those of you who like terminology, the three dots are called an *ellipsis*.) You don't need to place an ellipsis if you've taken out an *um* or a stuttered repetition. Use it only for important omissions.

4. **Add words as necessary to make the meaning clear.** Place the added words inside brackets so the reader will know that the bracketed words come from you, not from the person you are quoting.

When you clean up a quotation, take care not to alter the meaning or intention of the speaker.

Here's a possible quotation from the transcript at the beginning of this section:

> I'm glad you asked about the blue whale. A couple of years ago I went to my boss . . . to say that I thought we should study the blue whale's teeth to see whether cavities were a problem. He told me not to bother because blue whales don't have teeth. [Blue whales have baleen, a structure in the mouth that strains bits of food as the water passes through.] The great white shark might be [a better subject for the study].

Notice that three dots follow the word *boss* because substantial information (the name of the boss and an evaluation of him) has been left out. No dots indicate that *he* has replaced *he he er* because those words are not important. The words in brackets add information not in the original quotation — a definition of *baleen* and an ending to the sentence about the great white shark. Don't overuse brackets; save most of your comments for sentences before and after the quotation.

Sic of grammar?

One of the handiest words in the language is *sic*. If you are quoting someone who has used improper English, you run the risk of appearing ungrammatical yourself. Okay, not the worst fate in the world, but one you want to avoid. (As an English teacher, I place "appearing ungrammatical" below bubonic plague but above paper cuts on my list of disasters.) Fortunately, *sic* comes to the rescue. Just place those three little letters in brackets after the incorrect words in the quotation. *Sic* tells the reader that the speaker made the mistake, not the writer. Here's an example:

> Mr. Henhuff explained, "I loved to studied [sic] and spent almost all my free time reading grammar books."

Part III

Collecting Pearls of Wisdom: How to Take Notes

The 5th Wave   By Rich Tennant

"Well, kid, if your paper's as good as your notes, you're getting an 'A' from this gang."

In this part . . .

You've got books and articles. You've downloaded from some great Web sites. Maybe you've conducted an interview or two. Now your office (cubicle, desk, dining room) looks like a recycling plant that never got around to processing ten years' worth of paper. So what do you do? You take notes.

But before you take *notes,* take *note* of the best work methods. A few minutes of attention to note-taking habits at this stage saves a few dozen hours later, when you're writing the paper. In this part I explain how to find the best note-taking method for your personality. I tell you what to write down and what to ignore. Finally, I discuss how to keep the note taking (and later, the quoting) legal.

Chapter 8

One Size Does Not Fit All: Note-Taking Methods

As far back as stone slabs and as recently as handheld computers, human beings have found ways to take note of information that they do not want to forget. And now that we're officially in the Information Age, which in my opinion should be called the Age of Too Much Information, good note taking is even more important because of the ever-increasing number of sources and amount of information available to a researcher. But the method that suits someone who cherishes a fountain pen and a yellow legal pad is *not* the right method for the person who can't travel more than four feet from a computer without experiencing withdrawal.

In Chapter 9 I discuss *what* to write down, but in this chapter I tackle *how* to take notes. Specifically, I explain the most efficient note-taking methods for cards, notebooks, and the computer. I even give you a method that combines the computer *and* a notebook or cards. I also tell you how to keep track of sources so that you save the most valuable commodity — time — when you prepare documentation for your paper.

Carding — the Old System

Once upon a time when I was a kid (When? A dinosaur lived next door!), researchers always took notes on index cards and stored the results in shoeboxes. Note, or index, cards are still around, and some people swear by them. If you take notes on index cards, you can

- ✔ Carry a couple in your pocket, so you're always prepared to whip up a few notes during a free moment
- ✔ Literally, lay your cards on the table to get an image of the shape and structure of the information you've gathered (Very helpful to people with a strong visual sense!)
- ✔ Sort the cards into subtopics
- ✔ Re-sort the cards if your vision of the paper changes
- ✔ Arrange the cards of each subtopic pack in the order that you intend to use them
- ✔ Keep good records of your sources

However, cards are not for you if you

- ✔ Hate writing by hand or have trouble reading your own handwriting
- ✔ Don't like interrupting the flow of ideas in order to change cards
- ✔ Tend to lose small pieces of paper
- ✔ Go barefoot a lot, thus having no shoeboxes for card storage

Just kidding about the last one. But seriously, experience tells me that people either love the index-card method or hate it with a passion. Suit yourself! If you do take notes on index cards, here's the most efficient way:

1. **Whenever you begin taking notes from a new source, give the source a number.**

2. **If you work from a lot of sources, use letters as well as numbers to keep track of them.** On the bibliography card (or, with computer notes, in the master list file of sources) give each source a number and a letter.

Here's a simple system to use: Code books as B1, B2, B3, and so on, and magazine articles as M1, M2, M3. Newspapers get the prefix "N," and downloads from the World Wide Web may be labeled with a "W." "A" is for audiotape, "V" for video, and "I" for a personal interview. These prefixes save you time when you return to a source for more information. You can go directly to the Internet, to the book pile on the corner of the bed, or to the messy stack of photocopies falling off your bookshelf. Okay, I know we're not talking about saving hours here, but those minutes do add up!

3. **Before taking any notes from a source, create a bibliography card.** Put the number of the source (with a letter prefix, if you're using letters) in the upper left-hand corner. On the card, write all the information you need to supply in the *bibliography* of your paper. (See the "Documenting Your Sources" section later in this chapter for an explanation about what bibliographical information you need to collect while you take notes.)

Also, see Chapter 18 for all the details about creating a bibliography for your paper.) If you borrowed the source from a library, write the *call number* (the little number on the cover of the item that determines where it is shelved) and the name of the library. If you need the item again, you can easily locate it.

4. **Put the bibliography cards in a safe place and begin to take notes on a new set of blank cards, writing one fact or idea or quotation — and *only one* — on each card.** In the upper left-hand corner of every card, write the number of the source. Next to the source number, write the page number that you're working from. See Figure 8-1 for an example of a note card.

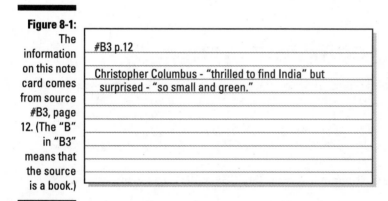

Figure 8-1:
The information on this note card comes from source #B3, page 12. (The "B" in "B3" means that the source is a book.)

#B3 p.12

Christopher Columbus - "thrilled to find India" but
   surprised - "so small and green."

5. **Place each new fact on a new card, which always contains the identifying source and page number.**

6. **When you have a number of cards, perhaps half of the cards needed for your paper, read through them.** Begin to think about subtopics. (For more information on defining subtopics, see Chapter 13.) For example, if you're working on a paper about political cartoons, you may decide to organize the material by centuries. Mark the top of each card with a colored line that corresponds to the individual century — the eighteenth-century cards may be red, the nineteenth-century blue, and the twentieth-century green. When you take additional notes, color-code the cards as you write them.

Color-code the cards on only one edge. Later, if you change your mind about the subtopics (choosing to organize the paper according to the subject matter of the cartoon instead of chronologically, for instance), you can color-code the cards on a different edge.

The subtopics and structure of your paper work together to make a strong, logical argument. As you choose a structure for your paper (explained in Chapter 12) and create a working outline (see Chapter 14), your subtopics may change.

7. **After your notes are complete, read them through again to be sure that the cards are sorted correctly.** Taking one subtopic pile at a time, place the cards in order. The first point that you want to make in the paper is the top card, the second point is the next card, and so forth. Some people like to spread all the cards from one subtopic on the floor or on a table at this point to make the sorting process easier.

8. **Create an outline and then begin writing once all the subtopic sets are in order.**

9. **Place the bibliography cards in alphabetical order and create the bibliography.** Use the bibliography cards for footnotes, endnotes, or parenthetical notes. See Chapter 18 for information on the format of footnotes, endnotes, parenthetical notes, and the bibliography.

Note Taking on the Computer

Do your fingers cramp up when you write more than three sentences at a time? Don't despair. The computer is your friend. If you take notes on a computer, you may be able to

- Download information from Web sites or other electronic sources directly into your note file

- Cut and paste quotations or data from your note file into the paper

- Move the information around electronically to create an outline

- Have a perfectly legible set of notes, regardless of your handwriting skills

- Cut and paste bibliographic information into the bibliography and footnotes, endnotes, or parenthetical notes

Alas, computers have their disadvantages. Taking notes on the computer means that you have to

- Work wherever the machine is, unless you have a laptop and are willing to lug it around

- Discipline yourself to back up all your notes every single time you end a session at the computer (Paper Assigners greet "the computer deleted my notes" the same way they welcome "the dog ate my homework.")

- Scroll around the file and see only a portion of your notes at one time, until you have a chance to print the file out

- Spend a lot of time moving bits of information around with the "cut" and "paste" commands, until the ideas are in an acceptable order

- Interrupt your reading of a book or an article to go to the computer to type in a note

Programming notes

In 1980 when my husband first saw a personal computer in action, he said, "I have seen the future, and it is good." Shortly after that announcement we bought a computer so big that it took up a whole corner of the living-room floor, even though it had less memory than one of today's handheld models. Since that time I've taken notes and written tons of stuff on computers, with the help of two types of programs. *Word processors* are programs that allow you to move, delete, add to, and change your text endlessly. Word processors also check your spelling and grammar (though they miss tons of errors and will never replace the human brain), suggest synonyms, count words, and format any margin, font, and note that you want. Most computers come equipped with a word-processing program, though you may choose to add another. As you word process, you save your work on a floppy disk *and* on the computer's built-in storage area, the hard drive. (Saving in two places saves *you* if the computer breaks.) Another useful type of program, a *database*, helps you keep track of information by sorting it into categories according to your commands. Think of a database as a set of electronic index cards that magically plops each note into the subtopic pile — a *field,* in computer lingo — that you define.

Writing notes by hand can be such a pain that more and more people are taking notes on the computer. If you choose this method, which is the one I use, a couple of things make life much easier:

- ✔ Whenever you begin using a new source, give the source a number. Keep a master list of sources in a separate file. Back up the master list every time you enter new information and print it out from time to time, storing the paper in a safe place.

- ✔ If you're researching from a book or article, don't type the notes into your file right away. Keep a pad of self-stick paper at hand. When you find something valuable, stick a piece of paper over the spot. (Or, if you own the book or have a photocopy of the article, highlight or circle the information.) When you finish a reading session, go back to each spot where you found something worth writing down. Type the notes, placing the number of each source and the page number next to each idea. For example:

#B6 p. 2: Langston Hughes and Zora Neale Hurston — two of the best-known writers of the Harlem Renaissance.

#B6 p. 6: During the Harlem Renaissance, many whites paid attention to African-American art for the first time.

The notations indicate that these two facts came from source #6, a book. The first note comes from page 2 and the second from page 6.

✔ When you find information online, select it and use the command to "copy" the information. Then open a note file and "paste" (another command) the information there. Label every fact with a source number (perhaps with the prefix "W" for the Web).

✔ In a separate master-list file of sources, create a bibliographical record for that source. Write down the *URL* (uniform resource locator, also known as the Web address) where you found the information and everything that you can find on the Web site about the date, author, original publisher, and so on. Also note the date and time you accessed the Web site. (See the section "Documenting Your Sources" later in this chapter for every boring little detail about this topic.)

✔ When you have plenty of information in your note file, print it out, read it through, and begin to think about subtopics. Go back and place a keyword at the beginning of each fact or idea. For example, if you are writing about Shakespeare's *Hamlet,* your subtopics may be the concept of honor, the idea of revenge, and the hero's flaws. In front of each idea in your file, type *"HONOR," "REVENGE,"* or *"FLAW."* Then by using the "cut" and "paste" commands, sort your notes into those three sections.

You can also sort notes with the help of a database program. Databases allow you to create categories called *fields.* Suppose you're researching the Greek gods. You may have a field for Zeus, Hera, Athena, and others. As you take notes, you tell the computer that a particular item belongs in the "Athena" field, perhaps, and the next item is part of the "Zeus" field. When you're done, a couple of clicks will tell the computer to sort your notes and retrieve whatever you want. So when you're ready to write about Athena, for example, all the "Athena field" notes and none of the unnecessary information will pop up on the screen.

✔ When you write the paper, use the "copy" and "paste" commands to insert quotations into the text.

✔ Every time you insert a quotation or a reference that must be documented, "copy" and "paste" information from the master source list.

✔ When you're done writing, open the source-list file and put the entries into proper bibliographic form. (Chapter 18 explains how to do so.)

Can't We All Get Along? Combining Note Cards and Computers

In the preceding two sections of this chapter, I describe two radically different methods of taking notes. One relies on index cards and the other depends upon the computer. Now it's time for me to confess: I combine a little of each method when I'm taking notes. First, I type as much as I can from books and magazines and download everything I need into a computer file. (See the preceding section, "Note Taking on the Computer," for more specifics.) Then

I print out the file. I read it and choose some logical subtopics. Next, I hit the stationery store and buy a set of multicolored index cards. I slice my printout into pieces, taping each fact (labeled, of course, with the number of the source and the page) onto the appropriate color card. Then I proceed with the method I describe in the section entitled "Carding — the Old System" earlier in this chapter: I sort the cards, put each subtopic in order, and create an outline. When the time comes to format the bibliography, I go back to the computer and open the master source-list file. I "cut" and "paste" the sources until they're in order.

I believe that my hybrid method gives me the best of both worlds. But this method is not for everyone. I happen to like kindergarten-level art projects (little round-tipped scissors, lots of different colors, double-sided sticky tape). But if the thought of little bits of paper drives you nutty, don't try this combo method. Stick with index cards *or* the computer. You'll be happier.

The combination system I just explained has image problems. Your boss may not appreciate an employee who cuts out little pieces of paper. A passing supervisor may deem you more efficient and professional if you're typing on the computer instead of playing with scissors, even if accomplishing the task on the computer takes more time. Moral: Know your enemy — er, boss — and behave accordingly.

Another hybrid method, one I use often, dumps both the index cards and the process of electronically sorting notes. I print out a copy of my notes from the computer and then color-code the facts with markers, one color for each subtopic. (A little slash mark in the margin works fine.) When I'm ready to create an outline, I read through the notes of one color — blue, for example. Then I number the blue notes — "1" for the first point I wish to make, "2" for the second, and so on. As I write the rough draft, I look at each blue fact in order.

I found a Russian hut!

While you're plowing through miles of notes, you may find it hard to imagine that research can be fun. Research can be a scavenger hunt, the quest for the Holy Grail, and a detective story all rolled into one big package. Actually finding what you are looking for is quite a thrill, as I found a few years ago when I was helping a student with a paper on the Russian Revolution. She became more and more involved in reading about the peasants, and her curiosity about their lives grew. In book after book, she gathered facts. But the big breakthrough — an image of their homes — escaped her. Then one day she came running down the hall crying, "I found a Russian hut! I found a Russian hut!" No, I didn't take her to a Nerds Anonymous meeting, because at that moment I was running towards her yelling, "That's great! That's great!" And no, the other people in the hallway didn't dial 911. They just giggled a little. It's a good school.

I find this method works well if I have no more than 10 to 15 pages of notes. If I have more than 15 pages, I can't keep track of all the information. I have to start cutting and pasting, either virtually or for real. You may find that you can deal with more pages (or fewer) than I can.

Highlighting and Indexing

Don't read this section if you work from printed materials that the library owns; nobody wants to take a book or magazine out of the library and see somebody else's yellow highlights all over it. But if you own the books you're working from, or if you've made photocopies of the articles you need, highlighting and indexing may be the fastest way to take notes.

Here's what you shouldn't do: Highlight everything that looks good and then go hang gliding. I have nothing against hang gliding, but I have *a lot* against fruitless searches through piles of photocopies or hundreds of pages of books. Highlighting alone, without indexing, is counterproductive. You waste countless hours searching for the information you need.

Highlighting in partnership with indexing, on the other hand, is the research equivalent of an expressway. Your work will zip by so speedily that you'll have enough time to practice for that big hang-gliding tournament you've been dying to enter.

Here's the deal on highlighting and indexing:

- ✔ Highlight everything you want to remember in one article or one section of a book.

- ✔ On a set of index cards or in a computer file, create a master list of sources. Write down all the information you'll eventually need for the bibliography. (See the "Documenting Your Sources" section in this chapter.)

- ✔ On an index card or in a computer file, write the source number, page number, and a few words describing the content of your highlights. Figure 8-2 shows an example of how to code your highlights.

- ✔ When you're ready to create an outline, look through the index cards or read the computer file. Refer to the books or photocopies to refresh your memory as needed. Next to each item on the outline, write the source number and page.

- ✔ As you write the rough draft, pile all the books and photocopies on or near your desk. When the outline calls for, say, a quotation on lightning from old Ben, you know that you have to turn to page 12 of book 2. (In case you've forgotten which book is #2, check the master source list — the index cards or computer file.)

Figure 8-2:
This card (or note in a computer file) tells me that on page 12 of book #2 I've highlighted a good quotation from Ben Franklin about lightning.

#B2 p.12

Quotation - B. Franklin - lightning

Indexing Audio-Visual Sources

Are you working from an audiotape of a live interview? Have you found a helpful videotape? If you replay the whole thing every time you need a quotation or a fact, the hours will just float away. You may have to give up some of life's frills, such as eating and sleeping.

An easier way to work with an audio-visual source is to *index* the material. Here's how to index:

1. **Before you do anything else, take an index card (Handy name, don't you think?) and write down everything you need to identify the source you're using.** (The next section, "Documenting Your Sources," tells you what to write.) Or, add the identifying information to the master list of sources on your computer. Give the source a number, perhaps with the prefix "A" for audio or "V" for video.

2. **Play the tape (audio or video).** The little numbers that roll on the player, indicate how far into the tape you've traveled. Be sure that the tape counter is set to 0000 before you start; if it isn't, press the reset button.

3. **When you hear or see something worthwhile, stop the machine.**

4. **On an index card or in a computer file, make a note of the number that appears on the machine.** Add a keyword or phrase describing what you've heard or seen. Check out Figure 8-3 for an example.

When you write the paper and need a comment from Bernstein about *West Side Story,* simply fast forward the tape to 5132.

Figure 8-3:
The information on this card tells you that at 5132 on videotape #2 Leonard Bernstein talks about *West Side Story,* for which he composed the music.

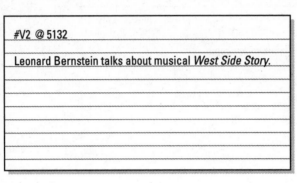

#V2 @ 5132

Leonard Bernstein talks about musical *West Side Story.*

Those handy numbers differ from machine to machine. So if you index the tape on one player, you have to stay with that player for the whole project.

Documenting Your Sources

No matter which method you use to take notes, you have to cite your sources. Inside the paper, you give source information in footnotes, endnotes, or parenthetical notes. At the end of the paper you create a bibliography or a list of works cited. Why do you have to let the reader know where the information comes from? For a couple of reasons. Simple honesty — not to mention a couple of laws and a ton of academic rules — requires that you not take credit for someone else's work. Also, if the reader doubts the information in your paper or becomes intrigued by the material, he or she should be able to read the source personally. Finally, providing a list of sources shows the person who is evaluating your work that you are thorough, earnest, and generally deserving of a pat on the back.

In Chapter 18, I go into excruciating detail on how to format footnotes, endnotes, parenthetical notes, and bibliographies. Here I just tell you what you need to write down as you take notes. (I recommend that you keep a numbered, master list of sources. See the sections on note taking earlier in this chapter for more information.)

Books

In general, all the information that you need to record for citation purposes is on the title page and the back of the title page, where the copyright and other publishing information appear. Write the title, subtitle (if there is one), volume number (if the book is published in more than one volume), author(s), translator (if applicable), editor (for a collection or series), publisher, place of publication (usually a city), date of publication, and edition (if specified). If the book is a collection of writings by several authors, write the title of the section or chapter, the first and last page numbers, the author of the section or chapter, as well as the title and editor(s) of the entire book. If the book quotes *another* source, write down all the information for that source as well. Also, keep track of the specific page numbers for each of the facts or quotations you use.

If you've read the book online, note the URL of the site where you found the book. Note the date the book was posted (if given) and the date you read the material. Also note the person or organization running the Web site.

Magazine, journal, and newspaper articles

The cover of the publication or the first page probably contains the relevant information. You may also have to check the *masthead,* the listing that names the publisher of the magazine, the editor, and so on. The masthead usually appears on a page near the table of contents. Record the name of the publication, the date, the volume and issue number (if given), the title of the article, the author(s), the page number, and the edition (if given).

If you read the article online, write the URL of the Web page where you found the article, as well as the URL of the site's home page, and the person or organization responsible for the site. Note the date the article was posted and the date you accessed the site. If you obtained the article through an online database, note the name and URL of the database and the keyword that you used to find the article.

Pamphlets and unpublished documents

If you're working from a pamphlet, write the title, author (if given), and date (if the pamphlet has one). Note the name of the organization that issued the pamphlet.

Unpublished documents, which are usually kept in library collections, may have an identifying number issued by the library. Write all the identifying information you can find: the type of document (such as a letter or journal), the author (if known), the name of the collection (*Letters of Bunsen X. Burner,* for example), the library number (if available), the date (if known), and the name of the library.

If the source is an unpublished dissertation or thesis, write the title and author(s), the type of paper (Master's thesis or Ph.D. dissertation, for example), the institution granting the degree, and the date.

Electronic sources

If you read an article online, either from a Web site or from an online database, write down (or "copy" and "paste" with computer commands) all the information listed in the previous paragraph about magazine, journal, and newspaper articles. In addition, include the date and time you downloaded the information and the URL. If the Web site tells you when the information was posted, write that date and time. If the site identifies who posted the information, note the individual's name and title.

URLs are long and tedious to type, and if they are not *exactly* correct, they're useless. Use the "copy" and "paste" commands on your computer to insure accuracy.

Audio-visual sources

If you made the tape yourself, note when you recorded the material. If the tape contains an interview that you conducted, note the location of the interview and whether you met personally or spoke on the phone with the subject. If you taped a live performance, note the time, date, place, and performers, as well as the sponsoring institution. For a homemade tape of a television or radio show, watch the opening and closing credits. Write the title of the program, the name of the series, the writer, when the program was aired, the name of the producer and director, the copyright date (usually appears in the closing credits), and the call letters of the station that broadcast the show.

For commercially produced films, CDs, DVDs, tapes, and records (Do they still make records?), note all the information in the preceding paragraph. Some of this information appears on the box, and the rest may be on liner notes or on the tape or film.

Special cases

As if there weren't enough documentation rules already, a few sources rate special treatment:

The Bible

Write the name of the book, the chapter and verse, and translation of the Bible you're using (King James, for example). Note all the other publishing information: publisher, place, and date of the edition.

Plays and poetry

Besides the publishing information of the book or magazine printing the literary work, record the act, scene, and line number (if given) for plays and the line number (if given) for the poem. If you read the play or poem online, record the URL of the page where you found the work and the home page of the site. Also note the date the poem or play was posted (if given) and the date you read it.

Government documents

Note the name of the agency or body issuing the document. Identify the title, author (if given), date, and publisher (if different from the agency responsible for the report). Some government documents are numbered; note the number. If you read the material online, record the URL of the page where you found the document and the home page of the site. Also, note the date the document was posted (if given) and the date you read it.

Laws and court decisions

Legal citation is a world of its own — with an entry fee of thousands of dollars for law school tuition. I'm not going to go into a lot of detail here. (You'll have to hire a lawyer! Or, you can delve into a book published by the Harvard Law Review Association, an exciting tome entitled *A Uniform System of Citation.*)

Here are the bare bones. In general, if you're quoting a law, write the number of the law, which is usually at the beginning or the end of the document. The section of the law may also have a number. If you know the type of law — federal, state, and so on — note the information. Also write down where you found the information. If you're quoting from a court decision, record the level of the court (Supreme Court or Circuit Court, for example), the name of the case, and the date.

Chapter 9

Note Taking: What to Write, What to Skip

● ●

In This Chapter

▶ Reviewing source material and taking preliminary notes

▶ Focusing your notes on useful information

▶ Avoiding repetition

▶ Omitting unnecessary words

▶ Writing clear and specific notes

● ●

During my teaching career I've read hundreds and hundreds of student notes (the kind that say "the new kid over in the third row has the hots for Dennie," as well as the ones that actually have an educational purpose). Far too often student notebooks leave me with one main idea: wasted time. Not only mine — the student's also! Some notebooks contain pages and pages of irrelevant information, and others are so cryptic that not even the writers know what they were trying to say.

In this chapter I tell you how to avoid writing (or downloading) too much and too little information in your notes. I give you strategies for focused, efficient note taking so that you don't end up copying a lot of useless stuff. I also provide sample sources and the notes drawn from them. Just don't look for any of these sources in your library; I made them all up!

Surveying the Field: Preliminary Notes

When you begin a research paper, you seldom know exactly what to focus on. You may have a vague idea of the subject (modern art, perhaps) and even a topic (Pablo Picasso). But you probably haven't narrowly defined what you're writing about (the "blue period" of Picasso's career). You certainly don't have a thesis statement ready. (For definitions of subject, topic, and thesis, see Chapter 3. For an explanation of how to write a thesis statement, see Chapter 11.)

As the topic of your paper evolves, so should your note taking. This section tackles preliminary notes. In the next section, "Note Taking with Focus," I explain how to take notes when you've settled upon the main idea of your paper.

In the preliminary stage, you've got the subject of your paper — modern art. You go to the modern art section of the library and leaf through a couple of books. Maybe you flip the pages of a reference book on modern art or skim a children's book on the subject. Or, you type "modern art" in a search engine or two and look at some Web sites. *At this stage you shouldn't take notes at all.* Just bookmark any interesting Web sites and record bibliographic information (title, author, and so on.) of any books that appear helpful. For library books, note the *call number* (usually found on the spine of the book or on one of the covers). If you borrow material from more than one library, write the name of the library where you found the material. For more information on record keeping, see Chapter 8.

After a few browsing sessions, you decide that Pablo Picasso rocks. Now you go back to the bookmarked Web sites and art books. If you find anything on Picasso, keep the source. If a Web site or book has nothing on this artist, dump it.

You may be tempted to begin taking notes at this point. Bad idea! You'll take notes about Picasso's cubism, his love affairs, his protest against the Spanish Civil War, the prices that his works command today, his daughter's jewelry designs, and a host of other things that won't be included in your final paper. So instead of recording information about Picasso, *record where the information is.* In other words, make an index.

Here's how to create an index of research materials:

1. **As you begin to read a new source, give it a number and record all the relevant information about the source so that you can find it again.** (Chapter 8 tells you how to do this.)

2. **Create an index by writing the number of the source and a brief description of what the source contains.** If the source is very short, one note does the job. For example:

   #M9 short article on the return to Spain of Picasso's painting "Guernica"

3. **For most sources, write several entries, such as:**

   #B7 chapter 2: Picasso's friendship with other artists

   #B7 chapter 3: All about blue period style

   #B7 chapter 4, pages 43-60: Explanation of cubism

   #B7 chapter 4, pages 61–78: Analysis of P's cubist paintings

By now you probably see the advantage of creating an index. After you've narrowed your topic to Picasso's blue period, you can ignore magazine article #9 and go back to book #7. Take notes on chapter 3, ignoring chapters 2 and 4 completely. Had you taken full notes at this stage in the research process, you'd have written a lot on Picasso's "Guernica," his artistic circle, and his experiments with cubism — all useless once you decided to write about the blue period.

As soon as you narrow the focus of your paper, narrow the focus of the index as well.

Note Taking with Focus

Think of your research as a flashlight, not a reading lamp, when you've progressed beyond the preliminary stage. You know what you're writing about, so the focus is narrower, although you haven't nailed down every little detail yet. Continuing the example from the preceding section, "Surveying the Field: Preliminary Notes," you've decided to write about the blue period of Picasso's artistic career. However, you haven't yet formulated a thesis statement. (See Chapter 11 for more information on thesis statements.)

At this stage, you should take notes on everything about the blue period, including:

✔ Details of Picasso's life during this period

✔ Characteristics of his blue period style

✔ Names and descriptions of his blue period paintings

Later, when you have a thesis, your note taking becomes even more focused. It resembles a laser beam rather than a flashlight. For example, a thesis about Picasso's blue period may state:

> The somber shades of Picasso's blue period complement his subject matter — the downtrodden of society.

When you decide on this thesis, you take note only of material that helps you make a case for the relationship between the colors in Picasso's blue period paintings and the people depicted. You should also record ideas or information that hurts your case, so that you can refute them in the paper. The index you created in the first stage of your research (see the preceding section, "Surveying the Field: Preliminary Notes," for directions) helps you choose relevant sources.

Got the idea? Once the preliminary stage — general reading and indexing of possible sources — is over, you take notes. But as you write each note, think about the paper you'll ultimately write. The topic and thesis of the paper will emerge gradually, and your notes will also gradually become more and more focused. Don't waste time writing things you won't need!

Time to put these note-taking techniques into practice. Check out Figure 9-1, a totally fictional article entitled "Kong: Top Banana Once Again?" The following sections provide a guide for taking notes from the article in Figure 9-1.

Hollywood Daily Press June 2, 2002

Kong: Top Banana Once Again? by Feigh Reigh

The fur is a little grayer and the shoulders are a tad rounder, but even his thick brow ridges can't conceal the youthful enthusiasm that twinkles in his giant brown eyes. At an age when many actors retire to the golf course, Kong, the fabled actor who starred in *King Kong*, is attempting a comeback. "That's 'Kah-Nng," he states forcefully. "The studio changed my name when they gave me the part." Kah-Nng reclaimed the original spelling about fifteen years ago when he returned to the island where he was born, in an effort, he says, "to rediscover his roots."

Speaking from the lot of Mega Studios, now planning a remake of the classic film, Kah-Nng quickly scaled a light fixture to show that he still has what it takes for the role that first made him a star. However, Kah-Nng admits that revising the role of Kong, if he gets the part, will be tough. The original role required Kah-Nng to fight airplanes, destroy subway cars, and climb the Empire State Building. He couldn't object, he says, because the studio would have fired him, even though he needed three operations on his knee because of the final scene, in which he fell from the skyscraper. "Some of the stunts in the remake will be done by a double," he says. "That's how they do it now. But I'll do some of them, no problem. I'm stronger than ever. I lift weights, I jog, and I keep the fur in good shape. I know I've still got it."

Reflecting on the original, Kah-Nng explains, "I had reservations about the role. I knew right away it was a career maker, but I also knew that the public would hate me. You get typecast, you know? I mean, they see this giant primate and they think 'monster.'" He pauses for a moment and then does two quick, astonishingly accurate impersonations of Adam Sandler and Robin Williams. Grinning in triumph, he says, "See? I could have played a clown, a spy, a lover, a chef. . .but casting directors never gave me a chance." He continues, "I almost didn't take the part when it was offered. But the money was too good to pass up. And the working conditions were great. The studio built that whole set, you know — though we did go on location for the Empire State Building scene. And everything was first class — the food, the trailers. . .of course, I didn't need costumes, but the hairdressers took good care of my coat." He adds, "I loved my co-stars. They were pros — all on long-term contracts, and they got a bonus for acting in King Kong. Not that it was about the money. They were truly committed to their art, as was I. I had a wonderful time on the set."

Kah-Nng began acting at an early age. His father, a banana gatherer, opposed his son's career choice. But his mother was star struck. She was an extra in three of the Tarzan movies, and in two of them she carried her son onto the set. Kah-Nng's first auditions, for small roles in *Hamlet* and *Miracle on Thirty-Fourth Street*, were discouraging. "This one guy controlled all the parts. He told me that I was good but that my 'physical type' would be a problem. I never even got to meet the director," Kah-Nng says. But Kah-Nng never lost his belief that he was destined for stardom. He was waiting tables when someone showed him the script for what was then titled *Giant Gorilla*. He immediately strode over to the studio, and the rest is history.

According to Kah-Nng, the remake presents a more complex character. "The new Kong has a softer side too. He's done some therapy, he's in touch with his feelings, and he really agonizes about that subway car he wrecks!" Asked about Kah-Nng's chances, studio officials would say only that many actors are competing for the part.

Figure 9-1:
A fictional
article.

The preliminary stage

You're vaguely interested in old movies, and you're checking possible sources. You come across "King: Top Banana Once Again." If you are indexing it, you may write

> #M1 Actor Kong trying to make comeback — comments on making original *King Kong,* studio, working conditions, his career

Because the article is short, one listing is enough and no page number is required. However, note the bibliographic information (title, author, publication, and so forth) on another card or on your source list.

Zeroing in on a topic

After you choose a topic — the classic film *King Kong* — you're ready to write more. Here are some notes for that topic, all labeled with the source number:

> #M1 Studio changed name of actor from Kah-Nng to Kong
>
> #M1 Kong fights planes, destroys subway cars, climbs Empire State Building
>
> #M1 Hurt knee (operated 3 times) in fall from Emp. St. Bldg.
>
> #M1 Had to do own stunts — couldn't object
>
> #M1 Kong almost didn't take part — typecasting bothered him
>
> #M1 Good working conditions, good salary
>
> #M1 Studio built set, except location for Emp. St. Bldg.
>
> #M1 First class — food, trailers
>
> #M1 No costumes for Kong, but hairdresser for coat
>
> #M1 Kong's co-stars on long-term contracts
>
> #M1 Co-stars and Kong committed to art
>
> #M1 Kong enjoyed time on the set
>
> #M1 Kah-Nng tried for roles in Hamlet + Miracle/ 34th St.
>
> #M1 Originally titled *Giant Gorilla*

Notice that these notes omit all the information about actor Kah-Nng's comeback attempt. Because the paper focuses on the original film, that information is irrelevant.

Now suppose your topic is even narrower — "the role of the studio in the making of the classic film *King Kong.*" If you take notes on the article at this point, you don't need to write anything about Kong's prior acting experience or his commitment to art, and you may omit the information about the film's original title as well. You'd probably include everything else:

#M1 Studio changed name of actor from Kah-Nng to Kong

#M1 Kong fights planes, destroys subway cars, climbs Empire State Building

#M1 Hurt knee (operated 3 times) in fall from Emp. St. Bldg.

#M1 Had to do own stunts — couldn't object

#M1 Kong almost didn't take part — typecasting bothered him

#M1 Good working conditions, good salary

#M1 Studio built set, except location for Emp. St. Bldg.

#M1 First class — food, trailers

#M1 No costumes for Kong, but hairdresser for coat

#M1 Kong's co-stars on long-term contracts

When you have a thesis statement

When you know the topic, you can start moving towards a *thesis* — the idea you will prove in the paper — and a *thesis statement* — the sentence that expresses what you are going to prove. With a thesis statement in mind, your note taking becomes even more focused. Chapter 11 explains how to create a thesis statement.

Here's one possible thesis statement for a research paper on *King Kong:*

The studio had total power over Kong during the making of *King Kong.*

If you read the article now, here's what you write:

#M1 Studio changed name of actor from Kah-Nng to Kong

#M1 Kong fights planes, destroys subway cars, climbs Empire State Building

#M1 Hurt knee (operated 3 times) in fall from Emp. St. Bldg.

#M1 Had to do own stunts — couldn't object

#M1 Kong almost didn't take part — typecasting bothered him

Don't bother writing about what happened before or after the movie or about the co-stars, because those facts aren't relevant to the case you're trying to make. Also, skip the notes on the set, hairdressing and costumes, and food and salary; those facts show the benefits the studio provided, but they don't have anything to do with power, and your thesis concerns power. You still note the name change and the tough stunts Kong was forced to do because these events show the studio's power over Kong.

You may or may not need the information about the knee operation. The injury resulted from the stunts Kong was forced to do (showing studio power), but the operation took place after the filming ended. When in doubt, write the note. Later, if you need it, it's there.

Note taking is not an exact science. As you write the paper, you may decide that a quote from Kah-Nng is perfect for the fifth paragraph. When you check your notes, you realize that you didn't write Kah-Nng's exact words — only that he couldn't object to dangerous stunts. No problem. The "M1" designation in your notes tells you which article contained this information. Just go back to the original source and collect your quotation. (You've been keeping accurate records, haven't you? Now all that work pays off.)

Notice that the amount of information you write, after the preliminary research stage, decreases as your ideas about the paper become clearer. You write fewer, but more useful notes.

Avoiding Common Pitfalls: Too Many, Too Few, and Repetitive Notes

Note takers too often fall into one of two categories: (1) those who take so many notes that they more or less recopy the entire source and (2) those who jot down so little that when they write the paper, they can't imagine what "sys — bld." means. (Don't ask me; I have no idea either.) A third category, which often overlaps with the write-too-much type, is the repeater. The repeater dutifully notes that Columbus reached the New World in 1492 — and then notes it again and again and again.

Never fear: In this section I explain how to avoid the common pitfalls of note taking.

Overwriters and repeaters

If you write too much information when taking notes, the best way to cut down is to focus your note taking, as I explain in the preceding section, the cleverly titled "Note Taking with Focus." But focus is not the only way to put your notes on a diet. Omitting unnecessary words also saves a lot of ink (or electrons or whatever it is that places words on a computer screen). Here's the deal for overeager note takers:

✔ If you quote a source, you usually need to write every word and punctuation mark exactly as it appears in the text. However, if part of the quotation is irrelevant, you may leave it out. Place three dots in the text to show that words are missing. If you drop words at the end of a sentence, place four dots @ three to show that words are missing and one for the period at the end of the sentence. (See Chapter 16 for every little detail on how to punctuate quotations.)

✔ If you aren't quoting the exact words, drop the unimportant stuff. **Remember:** You still need to cite the source! *Articles,* the grammarians' term for *a, an,* and *the,* should definitely go. Sometimes you can also omit parts of verbs or descriptive words and phrases without a great loss of meaning.

✔ A common pitfall, especially for a project that you work on over a period of several weeks, is repetition. The most common scenario goes like this: When you review your notes prior to writing, you discover that you've jotted down the name of Picasso's first blue period painting no fewer than nine times, once for each source that fact appeared in. For the most part, repetition is easy to avoid. Just quickly review your notes whenever you begin to read a new source. Unless you have a truly terrible memory, the name of Picasso's first blue period painting should look familiar to you. A quick glance back tells you that you don't have to write it again.

Underwriters

No, I'm not talking about jobs in the insurance industry. I'm talking about people who write too little. (Sounds like an Oprah show, doesn't it? People Who Write Too Little, and Those Who Love Them! Today at four!) This label applies to you if you find yourself desperately thumbing through photocopies or surfing the Internet when you're supposed to be writing the paper. True, a certain number of U-turns are inevitable when you're creating a research paper. Writing is a form of thinking, and until you actually do it, you can't know exactly what you need. Some rechecking is appropriate. But if you're on a major search and seizure operation after you thought that the research stage of the process was over, you're an underwriter, at least in the field of note taking.

If I've just painted a portrait of you as an underwriter, don't give up. Read the preceding section of this chapter, "Note Taking with Focus," and attack your next project with a couple of resolutions. Make a good index of sources, move from subject to topic to thesis as quickly as you can, and focus your attention on material that is likely to help prove your thesis. Then take a few more notes than you think you need.

A second type of "underwriting" comes from a researcher who would really prefer a career in espionage. Cryptic phrases with no context, abbreviations that make sense only on the planet Uranus, and all kinds of symbolic doodles with no labels characterize this researcher. This problem may be tough to correct. I speak from experience because I've found some of my own notes unintelligible, always when I most need them. (If anyone can figure out what "342 BCE — shrd" means, give me a call.) Whenever I'm drawing an arrow or jotting down a shortened phrase, I'm absolutely sure I'll remember what it means. But sometimes, I don't.

The answer to this problem is *not* to write in full sentences. You don't want to swing from underwriting into overwriting, without even a pause in the "just right" slot. It's okay to drop words that really are unnecessary. Don't give up on abbreviations either; they do help the harried note taker, no question. (The next section — "N Tkg W/ Abbr." — tackles this topic.)

Here's the bottom line for the CIA types out there: Provide enough detail to remember, even weeks later, what the note means. Test yourself a little: Every time you sit down for a work session, reread the stuff you wrote the day before. Intelligible? Random letters? Adjust your note taking accordingly.

N Tkg W/ Abbr.

Note taking is not exactly the world's most exciting activity. In a nanosecond or two, you can probably find something more interesting to occupy your time — counting the number of seconds between drips from the faucet, perhaps, or taking the lint out of your coat pocket. So it makes sense to spend as little time as possible taking notes. Enter abbreviations.

You probably know quite a few abbreviations already — weights and measures, countries, cities and states, and titles. In this section, I give you some abbreviations you may not know, all real timesavers.

Common words

Many common English words may be shortened. Check out these abbreviations, tried and found true by researchers:

& = and

anon = anonymous

~ = approximately (referring to amounts)

assn = association

@ = at

b/c = because

biog = biography

bk = book

c = circa (about, referring to dates)

concl = conclusion

cong = congress

esp = especially

ex = example

♂ = male

fig = figure

fl = flourished (used for dating the high point for something or someone when the exact dates aren't known)

e.g. = for example

gen = general

gov't = government

> = greater than

intro = introduction

irreg = irregular

< = less than

♀ = female

misc = miscellaneous

= number

org = organization

p = page

pps = pages

NB = pay special attention here (comes from the Latin words for "note well")

pseud = pseudonym (pen name)

? = questionable information

Q = quotation

s/b = should be

v. or vs. = versus

w/ = with

w/o = without

Personalized abbreviations

Why let the experts have all the fun? As you delve into your research, look for certain words or phrases that pop up frequently. Create your own abbreviations, but keep a master list somewhere in case you forget what the abbreviations stand for. Here's a partial list for a paper on the Revolutionary War:

> RV = Revolution
>
> G3 = King George III
>
> GW = Me (sorry, just kidding) George Washington
>
> BH = Bunker Hill

Don't abbreviate in the finished paper unless the Authority Figure reviewing your work has specifically stated that abbreviations are acceptable. Even then, take care to use only the abbreviations that he or she allows. If you're not sure about an abbreviation, write the whole word.

Acronyms (the first letter in each significant word of a name — EPA for Environmental Protection Agency, for example) are always acceptable in notes, and usually acceptable in writing. The first time you mention the name, write out all the words and place the acronym in parenthesis after the name. From that point on, use the acronym. For example:

> Senator Louella joined the Society for the Preservation of Elderly Senators (SPES) last year. When Louella turned 90, the SPES threw a party for him.

Taking Proper Notes: An Example

If you've read this whole chapter, you probably never want to hear the word "note" again. However, even if you're now allergic to the term, you still have to take proper notes if you want to turn out a good research paper.

In this section I provide a sample set of notes, drawn from "LeMeout's Principle: Discovery and Application" by Si Fai, from a science text entitled *Principles of Science.* (You can read Si Fai's masterpiece in Figure 9-2. Don't look for it in the library; I made it up.)

Imagine that your physics teacher asked for a paper on an important scientific principle. You found this source on "LeMeout's Principle" the first time you went to the library. Figure 9-3 shows what the bibliography card would look like.

"LeMeout's Principle: Discovery and Application" by Si Fai, from **Principles of Science,** *edited by Bunsen X. Burner. Publisher: Big Ben Books Ltd., London, 2003. All quotations drawn from the Journals of LeMeout.*

In 1722, Puhliz LeMeout proposed a fundamental principle of walking, now known as LeMeout's Principle. LeMeout came to his great discovery while the local barber was setting his nose, broken for the third time as a result of an unfortunate collision with a sidewalk. LeMeout realized that he "had never fallen Up in conseyquence of a Trippe" and that not falling up "might be Important." LeMeout, a methodical man, immediately hired "three or four Ruffians and Layabouts with Nothing Better to Do" to trip on the sidewalk as he meticulously took notes. The great scientist described the experiment in this way:

> They did fall certainly Down to the Ground, moaning instantly in Payne, and none did fall Up. I pushed Each again to cause a Greate Loss of Balance, whereupon he did fall again Down.

LeMeout also noted in his journal that he paid for the setting of

> one nose, an Arme (left), and a small pointer fynger, Two of these Brokeyn Bones on one Ruffian, he squealing like a Pig in heat from the Payne, for which I payed three pounds plus the barber's fees for bone settyng.

Page 34

Today, LeMeout's Principle is recognized as fundamental to our understanding of the physical world. It may be stated thus:

> A body tripping on a sidewalk falls in a downward direction, unless an exterior force intervenes and changes the trajectory.

In applying LeMeout's principle, define a "body" as any human or, in some cases, animal entity. The sidewalk may be straight, curved, or inclined; the genius of LeMeout's Principle lies in its universality. Any motion away from the apex of verticality constitutes a downward direction, although excessive movement forward may be considered a diagonal, still ending in LeMeout's observation of contact with said sidewalk. The exterior force, not observed in LeMeout's original experiment but rather in a follow-up series with unemployed milkmaids, was generally a supportive arm catching the body before contact with the sidewalk. In one case the milkmaid's trajectory was changed by collision with a large oak tree. LeMeout observed that the tree's opposing force equaled the downward momentum initiated by the trip, hence bringing movement of any kind to an end. (The milkmaid, however, did sustain "a brokeyn nose" as surely as her colleagues.)

Page 35

Figure 9-2:
A sample pulled from a fictional science text.

Figure 9-3:
A sample
bibliography
card for
Figure 9-2.

> #B4 pages 34-35
>
> "LeMeout's Principle: Discovery and Application"
> by Si Fai, from *Principles of Science*, edited by
> Bunsen X. Burner. Publisher: Big Ben Books Ltd,
> London, 2003.

After reading the essay, you decide that the topic of your paper will be LeMeout's Principle. (You don't yet have a thesis.)

Here are the notes:

#B4 p. 34: 1722 — Puliz LeMeout — fell, broke nose on sidewalk, while barber set discovered principle

#B4 p. 34: Tested principle — three "ruffians and layabouts" — pushed them — all fell ↓ none ↑

#B4 p. 34: LM: "They did fall certainly Down to the Ground"

#B4 p. 34: LM's journal: "ruffians" broke arm, nose, finger — LM pd. $

#B4 p. 35: Principle = body tripping on sdwlk falls ↓, unless exterior force intervenes

#B4 p. 35: Excess movemt. → = diag.

#B4 p. 35: Exterior force in follow up exp. = arm or tree

#B4 p. 35: No movemt then "tree's opposing force" = ↓ ward trip momentum

Can you read these notes? Many of the words have been shortened and a couple of symbols have been inserted, but they should still be understandable. Check out these features:

✔ The first time a name appears, it's spelled out. After this first mention, the name is expressed by initials ("LM" for LeMeout).

✔ Three of the notes contain quotation marks and the exact words. The first is labeled "LM" to indicate that the words come from LeMeout, not from the author of the essay. The second is labeled "LM's journal" to identify the source more specifically.

✔ Arrows and equal signs save words.

✔ Only important words, those expressing the main idea, appear in the notes.

✔ The common word *movement* is abbreviated ("movemt.").

These notes summarize the entire article. If you write the notes after formulating a thesis, omit those notes that didn't apply to your thesis. For example, suppose you choose this thesis for the paper:

> LeMeout's Principle is crucial for urban planners, particularly for those who design sidewalks.

With this thesis, all the details about LeMeout's discovery — broken nose, milkmaids, ruffians, and so on — are irrelevant. The only notes you may need to prove this thesis are the following:

> #B4 p. 35: Principle = body tripping on sdwlk falls ↓, unless exterior force intervenes

> #B4 p. 35: Excess movemt. → = diag.

> #B4 p. 35: Exterior force in follow up exp. = arm or tree

Keep in mind that note taking is not an exact science. For example, the last note in the preceding example deals with the "exterior force" in some of LeMeout's experiments. You may not need that note in the finished paper, but if you write about the issue of trees in urban planning, this fact may come in handy. Bottom line: Omit ideas certain to be irrelevant and include those that fall into the "possible" category.

Chapter 10

Staying on the Right Side of the Law

In This Chapter

▶ Avoiding plagiarism

▶ Quoting material

▶ Understanding when to cite and when not to cite sources

▶ Looking at copyright law

You and I both know that you can log on to the Internet, buy a fully formed research paper, and download it to your own computer. You've already rejected that option by buying this book. What? You say your mom bought it for you? Fine. But if you're reading it and she's not actually standing over you with a baseball bat, you've clearly chosen to write the paper yourself, staying on the ethical highroad and actually learning something at the same time.

Unfortunately, the ethical high road includes a lot of forks. Without a road map, you may accidentally take a wrong turn. In this chapter I explain why identifying the sources of information in your research paper is necessary. I show you how to distinguish between material that may be included without sources and material that must be documented. I also help you decide where to put those pesky little quotation marks and discuss how to stay on the right side of the copyright law.

Avoiding Plagiarism for Fun and Profit

Plagiarism is intellectual dishonesty — taking another person's idea or research and claiming it as one's own. Plagiarism is stealing in the same way that swiping a wallet is stealing. The only difference is that plagiarism is the theft of thought, not of goods. No matter: As you heard first in the sandbox, taking something that doesn't belong to you is a no-no.

If you're a student, one important reason to avoid plagiarism is self-protection. Students have been ahead of the curve in exploring — and exploiting — the Internet, but the old geezers on the teacher's side of the desk are catching up. A number of Internet sites allow a teacher to check a sentence, a paragraph, or a whole paper for plagiarism. (Plagiarized material from written sources can be verified also, usually with a little stroll through the library.) The odds are better every day that the student plagiarizer will get nailed — and if that happens, the paper will receive an F. Depending on the school's policy, the student may also be suspended or expelled.

Business writers also have good reason to avoid plagiarism. If your job description includes research, your boss expects you to know how to do research and to do it honestly. (Okay, maybe not. But if you work for a crook, time to read the want ads.) A list of sources shows your boss that you accomplished the task that the company is paying for. And if the paper you write is eventually published, you know that you and the boss won't have to go to court to defend against a charge of copyright infringement. Avoiding lawsuits is always a plus.

Both students and professionals have still another reason to stay on the straight and narrow path of intellectual honesty. To identify the sources of the information in a paper is to share the responsibility. Imagine that you quoted a statistic that turns out to be wrong: Ninety percent of all cookie eaters gobble the filling first. If you identified your source — an article entitled "Crumb or Icing?" by Ita Lot, published in the *Cookie Filling Manufacturers' Journal* — the author of that article takes the rap for the error. You may draw some displeasure from the Authority Figure reading your paper because you relied on erroneous material, but you're off the hook for the error itself.

Okay, now that you know why you shouldn't plagiarize, it's time to explain (in excruciating detail) how to stay out of trouble.

Quote Unquote

When you include an author's exact words in your paper, you must surround those words with *quotation marks,* the punctuation mark indicating (What will they think of next?) that you are quoting. If you include someone else's words in your paper, presenting them as if they were your own, you're plagiarizing. Go directly to jail; do not pass Go. Here's an example. Run your eyeballs over Figure 10-1, an excerpt from that famous (actually, nonexistent) book, *Investment Opportunities in Exploration: A Guide for Monarchs,* by Queen Isabella of Spain.

Excerpt from Investment Opportunities in Exploration: A Guide for Monarchs
by Isabel, Queen of Castile, Spain. Zaragoza, Spain: Fernando Vil, Inc., 1502.

- -

The running of a successful state is a burden that every monarch accepts, nay welcomes. An appropriate income capable of supporting royalty in a luxurious manner befitting their status is crucial. The people must be inspired to awe by the sight of their rulers! Castles must impress, and royal clothing must take the peasants' breath away. Hence every monarch, myself included, must raise revenue. Exploration has proved itself to be a profitable, though somewhat risky, investment.

A few years ago an Italian, Christopher Columbus, approached me and asked for funds to mount an expedition to the Indies. Spices, silks, and other treasures have always sold for enormous sums in this kingdom, and securing a trade route would give my kingdom a secure fount of income for the foreseeable future. My husband, Ferdinand, spoke with him first, but Ferdinand was not swayed by the Italian's arguments. I, on the other hand, immediately saw the appeal. First, I could finance the voyage by ridding myself of unattractive jewelry that my husband's family had bestowed upon me at our wedding. Selling those necklaces and bracelets to raise money for exploration — firmly, I would claim, to return ample funds to the state — was a proposition even Ferdinand's mother could not refute. Second, the Italian seemed to be onto a new idea: a round earth. While most look at the land beneath their feet and see flatness, I perceive that buildings at a distance appear gradually as one nears them. A ball, rotated thusly, behaves in the same way. I thought Columbus's idea might be right. Third, if the Italian proved wrong and fell off the side of a flat earth, I'd have lost little but a hideous ornament for which I had no use anyway.

Before I go any further, I wish to state several principles of sound investment in exploration, for the guidance of monarchs wishing to proceed down this path:

Do not fund journeys into areas already known; if revenue were available there, it would already be flowing into your coffers. You cannot discover what has already been explored.

Look for energetic young captains. They may be wrong and perish in the attempt, but they will amuse you with their presentations, and the chance of success, though slim, is greater because of their daring.

Do not risk funds you cannot afford to lose. Our maps include areas clearly labeled, "Here be monsters." Monsters may kill your captain and, therefore, the investment.

You must think about long-term profits. To sail into the unknown takes time, and then to sail back with something that produces income takes still more time. If you need money immediately, raise taxes or invade a nearby, unfortified country. Exploration yields its riches more slowly.

Finally, insure the explorers' loyalty by promising a percentage of the profits to successful crews. If money is tight, you can always break your promise (a time-honored privilege of high rank) or arrange a suitable death for the returning voyagers.

Figure 10-1:
An excerpt from a sample (non-existent) text on investment.

For those of you who threw spitballs during history class the day they covered Isabella, she's the one who financed Columbus's voyage to the New World, which he stumbled over while he was trying to find a trade route to India. Imagine that you're writing a paper on the economics of exploration. You write the following paragraph:

> It is no accident that the great age of exploration coincided with the age of absolute monarchs in Europe. Exploration investment is risky, and democratic rulers have to convince the people and their representatives that the investment is sound. Absolute monarchs, on the other hand, don't have to justify their actions to anyone; they can simply act. Monarchs have good reason to finance explorations. An appropriate income capable of supporting royalty in a luxurious manner befitting their status is crucial. The people must be inspired to awe by the sight of their rulers! Castles must impress, and royal clothing must take the peasants' breath away.

The last part of the preceding paragraph is lifted, word for word, from Isabella's book, but you've given no indication that those words are any different from the rest of the paragraph, which truly is your own. Time to bake a cake with a file in it, because you're going up the river to the plagiarism penitentiary. How do you avoid trouble? Easy. Just put the words you took from the book in quotation marks and identify the source:

> It is no accident that the great age of exploration coincided with the age of absolute monarchs in Europe. Exploration investment is risky, and democratic rulers have to convince the people and their representatives that the investment is sound. Absolute monarchs, on the other hand, don't have to justify their actions to anyone; they can simply act. Monarchs have good reason to finance explorations. As Queen Isabella writes in *Investment Opportunities in Exploration: A Guide for Monarchs,* "An appropriate income capable of supporting royalty in a luxurious manner befitting their status is crucial. The people must be inspired to awe by the sight of their rulers! Castles must impress, and royal clothing must take the peasants' breath away."

Now the reader knows which words are yours, and which aren't.

In Britain, quotation marks are called *inverted commas.* In American English, double quotation marks are your first choice, with single quotation marks for quotations inside other quotations. In Britain, the system is reversed. For more information on the punctuation of quotation marks, see Chapter 16.

To be legal, you also need to identify the source of the quoted material by providing a *citation.* A citation in the real world is that dreaded piece of paper the traffic cop gives you for saying things like "There was a stop sign on that corner? You're kidding!" A citation in the world of research papers is an identification tag. It tells the reader where you got the information — the Web site, article, book, or person that provided the material you are weaving into your paper.

When you cite material in a research paper, you provide information about the source in parentheses, in a footnote, or in an endnote. You provide even more information in a list of sources — often called a *bibliography* — at the end of the paper. Using the list of sources and the individual citations, the reader should be able to retrace the writer's steps and find the information exactly as the writer did. Parenthetical citations provide the page number where the material was originally found and just enough information to identify the source — usually the author's name, if it doesn't appear in your text. Footnotes and endnotes tuck a little number next to the sentence. At the bottom of the page (for a footnote) or at the end of the paper (for an endnote) the source is identified and the page number is specified.

I won't explain all the rules of citation here. Actually, I won't explain *all* the rules anywhere. If I did so, *Research Papers For Dummies* would be one of those books that you have to roll around on a cart. In Chapter 18, I go over the basics, enough to get you through most normal situations. For those of you who have to go beyond the basics, Chapter 18 also tells you which hundred-pound book to wheel home from the library. Under no circumstances should you learn the rules on how to cite information. All they do is clutter up your brain. Simply look them up when you need them.

Deciding When to Cite Sources

Putting quotation marks around someone's exact words is easy. Apart from the niceties of punctuation, you have no decisions to make. But a typical set of notes for a research paper includes more than exact quotations. In fact, most of the notes are a hodgepodge of ideas and facts harvested from books, Web sites, journals, and so on. Your research paper will certainly incorporate much of that information without quoting exact words.

When you stray from direct quotations, the question confronting you is this: To cite or not to cite. In this section I take you through a couple of common situations and explain when the rules require you to cite your sources.

Ideas

Even if your paper relies most heavily on statistics and other sorts of facts, you probably include some ideas as well. After all, most of us have a few notions floating around in our brains: "Recess is good," "buy wholesale whenever possible," "pollution is bad," and so forth. So what happens when you take an idea, not a fact, from a research source? Do you have to cite the idea? The answer is a definite maybe. (Don't you love these clear-cut guidelines?) Here's the deal: If the idea is one that is likely to occur to almost anyone (drug abuse is bad or homelessness is a problem, for example) you probably don't have to cite it, so long as you express the idea in your own words.

But if the idea is clearly original or creative, you must cite the source, even if you use only your own words to express it. For example, in her non-best-selling book, *Investment Opportunities in Exploration: A Guide for Monarchs* (see Figure 10-1), Isabella of Castile discusses how monarchs raise money from exploration, taxes, and war. If you include that idea in your paper without crediting Isabella, you're in trouble.

You must cite sources for original ideas even if the sources are not written. Imagine that you and your buds are sitting around eating your hamburgers when someone comes up with a theory about the relationship between hamburgers and modern art. You include the theory in your research paper "The Aesthetics of Fast Food." You have to cite your friend. (How? See Chapter 18 for information on how to cite sources.)

You may think you're off the hook if you restate ideas in your own words. Nope. You still need to credit the person who first came up with the ideas. Check out this paragraph drawn from the last five paragraphs of the excerpt from *Investment Opportunities in Exploration: A Guide for Monarches.* Notice how the writer incorporates most of Isabella's ideas, while changing the order of and expressing the ideas in different words:

> Kings and queens should avoid backing explorations into settled areas because those areas are not open to discovery. Monarchs should not gamble with necessary funds because exploration is, by its nature, risky. Also, although money may be made from explorations, it takes a long time for profits to materialize. To realize a quick gain, a ruler should choose war. The best expeditions, from an investment point of view, are those captained by lively young leaders. Rulers should promise to pay the explorers well, even if the promise cannot be kept.

You can place such a paragraph in your research paper, *if and only if* you cite the source. You may cite the source in the text, as in the following paragraph:

> In *Investment Opportunities in Exploration: A Guide for Monarchs,* Queen Isabella of Spain makes several suggestions for her colleagues. According to Isabella, kings and queens should avoid backing explorations into settled areas because those areas are not open to discovery. Monarchs should not gamble with necessary funds because exploration is, by its nature, risky and it takes a long time for profits to materialize. To realize a quick gain, Isabella writes, a ruler should choose war. The best expeditions, she goes on to explain, are those captained by lively young leaders. She believes that rulers should promise to pay the explorers well, even if the promise cannot be kept (32).

The revised passage clearly credits Isabella. Her name is not in every sentence, but scattered throughout the passage. The reader understands that all the ideas come from *Investment Opportunities in Exploration: A Guide for Monarches,* page 32.

If you cite a source in the text, be sure to list the source and all the identifying information in a bibliography at the end of the paper. See Chapter 18 for complete details.

When you cite the source for an idea expressed in your own words, take care not to confuse the reader. The reader must be able to determine which ideas come from the source and which are your own. Here's another passage from a research paper on the economics of exploration:

> Most voyages of exploration are quite expensive. Providing ships, food, and equipment for a hundred sailors is not cheap. Yet rulers who skimp on the basics may lose the entire investment to starvation or disease. To entice reluctant sailors, rulers should promise to pay the explorers well, even if the promise cannot be kept. Monarchs should not gamble with necessary funds because exploration is, by its nature, risky. Also, although money may be made from explorations, it takes a long time for profits to materialize (Isabella 32).

The citation in parenthesis tells the reader that information has been drawn from page 32 of Isabella's work. But the parenthetical note doesn't tell the reader *which part* of the paragraph is being attributed to Isabella. The seam between Isabella's words and the rest of the paragraph actually begins with the fourth sentence, but the reader has to check the original — or employ a mind reader — to figure out who wrote what. A reference in the text — "according to Queen Isabella" — may show the reader where the writer's ideas end and the source material begins. If the entire paragraph comes from one source, the citation alone is okay.

Train of thought

You also have to credit the original author if you include a whole pattern of logic, a "train of thought" that he or she created. Suppose you're writing about environmental issues, and you find an article by Cookie LeBeef entitled "Fruit Cocktail: The Next Frontier for Environmental Politics." In your notes you jot down the author's main points, an amazing set of linked ideas, as follows:

> Cherries grow on trees.
>
> Trees need soil to grow.
>
> If we pave over all the orchards to construct more superhighways, the trees will die.
>
> The lack of trees will ruin the cherry harvest.
>
> Fruit cocktail manufacturers will have to replace the cherries with hydroponic lettuce.
>
> Fruit cocktail fans, who generally dislike lettuce, are natural targets for recruitment into environmental organizations.

You write a research paper organized around this train of thought:

Apples grow in orchards.

Orchards die when cement is poured over them.

The more superhighways we construct, the more orchards will die.

The smaller number of orchards will lead to a shortage of apples.

Pie bakers will have to substitute lima beans for apples.

No one wants to eat a lima-bean pie.

Pie lovers will support environmental organizations.

The details in your paper are different, but the logical thread is the same as the one in Ms. LeBeef's article. If you don't acknowledge her contribution to your work, you've plagiarized. How do you credit Ms. LeBeef? The best way is to include the article in your bibliography and to make a reference to it in the text:

An untapped constituency for environmental causes is the eating public. Cookie LeBeef, in her groundbreaking analysis entitled "Fruit Cocktail: The Next Frontier for Environmental Politics," traces the links between cherry trees and opposition to superhighway construction. Similarly, apple-pie lovers. . . .

You may also credit the source in a footnote, as follows, with complete publication information in the bibliography:

The specter of lima-bean pies sitting uneaten on the supermarket shelves may galvanize the environmental movement.[2]

[2] For her analysis of the link between the eating public and environmental causes, I am indebted to Cookie LeBeef's ground-breaking study "Fruit Cocktail: The Next Frontier for Environmental Politics."

Unique phrases

What should you do if almost everything you write in your paper comes from your own brain, but one or two interesting words do not? For example, suppose you're writing about Queen Isabella's life and her impact on history. (Imagine that Figure 10-1, an excerpt from Isabella's book on investing in exploration, is one of your sources.) Here's a passage from your paper:

Isabella of Castile married Ferdinand of Aragon, but she did not surrender her power or rights, and she certainly saw herself as Ferdinand's peer. However, she was not above trickery. She sold some of her wedding presents, including a hideous ornament, to finance Columbus's voyage to the Indies.

See the phrase "hideous ornament"? That phrase comes from Isabella's book. She chose those words, which reflect her feelings and reveal her way of expressing herself. To lift the phrase without crediting her is plagiarism. You probably have not seen and evaluated the jewelry; even if you have seen the thing, the judgment is still the queen's and should be so labeled. Following are two ways to correct the problem

Example #1:

> Isabella of Castile married Ferdinand of Aragon, but she did not surrender her power or rights, and she certainly saw herself as Ferdinand's peer. However, she was not above trickery. She sold some of her wedding presents, including one she called "a hideous ornament," to finance Columbus's voyage to the Indies (Isabella 32).

Example #2:

> Isabella of Castile married Ferdinand of Aragon, but she did not surrender her power or rights, and she certainly saw herself as Ferdinand's peer. However, she was not above trickery. She sold some unattractive wedding presents to finance Columbus's voyage to the Indies.

In the first sample passage, Isabella's phrase is now in quotation marks and cited. The reader knows that "hideous ornament" is Isabella's way of describing the gems. In the second sample passage, "unattractive wedding presents" is not attributed. In her book, Isabella did use the word "unattractive." But "unattractive" is a common, everyday description, not a unique or distinctive expression. The passage is okay without quotation marks or a citation.

Unique or not unique? The answer is a judgment call. If you have any doubt at all, place quotation marks around the words that aren't your own and cite the source.

Structure

Even if you cite all the ideas and information in your paper, you have to think about structure, too. The information in your research paper is like the clothing in your closet. The structure of the paper is like the clothes pole and the hangers that arrange the clothing in an orderly way. (Unless your closet looks like mine, of course.) Structures are creations, like everything else in your paper. The Authority Figure assigning the paper may define the structure for you, or you may use a garden-variety, everyday sort of structure — comparison, chronological order, and so forth. Writing a paper that follows an assigned structure or a commonplace framework is not a problem.

But if you lift a *unique* structure from someone else's work, you're plagiarizing. For example, John McPhee, a wonderful nonfiction writer, once profiled two tennis players about to square off for an important match. He described one player, and then the other, and then returned to the first, and back to the opponent, and so on. The structure of his writing resembled a tennis match — a creative way to organize the information. That structure belongs to John McPhee and shouldn't be imitated in your essay on ping-pong players.

Similarly, you shouldn't copy the *specifics* of another author's structure. If you are writing a report on plagiarism, for example, you shouldn't discuss the issue in exactly the same order as I have in this chapter.

You can't get off the hook for copying structure, because there's no truly acceptable way to cite it. The best solution is to take pains to create your own structure. If you're using more than one source — and you should be — the task is easier, because chances are the authors arranged their material differently. Chapter 12 discusses how to create a suitable structure for your paper.

The Authority Figure who assigned your research paper will expect some degree of originality from you, even if the originality only comes from combining ideas from a number of sources. (All properly cited, of course.) If you have only one source for your paper, you're essentially rewriting what someone else already wrote. Penalty Box! To avoid this problem, be sure that you gather information from several sources. See Chapter 4 for a discussion of the number of sources needed for your research paper.

Facts

Cite all information that you take directly from a source, even if you express the information in your own words. (The exception is information that is common knowledge, explained in the "What You Don't Have to Cite" section, later in this chapter.)

A few examples of the kind of information that should be cited include:

- ✔ **Arts**
  - • Observations about the type of brushstrokes in a particular painting
  - • Descriptions of how the critics reacted to a musical performance
- ✔ **History and social science**
  - • Provisions of a treaty or law

- The sequence of events leading up to a historic event, including steps not known to the general public

- The results of a sociological study

✔ **Literature and language**

- The reactions of critics to a work of literature

- Who bought the book and how the work was received

✔ **Science and technology**

- Flaws identified in particular computer programs

- The results of laboratory experiments

- A distinctive mathematical proof

Cite the source for statistics about competing companies, sales projections, product standards, and other such facts. If you tell the boss that the new toothpaste whitens 30 percent more than the competing brand, you must explain how you arrived at that figure.

Be especially careful to cite the source for all controversial statistics so that the reader may decide whether to accept the information or not. For example, if a study shows that lower taxes and increased government spending won't create a deficit, the reader may rightly ask, "Says who?" Knowing that a politician's staff conducted the study is helpful to the reader, especially if the reader also knows that the politician is campaigning on a platform calling for lower taxes, increased government spending, and a balanced budget.

Illustrations

If you create an illustration yourself, you don't have to cite it unless it includes information you got from a source. In other words, if you draw a diagram of a famous building *directly from your own measurements,* no citation is necessary because you're the source. However, if you create a chart illustrating sleep deprivation in paper-writing office-cubicle dwellers, you have to cite the source *for the information,* unless you did the research itself by asking everyone in the company how many minutes of sleep they managed to squeeze into the last 24 hours.

If you download graphics from the Internet, cite the Web site and, if known, the creator or artist. All that stuff on the Web is *not* free, at least in the citation world. Somebody put it there and should therefore get credit for doing so.

Seeing What You Don't Have to Cite

By now you probably think that all research papers are one giant footnote. Not true! You get a free pass (sort of a get-out-of-citation-jail-free card) for several types of information.

Common knowledge

In general, you don't have to cite material that is common knowledge — facts that everyone knows. If your term paper includes the brilliant observation that the world is round, you don't need to credit *Basic Exploration Techniques* by Christopher Columbus for that information. Except for the members of the Flat Earth Society (a real group, honest), everyone knows that the world is round. The biographical data of public figures, the dates of important world events, and basic scientific principles are other citation-free items.

Just to give you some guidelines, here are some facts that may be included in your paper without citing a source:

- **Arts**

  - Pablo Picasso's early works belong to his blue period.

  - Beethoven's Ninth Symphony includes the famous "Ode to Joy."

  - Matthew Brady, a famous early photographer, took many pictures of the Civil War.

  - Chiaroscuro is a technique of shading used in pastels.

- **History and social science**

  - Bill Clinton was the second American president to be impeached.

  - In the British parliamentary system, membership in the House of Lords is inherited.

  - Marie Antoinette was beheaded during the French Revolution.

  - The Oedipal Complex is a psychological term describing a very young boy's fixation upon his mother and conflict with his father.

- **Literature and language**

  - William Shakespeare's theater was called the Globe.

  - In Greek mythology, Arachne is a skilled weaver who is turned into a spider as punishment for her pride.

- An English sonnet is a poem of 14 lines, generally divided into three quatrains and a couplet.

- Spanish is called a Romance language because it is derived from Latin.

✔ **Science, mathematics, and technology**

- Computers store information on floppy disks or on hard drives.

- The area of a rectangle is determined by multiplying the length and the width.

- Photosynthesis is the process by which plants convert light into energy.

- Copper is an excellent conductor of electricity.

Information may be common knowledge even if you didn't know it until you started researching your paper. If a particular fact — that the currency of Japan is the yen or that Yellowstone is a national park, for example — seems readily available to the general public, you don't have to cite it, even if you yourself just learned it.

Your own ideas

While writing a research paper, don't cite ideas that you come up with yourself. Suppose you research the fuel efficiency of all the vehicles produced this year, citing sources for that information in your paper. After analyzing those statistics, you decide that a law will be passed requiring everyone to travel on motorized skateboards in order to protect the environment. You don't have to give a source for the skateboard statement. In fact, you *can't* give a source for that particular notion because it comes from your own brain. Uncited material in your paper is, by definition, yours and yours alone. (By the way, if you really do think that such a law will be passed, you've been riding that skateboard a bit too often without a helmet.)

Your Authority Figure's ideas

Sometimes the Paper Assigner gives you the main idea and asks you to prove it. In that case, you have to cite sources for the proof, but not for the idea itself. Here's an example of one such assignment from Professor McWork, whose latest novel sold seven copies, all to relatives:

> In a well-researched, well-documented, 169-page paper, prove that the character development in *Don't Cry For Me, Plutonia* is superior to that of Shakespeare's *Hamlet.* Include at least three references to critical reactions, showing that their negative comments are entirely unmerited.

If you come up with the main idea and the Authority Figure confers with you while you're in the process of writing the paper, you may or may not have to cite the comments that the Authority Figure made during your discussions. Bosses don't ordinarily want to be cited; teachers usually do. The solution: Ask.

Following the Golden Rule of Citations

You may have noticed, if you've managed to read other sections in this chapter without dozing off, that a lot of decisions about citing sources fall into the Gray Area, the legendary land where you have to make judgment calls. The problem with citations is that the wrong judgment sends you over a cliff. So here's the primary, most important, mother-of-all rule of citations:

> When in doubt, cite.

This rule is so crucial that I must say it again: If you are not sure whether or not you need to write a citation for paragraph ten of your paper, write a citation for paragraph ten. Better you should appear overcareful than risk plagiarism! The Authority Figure reading your work can always cross out a few unnecessary footnotes. *You* can't cross out a few unnecessary failing grades or negative employment reviews.

Staying on the Right Side of the Copyright Law

If you're not planning to publish your paper, the governing body for your work is largely academic, not legal. That's good news and bad news: You probably won't have to worry about being hauled into court (the good news), but academic rules are a lot stricter than actual laws (the bad news). But even if you do not aspire to be published, you should give some thought to legal issues before you download, photocopy, and retype from a published source. Each book, article, or Web site is someone's brainchild, and brain-children, like real children, are expensive. They are created with labor, time, and experience. Readers and researchers need to respect that fact.

I make this statement with a degree of passion because I'm actually writing a book at the moment — the one you're reading. Like any parent, I don't mind if you admire my child; borrowing bits of it, with proper citation, may be a form of admiration. However, I don't appreciate your taking my child home and becoming its new parent. In other words, you can use *Research Papers For Dummies* but not abuse it.

How do you use, not abuse, a work? You don't photocopy huge chunks of it to avoid plunking down cash for your own copy. You cite it as a source according to the rules set down earlier in this chapter. You don't extract so much information that you have essentially copied the entire book. You leave other readers a reason to buy the book, assuming they want the information it contains.

I'm not a lawyer, and I don't even play one on TV. (I am the mother of a lawyer, but little legal knowledge has rubbed off on me, despite any number of fascinating dinner conversations about torts.) So don't look to me for the definitive verdict on copyright law. Consult your own lawyer about any worrisome issues, especially if you intend to sell your work. All I'll mention here is one basic principle: You can't diminish the value of someone else's creation by hashing it up, putting your own name on it, and sending it out there so that it brings recognition, grades, or money back to you. Or, as they say in the sandbox, you have to play fair.

Part IV

More Than Sharpening Pencils: Preparing to Write

The 5th Wave   By Rich Tennant

"Although you have a good thesis statement, it belongs on the first page of the paper -- not on page 124."

In this part . . .

With a two-ton tub of notes on your desk, your first impulse may be to whip out a pen or turn on the computer and begin to write. Bad idea! Writing without a plan is the research-paper equivalent of driving off in a car without knowing all of the picky little details of driving — like where the brakes are and how to back up. Before you write, you should create a thesis statement (Chapter 11), choose a structure (Chapter 12), define subtopics (Chapter 13), and construct an outline (Chapter 14).

Chapter 11

Forming a Thesis Statement

You've got a subject ("human-bear interactions") and a topic ("the relationship between Goldilocks and the three bears"). Now it's time to come up with a thesis statement — the point that you want to make about Goldie and the furry guys. A couple of possibilities occur to you — "bears that hang around people end up eating porridge and sleeping in beds," "both blonds and baby bears like medium-firm mattresses," and "humans and bears share forest resources." As you tease out a few more ideas, you search for the middle ground, avoiding a thesis statement that is too broad or too narrow. You want one that, like Goldilocks's porridge, is "just right."

But how *do* you create a good thesis statement? And why does a paper need a thesis statement anyway? What about papers with topic sentences instead of thesis statements? How should those papers be handled? This chapter unlocks these mysteries and starts you on the road to a successful research paper.

Laying a Firm Foundation for Your Paper

The *subject* of your paper is what you're writing about, in the broadest sense. The *topic* is a narrow sliver of the subject. (For more information on subjects and topics, see Chapter 3.) The *thesis* is narrower still — the idea that you're trying to prove in your paper. Most research papers need a thesis. Just to finish off all the boring definitions, a *thesis statement* is a single sentence that expresses the thesis.

Research papers that are general surveys or simple reports of information don't need a thesis. Chapter 1 describes this sort of research paper, and the "Forming a Topic Sentence" section later in this chapter explains how to lay the foundation for a survey paper. Science research papers reporting the results of experiments have a hypothesis instead of a thesis. Check out Chapter 12 for more information on a science research paper.

One type of research paper, usually written on the college or postgraduate level, is called a *thesis*. In this chapter the word *thesis* always refers to the idea you're promoting in the paper, not to an entire research paper.

A thesis turns your paper from a simple report on information gathered into an argument supporting a particular interpretation of the facts. To choose a thesis, imagine that you're a lawyer making a case before a jury. Watch a couple of courtroom dramas to get in the proper mood. As the attorney (the paper writer), your job is to:

- ✔ Gather all the relevant information about the case (In Research-Paper World, which is *not* a new theme park, the case is the topic.)

- ✔ Analyze and come up with a reasonable interpretation of the facts

- ✔ Extract one main idea from the interpretation (the thesis)

- ✔ Express that main idea in a single sentence (the thesis statement)

- ✔ Organize the evidence (the facts you collected during the research process) to show how the evidence supports your thesis

- ✔ Answer in advance any likely objections from the opposing side (In Research-Paper World, this process is called "concession and reply." I explain how to write a concession and reply in Chapter 16.)

- ✔ Convince the jury (the Authority Figure who will evaluate your work) that your thesis has merit

Think of your thesis as the spine of your paper, the organizing principle. Everything that you say is connected to the thesis, woven together with a logical thread that leads the reader from "here's what I'm going to prove" through "I rest my case."

The Authority Figure may have given you a thesis as part of the initial assignment or checked the thesis you came up with. (Actually, running your thesis by the Authority Figure is a great idea.) Nevertheless, you still have to present strong, logical arguments and plenty of specific evidence in your paper. Without those two elements, your paper will be mediocre at best. No matter what the Authority Figure actually believes, pretend that you are presenting your material to someone who completely disagrees with you. Argue your case as if you were sparring with an opponent — politely, of course. You may find it helpful to conjure up an imaginary figure, the opposing attorney. Imagine that the opposing attorney is sitting at your desk while you work, probing for every weakness in your case. Your job is to make that guy lose!

Forming a Thesis and Writing a Thesis Statement

As soon as you've got a chunk of research, a deck of index cards, or a few files on the computer, take a few moments to reread your material. (Check out Chapters 8 and 9 for a lowdown on note taking.) Think about what you might prove with all those facts and quotations. A couple of techniques will help you decide.

Ask questions

As you review your notes, do any questions occur to you? Is your curiosity piqued by anything you've written? If not, check out the next sections, "If only," "I recommend," and "Relationships," or go back to note taking and try again later.

Any questions that pop into your mind arise from issues that are relevant to your topic, and issues are the breeding ground for theses. For example, suppose you're doing a psych paper on parental influence — specifically, how parental discipline affects children's behavior. You've read a ton of studies that attempt to describe the relationship between parents' actions and children's reactions. As you review your notes, you may find yourself wondering:

Do children of very strict parents behave better?

Does a child's reaction to strict parental rules change as the child grows older?

Does spanking affect children's self-esteem?

Does inconsistent discipline have a negative effect on children's behavior?

Not one of these questions is a thesis, but each is a possible starting point. I say *possible* because you can't cover them all in one paper. You have to choose. Right now, I select the second sample question to illustrate my point.

Suppose that the question of age interests you the most. Read your notes again with question two in mind. Look closely at every note concerned with discipline, age, and rules. Put little check marks next to information about children's behavior — the behavior of those children identified as having trouble in school or with the law, perhaps. If necessary, go back to the library or the Internet for more research on the relationship between discipline techniques, age, and children's behavior. If you can, do some statistical analysis to see which factors matter and which are simply coincidence.

After you've finished those tasks, you're probably ready to take a stand. Express that stand in a single sentence, perhaps this one:

> Children of very strict parents follow the rules diligently until adolescence, but not during the teen years.

Now you've got the basis for your paper: the thesis statement. (By the way, in the preceding paragraphs I'm making up an example, not stating a psychological truth. I have no idea what the relationship is between very strict parenting, age, and children's behavior! I have my own opinions, but I'll keep them to myself.)

If only

Another way to hunt for a thesis is to consider the "if only" spots in your paper. This method is particularly helpful for history projects. Again, start by rereading your notes. Look for moments when the entire course of historical events might have changed, *if only* one decision or one detail had been different. For example, suppose you're writing about a famous incident involving Humpty Dumpty. (To make my point, I'm pretending Dumpty's fall really happened. In fact, the event is an episode in *Through the Looking Glass,* the sequel to Lewis Carroll's *Alice in Wonderland.*) You've read eyewitness accounts, historians' analysis of the events, and doctors' descriptions of the injuries Mr. Dumpty suffered. Now you're ready to make a thesis statement.

For those of you who aren't familiar with the story, here are the "facts" of the case:

Victim: Humpty Dumpty, male egg

Physical description: Round but delicate build, oval face, pale complexion

Age: Fresh

Date of incident: Nineteenth century

Place: King's walled courtyard

Description of incident: Victim had a great fall from a wall approximately ten feet high. Bystanders called 911 immediately. King's horses and king's men arrived within ten minutes. Entire battalion of horses and men worked on the victim for 45 minutes, but could not put him back together again.

After reviewing all your material, you think

> If only the top of the wall had been shaped like an egg crate, giving Humpty Dumpty more stability
>
> If only Humpty Dumpty had eaten a calcium-rich, shell-strengthening diet
>
> If only the king's men had had more training in regluing than in military maneuvers

The last "if only" in the preceding list gives you an idea for a thesis, which you turn into a sentence:

> The emphasis on militarism in the training of the king's men led to the tragic demise of Humpty Dumpty.

I recommend

Depending upon your topic, another road to a thesis statement comes from the phrase "I recommend." This road is especially helpful if you're writing about science, social science, technology, or any area that looks toward the future. Review your notes and ask yourself what improvements you'd like to see in the situation or conditions. Then ask yourself what should be changed to bring about those improvements.

Here's this method in action. Suppose you're writing about fatal accidents. One of your sources is the Humpty Dumpty incident, described in the preceding section, "If only." As you scan your notes, think about the improvements that you would like to see — perhaps the prevention of shattering injuries caused by falls. What should be changed to bring about that improvement? The addition of calcium supplements to the water supply, a change in the design of palace architecture, additional training in egg gluing for emergency medical personnel, or something else? One of those ideas becomes your thesis statement:

> To prevent serious injury, architects should design safer walls.

Relationships

Another thesis catcher is the relationship question, especially helpful when you're writing about literature. As you're poring over your notes, look for events or ideas that belong together in one of these ways: cause and effect, contrast, or similarity. For example, suppose you're writing about the murder of the king in a modern drama, *Macbeth Revisited* (not a real play). You delve into English politics during the Thatcher era and decide that the factions portrayed in the play reflect the conflict between contemporary English political parties. Now you've got a "relationship" thesis.

> The strife between the Googrubs and the McAgues in *Macbeth Revisited* mirrors the conflict between the Labor and Tory parties in the late twentieth century.

Or, suppose you're writing about energy and pollution. You contrast fossil fuels with solar power, deciding on this thesis statement:

> Solar energy is less harmful to the environment than fossil fuels.

The thesis for most business writing falls into one of these categories:

- ✔ **Cause and effect:** If you're explaining to your boss why consumers can't find their favorite vegetable at the supermarket, your thesis is something like "the drought in the Midwest depressed the supply of spaghetti squash." The thesis has a cause (drought) and an effect (depressed supply).

- ✔ **Recommendation:** Which company should you invest in? Where should you advertise? How should the Department of Dumb Memos be reorganized? Your thesis statement expresses your recommendation: "Gingivital Brothers should merge with Decay Industries." "Fluorescent floss should be marketed on the Internet." "A 50 percent reduction in staff will streamline the Department of Dumb Memos."

- ✔ **Prediction:** Based on current levels of X, what is the future of Y? If Q changes, what happens to R? Frequently, the business of business is planning. Sales projections, proposals, and marketing plans look to the future, and so do your thesis statements: "Based on current levels of X, Y will decrease rapidly, recovering during the third quarter of the fiscal year." "Given that Q goes out of business, the market for R will expand rapidly."

Avoiding Potholes: Too Broad, Too Narrow, or Self-Evident Theses

When you're on the road to a thesis statement, steer around the potholes. Don't try to prove too much, or you'll need a tractor-trailer full of evidence to support your case. Furthermore, your paper will lack focus. Don't choose an overly narrow thesis either. If you can prove it on the back of a cocktail napkin, your reader tends to say, "So what?" Don't try to prove a self-evident point, or the reader will see your paper as a waste of time.

The best way to avoid the potholes of thesis writing is to recognize them. The following sections provide a field guide.

Too broad

Keep in mind that you have to prove every single part of your thesis. If your thesis statement has several parts, chances are you're aiming wide. For example:

> Human societies tend to form hierarchies in which each class has more power and prestige than the one below it and in which the upper classes frequently exploit the lower classes, leading to an overthrow of the ruling class.

Oh, my. To prove that statement you'd have to do all of the following:

✔ Survey a large number of societies from different time periods and different geographical areas

✔ Show that most, if not all, of those societies are organized hierarchically

✔ Explain the ranks in those societies

✔ Show how the higher ranks have more power and prestige

✔ Show that the higher ranks often exploit the lower ranks

✔ Survey societies that have experienced revolutions

✔ Show how the lower class's rebellion was directly linked to exploitation by the upper class

By the time you finish, you'll be eligible for retirement. So will the person who is supposed to be reading your paper.

Another clue that your thesis is too broad is the presence of general terms — *human societies* in the preceding example, and *art* and *politics* in this next statement:

> Art is often censored because of politics.

Really? What kind of art? Visual? Theatrical? Musical? Literary? And what do you mean by *politics?* The desire for certain politicians to stay in office? Political ideologies? In which countries? At which levels of government? And are you including personal political beliefs, or just the actions of official bodies?

By now you see the problem. To fix each of these overly broad statements, limit the terms of the thesis. Zero in on a time period, a group, or a subset of a larger general idea. Dump the wide-angle lens looking at all of human history or endeavor. Focus in on a smaller target. Here are two possible corrections. Both are imaginary examples, so don't look for them in real history or art books:

> In thirteenth-century Ocuiolo society, the upper class's exploitation of the lower classes led to the Rebellion of 1265.

> In thirteenth-century Ocuiolo society, the ruling Azzadas attempted to forestall rebellion by censoring visual arts.

Many overly broad thesis statements arise from a desire to make one sentence sum up everything you discover about your topic. But instead of looking for a sentence that covers *everything,* you should look for one that takes into account the *most important or most interesting aspect* of your research. During the early stages of writing a research paper, note taking is unfocused. Even later in the process, you'll probably write down a few things that don't mesh well with the rest of your material. Still later, you'll narrow your focus again, but even then you'll record some unneeded information. (See Chapter 9 for a complete explanation of note taking.) So, when you review your notes, you'll find that some don't fit. Not a problem! Those misfit facts simply won't appear in your finished paper. Remember, writing a research paper is a discovery process. No discovery comes from a straight-line journey; a few side trips are inevitable.

Too narrow

The academic world is infamous for discussing incredibly tiny issues in far too much detail. A friend of mine once told me that he dropped out of his graduate program in classics when he found that he would have to read two full-length books examining a single vowel sound. I tell you this story to illustrate the fact that it's rare to find a thesis that is too narrow; you're much more likely to come up with one that is too broad. However, overly narrow theses do exist, and if you create one, you'll have trouble writing a paper based on it.

How do you know that your thesis is too narrow? Here are some clues:

- ✔ You can't find much to say about your thesis, even though you have a ton of note cards or a long computer printout. Perhaps you've simply taken the wrong notes, but unless you have a love of research and lots of time to do more you may as well change the thesis.

- ✔ You have a lot of notes that relate to your thesis, but most of them simply describe the situation. They don't shed any light on the deeper meaning of events, people, situations, and so on.

> ✔ All the categories in your thesis — people, events, time periods, places, attitudes — refer to the smallest possible subgroup. For example, instead of talking about urban teenagers, you're talking about 15-year-old males who were born in Detroit during the month of January or February.

Examples of theses that may be too narrow include:

> In Ocuiolo society, the chief priest's theft of temple offerings outraged the middle-class artisans.

> Male English teachers in all-female independent high schools are very successful at raising reading levels of students who began the school term no more than two years below standard reading levels for their grade.

Depending upon how you handle the thesis and what information you've been able to gather, almost no thesis is impossible. What's too narrow for you may be okay for someone else who has access to different sources or who has time to research from primary sources. Judge your thesis in relation to your own abilities; if it's too narrow *for you,* dump it, even if someone else may be able to make a go of it!

Self-evident

In every dwelling, some sort of floor is present to support your feet. That fact is self-evident; except for Indiana Jones, no one walks into a room wondering whether the architect has installed a bottomless pit. When you choose a thesis statement, avoid ideas like "rooms have floors." True, you can prove it. But why bother when everyone knows the score?

Another form of self-evident thesis is the simple statement of fact. This sort of thesis is true and may even be quite interesting, but it doesn't lead anywhere. You make the statement, the reader reads it, and the conversation is over. You've got nothing to prove. To extend it into a paper is to waste the reader's (and your) time.

My favorite example of a self-evident thesis comes from an essay, not a research paper. After reading a short story describing a mutilated character, a student formed this thesis statement: "The character who has no nose at the beginning of the story still has no nose at the end of the story." As they say in the playground, "Duh-uh."

Here are some self-evident thesis statements:

> ✔ **Arts**
>
> Gauguin painted many works in Tahiti.
>
> Beethoven wrote music after he went deaf.

✔ **History and social science**

World War II pitted the Allies against Italy, Germany, and Japan.

Anthropologists study human society.

✔ **Literature and language**

Shakespeare's comedies always end happily.

The word *plagiarism* is derived from the Latin word for kidnapper.

✔ **Science, mathematics, and technology**

Computers allow extremely rapid calculations.

The scientific method relies on observation and the testing of a hypothesis.

Examining Quality Thesis Statements

It's not too broad and it's not too narrow. It doesn't state the obvious. Fine. That's what a quality thesis statement *isn't*. But what *is* it? Characteristics of a good thesis statement include:

✔ A complete sentence written in grammatically correct language

✔ A clear, unambiguous statement of an idea

✔ An idea that involves some degree of judgment

✔ An idea that may be supported with proof

Just to give you an idea of what you're aiming for, here are a few good thesis statements in each subject area:

✔ **Arts**

The visual art of the Navajo often reflects the traditional religion of the tribe.

The melodic line of songs in musical comedy emphasizes the emotions of the characters.

✔ **History and social science**

The invention of the cotton gin prolonged the existence of slavery.

Marbury v. Madison brought the three branches of government into balance by giving the power of judicial review to the Supreme Court.

✔ **Literature and language**

Homer's *Odyssey* differs in tone and content from the *Iliad.*

Jack Kerouac's novel *On the Road* illustrates the alienation of the youth of post–World War II America.

✔ **Science, mathematics, and technology**

SAT scores are closely related to the income level of the student's family.

Robots may approach but never reach true intelligence.

Notice that the preceding thesis statements are complete sentences. Each declares an idea, making it a *declarative* sentence. (English-teacher talk for a sentence that states something instead of asking a question.) Don't create a thesis statement in the form of a question, and don't write a partial sentence, which English teachers call a *fragment*. Some examples:

✔ **Bad thesis statement:** Was World War II responsible for ending the Great Depression?

Why it's a bad thesis statement: Don't ask the question! Answer it.

Better thesis statement: World War II was responsible for ending the Great Depression.

✔ **Another bad thesis statement:** How the choice of material influences the sculpture's form.

Why it's a bad thesis statement: The statement is not a complete thought and therefore not a complete sentence.

Better thesis statement: The choice of material influences the sculpture's form.

Forming a Topic Sentence

Some research papers simply survey information about a particular topic without taking a stand. These papers don't have thesis statements. Instead, a topic sentence serves as the foundation of the work. The topic sentence communicates the main idea of the paper. Think of the topic sentence as a telegram to the reader. It says, "Here's what you're going to read."

In some long-gone or all-too-present English class, you may have heard the term *topic sentence* defined as the sentence in each paragraph that expresses the main idea. In this section of *Research Papers For Dummies,* I'm using the term to refer to the main-idea sentence of the entire paper.

By the time you finish your research and prepare to write, your paper has heaps of ideas. How do you decide which one is the main idea? Easy. Think *shopping list*. Here's what I mean. Imagine that your shopping list contains the following items:

> Coffee filters
>
> Lentils
>
> Quart of milk
>
> Cheddar cheese
>
> Cookies
>
> Alfalfa sprouts
>
> Paper plates

What can you say about your shopping list? Check out these three sentences:

> I have to buy things.
>
> I have to buy food.
>
> I have to buy items for the kitchen.

Which one makes sense? The first sentence is so wide that it's almost meaningless. The word "things" covers too much territory. The second sentence looks better, but reread the list. "Food" doesn't take into account two of the items on the list: coffee filters and paper plates. The third sentence is the best. Coffee filters and paper plates relate to the kitchen, as do the other things you have to buy.

Think of the material that you plan to include in your paper as items on a shopping list. Choose the most specific sentence that takes into account all of the relevant information. Bingo: You've got a topic sentence.

Choosing a Title

At one time, no woman considered herself fully dressed without a proper hat, the finishing touch to an outfit. Your paper needs a finishing touch also — not a hat but a title.

Some writers like to choose the title after the entire paper is written. Only then, they say, can they be sure that the title reflects the content of the paper.

Bad idea. By the time you sit down to write the paper, you should already know what the content of the paper will be. A better strategy is to select a title shortly after you form a thesis statement or topic sentence, or, at the very latest, after you select all the evidence and arguments you are going to include. (See Chapter 13 for tips on organizing and selecting evidence.)

The title of a research paper is not the same as the thesis statement. The title is shorter, and it doesn't always express a position on the issues discussed in the paper.

Research papers that discuss scientific subjects follow the preceding rule on titles. However, science research papers reporting the results of original experiments do *not* follow this rule. See Chapter 12 for an explanation of how to title a science research paper.

The title should give the reader an idea of what content and approach to expect in your paper. It shouldn't be too broad, covering so much ground that the material in the actual paper is lost in vagueness. Nor should it be too narrow, describing only a portion of the contents of your work.

Here's an example of how to choose a title. Imagine that you're writing a paper on minor league baseball. After a great deal of research (not to mention hot dogs and visits to a bunch of games), you write this thesis statement:

> Minor league baseball, as it becomes more profitable, loses the best qualities of the game.

To support your thesis you've got information on player recruitment and salaries, fan reaction, the feelings of the coaches and managers, promotional events, profits and losses, and so on. Which title fits best?

Minor League Baseball

A Major League Business: Baseball's Minor Leagues

The Effect of Increased Profits on Minor League Baseball

If you picked door three, you've won a tour of the Midwest League. The first title is too broad. The reader doesn't know whether you're focusing on players' skills, the love Americans have for the game, or the history of the minor leagues. The second title is too narrow: It says that you're concentrating on the business aspect of minor league baseball, but it omits part of the thesis (that the best qualities of the game are lost as profits increase). The third title takes into account the idea of profits *and* the effect on the game. Clearly a home run!

Chapter 12

Choosing a Structure for Your Paper

*I*n a wildly and deservedly popular book about a teenage wizard, a magic spell removes the bones from the boy's arm. In that alternate universe, the school nurse tsk-tsks for a moment and then sets about regrowing the missing parts. Meanwhile, the poor fellow's stuck with a shapeless mass of muscles.

Nobody has to point out to young Harry Potter that skeletons are really useful items. And probably nobody has to point out to you that the skeleton of your paper — its *structure* — is essential. But you may *not* be aware of the many different structures available for your paper, and you may not have thought much about how those structures affect the reader.

In this chapter I define the most common structures and show you how to select the one that best fits the information you've gathered. I discuss how the structure of your paper works with your *thesis* (the idea you're proving) to convince the reader of the merits of your case. Finally, I show you how to organize a paper that doesn't have a thesis.

Marrying Form and Content: The Right Structure with the Right Thesis

Run your fingers down your rib cage. Feel the bumps? Now imagine that the number of ribs in your body suddenly doubled. Wouldn't you choose a longer sweater the next time you went shopping? Suppose that those ribs were rectangular instead of curved. I bet you'd redesign the chair you plop in at the end of a tough day. And just spend a moment rearranging the world to suit people whose arms sprout from the top of their heads. For one thing, all the expensive stuff in the grocery store would be on the top shelf.

By now I'm sure you see the point. The structure (those ribs, the arms) affects clothing, chair design, marketing, and a host of other factors. In the same way, the structure of your paper affects the way the reader perceives your arguments.

Sometimes the Authority Figure who is torturing you with the paper gives you a ready-made, required structure. That sort of assignment brings good news and bad news. The good news: You don't have to make any decisions about structure. The bad news: You have to tailor your topic, thesis, and research to fit the assigned structure.

If the structure of the paper is *your* choice, the good news/bad news blend is slightly different. You probably have more control over the topic and thesis, but you have to come up with a structure that enhances them, a structure that works *with* the point you're trying to make, not *against* it. For definitions of topic and thesis, see Chapter 3. For a complete explanation of how to write a thesis statement, turn to Chapter 11.

Science research papers that report the results of experiments that the author has performed have their own unique structure. (See Chapter 12 for details.) The information in this chapter applies to research papers written about scientific topics, not to reports of original experiments.

Before you decide on a structure that suits the thesis of your paper (or the opposite — a thesis that suits the assigned structure), consider all the things a structure does. The structure

- Determines the order in which information is presented
- Relates ideas to each other (cause and effect, opposing views, and so on)
- Ranks the ideas and information in order of importance (main ideas, subtopics, supporting evidence, and so forth)
- Creates a logical framework for all the evidence
- Presents readers with a pattern, a way to make sense of what they're reading

Considering the Options: Structures for Every Occasion

In the wonderful world of research papers, as in the stock market, you have to consider your options. In this section I describe the basic structures, the skeletons that give shape to every research paper.

Chronological order

Chronological or *time order* presents events in sequence, from the earliest incident through the most recent episode. You may find chronological order appropriate for a paper that shows how something develops or for one that describes a series of steps. Say you're writing about the changes in a writer's style. Your thesis is that with each novel the writer's language became more abstract. You begin by examining the writer's early works and then move forward in time to the later novels. Or perhaps you're writing about forestland after a fire. Your thesis is that the fire is the first stage of a natural cycle of regeneration. The paper examines each stage in order, from the burning through the first new growth, subsequent growth, and so on. You may also modify chronological order, perhaps beginning with the last step and then "flashing back" to the stages that led to the final moment.

Here are a few topics that mesh well with chronological structure:

- ✔ **Arts**

    The evolution of an art form during a specific period of time

    The rise or fall of a particular artist's popularity

- ✔ **History and social science**

    Changes in attitude towards a public figure during the course of his/her career

    Sequence of events leading up to a major historical change

- ✔ **Literature and language**

    Evolution of the meaning of a particular word

    Changes in literary style of one or more writers during a defined period

- ✔ **Science, mathematics, and technology**

    The developmental stages of an organism

    Steps involved in a scientific discovery

Cubicle dwellers may write in chronological order for the following:

- ✔ Accident or incident reports.

- ✔ Descriptions of marketing campaigns (initial advertising, follow-up to advertising, and long-range plan, for example). In this case the time order moves from the present to the future.

- ✔ Manuals for a process or procedure (steps for the employee to follow, described in chronological order).

- ✔ History of the company, the product, an executive's career, and so forth.

Comparison and contrast

I bet that at least once in your life you've said something like "both jobs pay fantastically well, but Growgrub Industrials has an all-you-can-eat doughnut cart. . . ." Comparing two things, showing how they are alike and how they are different, comes so naturally that this structure may very well be hard-wired into the human brain.

Comparison-and-contrast papers may be organized in a couple of ways. Suppose you're writing about the Industrial Revolution and the current Internet Revolution. (Okay, I made up that term, but I think the Internet really has changed everything.) Here are your options for comparison and contrast:

- ✔ Divide the body of the paper into two sections, the first describing the Industrial Revolution and the second describing the Internet Revolution.

- ✔ Create several subtopics such as time spent at work, type of work performed, and job satisfaction. Devote a separate paragraph or section to each subtopic. Within those subtopics, discuss both the Industrial Revolution and the Internet Revolution.

- ✔ Divide the body of the paper into two sections. The first section explains how the two revolutions are similar. The second section explains how the two revolutions differ.

Chapter 13 tells you how to define subtopics. Chapter 16 explains how to write the body of a research paper. Regardless of how you organize the body of a comparison-and-contrast paper, you need an introduction and a conclusion. Chapter 15 gives you the lowdown on introductions, and Chapter 17 tackles conclusions.

Although two is a natural number for a comparison-and-contrast paper, you may discuss more than two elements. Just add extra sections as needed.

So handy when the banks fail. . .

The newspapers of a by-gone era can give modern readers a unique perspective on the past . While researching a demonstration that took place during the Great Depression, I found a serious article explaining the workers' demands. Next to the article was a whimsical advertisement for a department store charge account. "So handy when the banks fail. . ." proclaimed a young woman dressed in the height of 1930s fashion. "I can still shop for the new fall fashions at Gimbel's, even if cash isn't available." Until I saw that advertisement, I had always imagined that everyone of that era understood the significance and the seriousness of what the nation was enduring. Not so! People were living their lives, just as they do now, and for at least some of them, the bank closings were not historic events but rather annoying interruptions in their quest for a new wardrobe.

Some good comparison-contrast topics are as follows:

✔ **Arts**

Paintings of the same scene by two different artists

Works on one theme in different media (film and stage play, for example)

✔ **History and social science**

Two economic systems such as communism and capitalism

Wars, inventions, laws, or court cases from two different countries or time periods

✔ **Literature and language**

Authors tackling the same issues in different time periods

One type of work (epic poems, perhaps) from different cultures

✔ **Science, mathematics, and technology**

Different explanations for a scientific phenomenon

Contrasting proofs for a mathematical principle

When you're seeking financing, investors want to know how your product or service differs from the competition's offerings. In a comparison-and-contrast structure, acknowledge the ways in which your company resembles others, but emphasize what your company will do differently. Show how that difference will cause consumers to desert the competition, flock to your doors, and return megaprofits for your investors, who will all retire to Margaritaville.

Cause and effect

Cause-and-effect structure predates language itself. The crying baby can't say or even think the word *hungry*, but the little one soon learns that crying (cause) brings a large, warm creature bearing milk (effect).

In writing with a cause-and-effect structure, you can go in one of two directions:

- ✔ Start with a description of the cause, explaining all the relevant events or factors. Then move on to the effect, clearly relating it to the cause.
- ✔ Describe the effect and trace the events backwards to the cause, again taking care to show how the events are connected.

Which one is better? Neither, really. Go with the one that feels right.

The introduction of a cause-and-effect paper mentions both factors. The thesis sentence says something like "Ughabuga is responsible for okaoka." The conclusion often refers to lessons learned and recommendations for the future. (See Chapter 11 for a complete discussion of thesis statements and Chapter 17 for everything you ever wanted to know about conclusions.)

Topics that lend themselves to a cause-and-effect structure include:

- ✔ **Arts**

    How a song or type of music influenced public opinion

    The reactions of artists to acts of censorship

- ✔ **History and social science**

    The effect of a law on human behavior

    Changes in spending habits as a reaction to taxation policies

- ✔ **Literature and language**

    The reaction of language to an invention (new vocabulary for e-mail, for example)

    Ties between an author's life and work (such as how a particular event affected the author's themes)

- ✔ **Science, mathematics, and technology**

    How a new chip expands or changes computer applications

    The effect of an invention or public policy on the environment

Proposals for changes in procedures often rely on cause-and-effect structure: "If we switch suppliers, we'll save $30 trillion on shipping charges. . . ." "Installing surveillance cameras will decrease doughnut theft by 30 percent. . . ." and so on.

Pro and con

No, this structure doesn't pair salaried athletes (pros) with those who get locked up every night (cons). Instead, this structure argues both sides of an issue, explaining the merits and faults of each position. Depending upon your point of view, pro-and-con papers are either wishy-washy (not courageous enough to take a stand) or mature (the situation is complicated and each stance has something to contribute towards a solution). You may handle pro-and-con papers in several ways:

✔ Explain each position separately and thoroughly in the body of the paper and choose one side in your conclusion. With this arrangement, your introduction may not have a clear thesis but instead simply present the problem or issue.

✔ Your thesis presents your point of view, and the body backtracks to the arguments on both sides. The conclusion explains why you find one side more compelling than the other.

✔ You avoid taking sides altogether, dividing the body into halves: pro arguments and con arguments. The introduction explains the problem or issue, and the conclusion simply presents the consequences you expect if each side prevails. Or, the conclusion attempts to define a third path, a compromise position.

✔ You divide the issue into subtopics and present the pros and cons of each subtopic in a separate section or paragraph.

However you decide to organize a pro-and-con paper, be fair. Don't pretend to show both sides and then stack the deck toward one or the other opinion.

Here are some topics that suit the pro-and-con structure:

✔ **Arts**

Public funding for art

An examination of an artist or a style hailed as original (the pro position argues that the work is innovative and the con argues that it is a rehash of someone else's work)

✔ **History and social science**

Current issues: gun control, abortion, censorship, and so on

Value of particular public programs (pro side argues that the program — drug prevention, perhaps — is effective, and the con side argues that the course of action isn't successful)

✔ **Literature and language**

Quality of particular works (pro = masterpiece, con = pop trivia)

Response to critical essays (agree or disagree with a critic's interpretation of a work)

✔ **Science, mathematics, and technology**

Examination of a scientific theory (such as a meteor wiped out the dinosaurs)

Statement about technology (for or against the idea that computers rival human intelligence, for example)

The person who pays your salary probably wants you to take a stand in your research papers: "Invest in Flubdub Detergent" or "Cancel the Office Football Pool." However, the boss might also want you to prepare a good summary of both viewpoints and leave the decision to the higher-ups. Ask!

Interest groups

This structure, a variation of "pro and con," is great for history or current events. It also works well for social issues. *Interest groups* are all those people who have a stake in the outcome of a specific situation. Looking through the lens of their own lives, interest groups react to the same elements in very different ways. Think: What's in it for me? Then answer that question from the perspective of all the participants. Bingo: You've got an interest-group structure.

Here's an example of an interest-group paper. Say you're writing about the westward expansion of the United States. Your subtopics examine expansion in relation to the resident Native Americans, the settlers moving into the area, the U.S. cavalry, traders, other colonial powers, and so forth. You discuss the attitudes of each group and examine the effect of the westward expansion on the group. Each interest group becomes a subtopic covered in a separate section or paragraph. The introduction to the paper describes the basic situation, presenting the facts and your thesis. The conclusion considers the implications for one or more of the groups you describe. Chapter 13 provides more information on defining subtopics. Chapter 15 covers introductions, and Chapter 17 tells you how to write a conclusion.

A variation of the interest-group paper considers one subject from the viewpoint of several disciplines. For example, a paper about drug abuse might cover the topic from the point of view of psychology, political science, economics, criminal justice, and biology. The thesis may be your assessment of the success or failure of the war on drugs. The conclusion may be your recommendations based on one or more of the viewpoints you describe.

A few possible interest-group topics:

- ✔ **Arts**

    What's the next frontier for the art world? Interest groups include artists themselves, art dealers, collectors, museum curators, and so on.

    Factors that make a play successful. Interest groups include playwrights, directors, actors, theater critics, and the audience.

- ✔ **History and social science**

    Relationship between rock music and the social upheaval of the 1960s. Interest groups include musicians, historians of the era, consumers (people who were teenagers in that era), journalists, and music critics.

    Reconstruction Era in the American South. Interest groups include former slave owners, poor whites, former slaves, middle-class African Americans, Northerners, and so forth.

- ✔ **Literature and language**

    Study of a theme within one novel. Interest groups include clusters of characters or a single character. For example, in Zora Neale Hurston's *Their Eyes Were Watching God,* the groups may be the residents of Eatonville, Janie, and each of her three husbands.

- ✔ **Science, mathematics, and technology**

    Any issue open to further research. Each avenue of study represents an interest group. For example, for a paper on the AIDS crisis, interest groups may include scientists attempting to create a vaccine, those studying protease inhibitors, the patients, the drug companies, and public health workers.

If you're writing a proposal for a new product, procedure, or marketing campaign, you may employ an interest-group structure for your paper. The interest groups are anyone affected by the change: the consumer, the factory workers, and the publicity department, for example. Each section of the paper considers the consequences of the change for one interest group.

Hypothesis, test, and results

The microscopers out there *must* use this structure to report on original scientific research. But those of you who don't know which end of a Bunsen burner to light may still find a hypothesis/test/result structure appropriate, even for a nonscience topic.

A *hypothesis* is an educated guess. A *test* is the means you employ to check the accuracy of your guess. The *result* is what you get when the test is over. Scientists, who take some sort of oath to avoid conclusive answers, never say that the results *prove* the hypothesis. They love the verb *support,* as in "the fact that 1,000,000 trials with dropped objects resulted in falls downward supports the hypothesis that gravity pulls things toward, not away from, the earth." Non-lab-coaters can go out on a limb and say that the results prove that the original hypothesis is correct.

Here's the basic structure of a science research paper. To illustrate my point, I describe an experiment my son performed for his fifth-grade science class. Each day he took a group of African violet plants into a separate, reasonably soundproof room and blasted loud music for an hour. One group of plants got a symphony, another group got heavy metal, and a third sat in a room full of country music. He watered and exposed each plant to sunlight in exactly the same way and then charted their growth rate by measuring height and number of leaves. (In case you're wondering, the classical group did the best, although the difference was not significant.) This science research paper contained the following:

- ✔ **The Title:** "The Effect of Different Types of Music on the Growth Rate of African Violets *(Saintpaulia Ionantha).*" Notice that the title summarizes what happened in the experiment without wasting a single word. Had I left out "growth rate," for example, the reader would not know what kind of effect was tested — flowering ability, color quality, cheerfulness, and so on. Had I omitted "different types," the reader would assume that one type of music was compared to silence. Also notice that the common name of the organism tested, African violet, is accompanied by the scientific name of the plant *(Saintpaulia Ionantha).*

- ✔ **Abstract:** The *abstract,* also called the *summary,* is the whole paper in capsule form. In only one or two short paragraphs, the abstract explains what you did, the method you used, the results, and your conclusions. Although it is very short, the abstract may take more time to write than all the other parts of the paper combined. A good abstract is more than worth the effort! Busy scientists may read nothing but the abstract and judge your work by it. Also, if you publish a science research paper, the abstract appears when a researcher types in the appropriate keyword to search a database.

✔ **Introduction:** This section of the paper contains background information, including the properly cited research of other scientists on the issue. The report of others' research is called a _literature review_. Begin the introduction with general statements and then go to specifics, ending with the hypothesis. For example, the hypothesis of the African violet experiment was as follows:

African violets plants _(Saintpaulia Ionantha)_ exposed to classical music grow at a faster rate than plants exposed to heavy metal or country music.

✔ **Methods and Materials:** This section explains _how_ you did what you did, and what you used to do it. Give enough detail so that another researcher working half a world away can repeat your work exactly. Include exact amounts ("The plants were watered daily with one cup of water mixed with 0.2mg of Shuregrower powder." "Group A was exposed to a tape of Beethoven's _Fifth Symphony_ for 60 minutes daily") .Notice that everything is in past tense, because the experiment is already over.

Some Authority Figures prefer passive voice (The plants were watered) and some prefer active voice (I watered the plants). Ask!

✔ **Results:** A report of the raw data. Summarize the data, but save the interpretation for later. Present the results in charts, graphs, and tables. Also mention the information in the text, referring the reader to the _figure_ (for charts and graphs) or _table_. Number the figures and tables separately. In the text, capitalize the first letter of _Figure_ and _Table_. As a caption, generally capitalize the entire word _(FIGURE 12, TABLE 3)_. For example:

Plants in group A sprouted an average of five new leaves per week (Figure 7).

✔ **Discussion:** Here's where you interpret the results, explaining to the reader what you think the results mean. Refer to your hypothesis and discuss whether your results support it.

Never say that you have _proved_ your hypothesis. Scientists are allergic to that word. Instead, say that the results _suggest_ that the hypothesis is true. However, if you've disproved the hypothesis, say so.

✔ **Literature Cited:** The bibliography of your paper. Every work you referred to in the paper must be listed here with identifying information, so that readers may locate a source and read it for themselves. Science and social science research papers generally follow the format of the American Psychological Association, even for nonpsych works. (See Chapter 18 for the whole story on format of citations and bibliographies.)

Give each section a heading (Abstract, Methods and Materials, and so forth) and center the heading. Also center the title.

Organizing a Paper That Doesn't Have a Thesis

If you're writing a *survey* or a *general report,* your paper may not have a particular point of view. In that case you don't formulate a thesis statement. Instead, you write a *topic sentence* — a more neutral statement that gives the reader the main idea of the paper.

The term *topic sentence* is also used for the sentence that expresses the main idea of a paragraph. Here I'm using the term to designate the sentence that contains the main idea of the entire paper.

For a survey paper or a general report, create a "sandwich." The "bread slices" are a general introduction and a conclusion. The "filling" consists of clumps of related information, the subtopics. For example, suppose you're writing a general report about ballet. After reviewing your notes, you see that you have information on the history of the ballet, famous choreographers, prominent dancers, training regimens for the ballet, physical challenges of the art, scenery design, costumes, and music. That list works fine as a set of subtopics. You may combine a couple (choreographers and dancers, scenery and costume design, perhaps). The paper moves from one section to another with the help of subheads or transition sentences. To read more about papers that don't have thesis statements, check out Chapter 3. For more information on defining subtopics, see Chapter 13. For tips on transition sentences, see Chapter 16.

Reading like a writer

As you ponder the perfect paper structure, explore quality nonfiction as a source of inspiration. (But take care: If you're inspired to copy someone else's structure, you may be in trouble. See Chapter 10 for the rules of intellectual honesty.) Here's how to read like a writer: When you sit down with a newspaper or a magazine article, think about *how* the author constructed the article. How does the author organize the material? What's where? What kind of information or statement is in the introduction? How many subtopics does the article have, and how are they connected? What point does the conclusion make? Chances are you'll pick up a writing tip here and there. How do you know whether an article is worth your writerly attention? Avoid periodicals that place all the words in little bubbles or that report Elvis sightings. (Nothing against comics or those entertaining supermarket tabloids; they just won't teach you much about writing.) Look for serious subjects; the writing quality is probably serious also.

A general report sometimes offers you the chance to have fun. One of my favorite writers, John McPhee, once wrote about Atlantic City. As you may know, the squares on the traditional Monopoly game are named for streets in Atlantic City. McPhee wove together a description of the city and an account of a Monopoly tournament. Each time a player bought a property, McPhee shifted to a description of the actual place. Very effective!

Personalizing a Structural Framework

The structures I describe in this chapter are good starting points, but they may not be the best place to end up. Depending on your topic and the point you intend to make about it, you may need to modify a standard structure to suit your material. Sometimes the best papers combine two standard structures. For example, you may describe a situation in chronological order and then point out the cause-effect links. Or, you may begin with a pro-and-con explanation of an issue and then compare and contrast the proposed solutions of each group. The bottom line is simple: The form should complement the material. As you construct an outline (a process I discuss in detail in Chapter 14), put yourself in the reader's place. Are you offering a logical framework, a way for the reader to understand the point of all your research? If a standard structure does the job, fine. If not, punch it into a better shape. After you've personalized the structure, check it with these questions:

- ✔ After reading the introduction, does the reader know what I'm writing about? Is the point I'm making clear?

- ✔ Does each subtopic advance my argument?

- ✔ Can the reader see the logical connection between my arguments and the main point?

- ✔ Does one subtopic lead naturally to the next?

- ✔ Is the conclusion clear? Does it make the reader think, "I see. . .that makes sense"? Does it open the door to the next logical thought?

If you've answered yes to these questions, pat yourself on the back and go dancing. You've got a structure to be proud of!

Chapter 13

Organizing the Information: Subtopics

*T*urning a carton of notes into a research paper is a lot of work, but chances are the material divides naturally into categories. In Research-Paper World, those smaller pieces are called *subtopics,* logical subdivisions of the topic you're writing about. Identifying subtopics makes writing easier because you have to think about only one small chunk of information at a time. Reading a paper with subtopics is also easier because the person hanging on your every word has to grasp only one idea at a time. In other words, subtopics have no downside!

In this chapter I explain how to mine your notes for appropriate subtopics and prepare your notes for writing. I also explain how to match subtopics and structure. The result may not be as entertaining as dinner with Cousin Herman (he's been known to launch pickles across the table), but it should be a sound basis for your research paper.

Mining Research Notes for Subtopics

Even before you finish all the research, ideas may flash through your mind. Some undoubtedly involve revenge on the Paper Assigner or the gigantic party you're going to throw when the thing is finally finished. Along with these ideas, a set of subtopics may appear somewhere between your ears.

Grab that set before it evaporates! Jot down possible subtopics in the margin of the paper, in a separate computer file, or on your elbow if nothing else is available. When the research is complete, check out those notes.

Now think about the *thesis* of your paper, the point you will argue. The subtopics are the arguments you make in support of your thesis. Each subtopic is one argument. The subtopics should carry your reader along the road from "hmm . . . interesting idea but I'm not sure I agree" to "of course, that's exactly right." Imagine each subtopic as one witness in a trial. No one witness sways the jury, but each has something to add to the case.

Next, consider the structure of the paper. The subtopics have to work *with* the structure, complementing its logic. For example, a paper written in chronological order often divides neatly into time periods — centuries, perhaps, or before and after a historic event. If you can't make the subtopics match the structure, something has to give. Change the structure, or change the subtopics.

For instructions on how to write a thesis, see Chapter 11. For an explanation of how to choose a structure for your paper, see Chapter 12. To see how subtopics fit into the standard structures, check out the next section in this chapter, "Matching Subtopics to Structure."

Writing a survey paper that doesn't have a thesis? No matter. It still needs subtopics. Even extremely short papers have subtopics, usually one for each paragraph. To find the subtopics for a survey paper, pretend that you're turning your research notes into a television series. Divide your material into episodes. Bingo! You've got subtopics. The "Sorting Notes: Placing the Right Idea in the Right Basket" section later in this chapter also works for non-thesis papers.

If you're writing a marketing report or business plan, the subtopics are standard. (Chapter 1 describes these business documents in detail.) For example, suppose you're working on a business plan for International Widgets, Inc. Every business plan contains a section that explains how the new company differs from the competition. What's different about International Widgets? Each reason is a subtopic of that section of the paper. The last section of this chapter, "Sorting Notes: Placing the Right Idea in the Right Basket," helps salaried folks and CEO wannabes, as well as the tuition payers.

A science research paper based on original research has a standard structure and standard subtopics. (See Chapter 12 for more information.) So if you're in the lab-coat crowd, concentrate on splitting the subtopics into logical pieces. For example, the results section of an experiment on plant growth may be divided into plant height, number of leaves, number of flowers, and so forth. Check out the last section of this chapter, "Sorting Notes: Placing the Right Idea in the Right Basket," for help in defining these smaller categories.

Matching Subtopics to Structure

Subtopics and structure are like a pair of tennis players bashing the ball back and forth. Each needs the other, or there's no game. But it doesn't really matter which player arrives at the court first, so long as they both get there eventually. Sometimes the subtopics appear first, and then the structure falls into place. At other times you choose a structure, and soon the subtopics reveal themselves. Occasionally structure and subtopics show up together, plopping into your mind like a divine revelation. Divine revelations, unfortunately, aren't all that common. You'll probably have to sweat a little to connect subtopics and structure.

In this section I show you how to make successful matches by providing examples — pairs of structures and subtopics. Each heading in this section has two elements: the structure first and then the subtopics. The examples work in two directions. If you've got the structure, check out the suggested subtopics. If you've got the subtopics, read up on the structure. (You can find more information on each structure in Chapter 12.)

Chronological order — time periods or stages

A paper in *chronological order* is organized by time, generally starting with earlier events and working toward later events. (I imagine that you can trace something backwards through time, but a paper in reverse order would be unusual, to say the least.) The subtopics for a chronological paper are time periods or stages.

In deciding where the breaks belong, look for turning points — moments when events achieve a new level or participants enter a new stage. For example, imagine that you're writing about the rights of American women. An important turning point is 1920, when women won the right to vote. Another turning point is 1970, when the modern liberation movement gathered steam. Or, perhaps you're writing about plant growth. The sprouting of the seed and the emergence of flowers are stages in the plant's life cycle, and each may be a subtopic in your paper.

Here are a few other examples:

✔ **Arts**

Topic: The evolution of an art form or an artist's career.

Subtopics: The stages of the evolution, each characterized by a new development in style or materials or level of success.

Other possible subtopics: Time periods — centuries, reigns of kings or queens, dynasties, before and after important events. For each time period, describe the common characteristics of the art. Show how the art is different from the preceding period or explain how the events of that period influenced the art.

✔ **History and social science**

Topic: The influence or evolution of a social movement.

Subtopics: Time periods, divided at points when conflicts are created or resolved, government policies change, people's attitudes change, significant laws are passed, or leaders rise or fall.

✔ **Literature and language**

Topic: Influence of an outside element on works of literature (such as the role of women, views of the supernatural, or rising nationalism).

Subtopics: Time periods, divided at points when roles or attitudes change.

✔ **Science, mathematics, and technology**

Topic: Development of an organism or evolution of a type of technology.

Subtopics: Stages, divided when the organism or technology achieves a breakthrough to a new level of ability.

Comparison and contrast — paired elements and their characteristics

Has your boss asked you to analyze the costs and benefits of two new manufacturing processes? Does your history professor want you to compare two radically different views of the Spanish Civil War? If so, you're writing a comparison-and-contrast paper, which, by the way, can be used to analyze more than two things. You just need more sections.

A comparison-and-contrast paper may be organized in one of three ways:

✔ You may make two giant subtopics (or more, if you're comparing more than two things). In the first subtopic, state everything about one of the elements you're comparing, and then in the second subtopic state everything about the other. In keeping with the examples I mention previously, each element would be one of the new manufacturing processes or one of the views of the Spanish Civil War.

✔ Make a list of the important characteristics of the elements you're comparing. Devote one subtopic to each characteristic. Within each subtopic, discuss each of the elements you're comparing in relation to that characteristic.

✔ Divide the paper into two giant subtopics. The first subtopic tells how the elements you're comparing are alike, and the second tells how they differ.

You've probably already figured out that giant subtopics are hard to handle unless you break them down into smaller parts. (Think *sub*-subtopics, a term that doesn't really exist, but should.) The sub-subtopics are characteristics of the elements you're comparing.

Here are some hints for each subject area. I don't bother listing the giant subtopics I mention in the previous paragraph because these subtopics are simply comprised of the elements listed in the topic. Instead, in the "subtopic" category I list some of the characteristics you may consider in your analysis:

✔ **Arts and literature**

Topic: Comparison of two or more works of art or literature

Subtopics: Style, technique, content or subject, theme, form, symbolism, effect on viewer or listener or reader, reflection of societal values

✔ **History and social science**

Topic: The effectiveness of two or more approaches to the same problem (for example, legalization versus the war on drugs)

Subtopics: Significant legislation, preventative measures, surveys of public attitudes, statistics of damage or benefit

✔ **Science, mathematics, and technology**

Topic: Two species living in similar environments

Subtopics: Survival rates, impact on the environment, life cycles, use of natural resources, interaction with human beings, relative success of adaptation to habitat

Cause and effect — actions and reactions

A cause-and-effect paper answers the *why* question, usually on two levels. For every event, the paper gives the immediate cause (action), but a good paper digs a little deeper and analyzes the roots of the problem, the background factors (also actions) that led up to the event or the reaction you're writing about. The section of your paper devoted to the effect (the reaction) may also work on two levels — the immediate and the long-range consequences. Most cause-and-effect papers focus more on one element or the other (the cause *or* the effect), not equally on both.

In choosing subtopics, divide the paper into two sections; one section explains the cause (the action) and the other the effect (the reaction). These two large subtopics will probably divide into smaller clumps of information, what I'm calling the sub-subtopics. The cause section splits into the immediate cause and the background factors. The effect section consists of the first reaction and then the long-term results. Just to give you an even better migraine, each of the sub-subtopics may split into smaller units. For example, you may identify three or four long-term results of a specific event. Each result is a separate paragraph or section of your paper.

Here's an example: Imagine that you're writing about the (imaginary) new performance artist, Louella Locket. After extensive research you decide to write a cause-and-effect paper with the following thesis:

> Louella Locket's arrest for creating a public nuisance was a direct result of pressure from the anti-fluoride-in-drinking-water lobby.

The basic facts are as follows: Louella had been receiving a great deal of publicity for her sugar-based performance art, in which chocolate, lollipops, gumdrops, and other confections were distributed to the general public. According to Louella, the message of her art was "seize the sweetness of life." Candy sales were at record levels, and dentists noted a sharp rise in cavities. Pressure to add cavity-preventative fluoride to drinking water grew, alarming the antifluoride lobby. On November 5, Louella, dressed as a candy bar, distributed 250 pounds of chocolate caramels to pedestrians on a downtown street. A riot broke out as people scrambled for the candies. Soon after, Louella was in jail, where she issued a call for action and asked her public to pelt the police with jellybeans to protest her arrest. Phone records showed that several members of the "No Fluoride for Us Society" (NOFFUS) called the mayor on November 4, shortly after Louella announced her November 5 candy-bar performance piece. An analysis of the minutes of NOFFUS meetings reveals that the group planned to "stop Louella by any means necessary."

The situation may be broken down into these parts:

> Immediate cause: NOFFUS calls the mayor.
>
> Immediate effect: Louella is arrested.

Background causes: NOFFUS's opposition to fluoride in drinking water, NOFFUS's campaign contributions to influential politicians, NOFFUS's stated view that a rise in cavities may sway public opinion in favor of fluoride additives, Louella's proven effect on candy consumption and the cavity rate.

Long-term effects: Backlash against Louella's arrest by the candy industry, campaign by public health officials to educate the public about proper flossing techniques, investigation of the relationship between campaign contributions and the actions of elected officials, decision by the city council on fluoride additives.

How do you put these in order? Several roads are open to you. Here's one: Begin with a "you-are-there" description of the caramel riot and the arrest and then move to the thesis about NOFFUS's pressure. Next, present the background causes, and end with a discussion of the long-term effects of NOFFUS's actions. For more information on putting subtopics in order, read Chapter 14.

Pro and con — opposite sides of an issue

Writing about abortion, gun control, drug laws, bilingual education, or another current issue? Considering such knotty questions as whether a meteor killed the dinosaurs or whether the works of Hilda Shakespeare (the Bard's imaginary sister) could have received a fair evaluation in Elizabethan England? Pro-and-con structure may be just what you need, and, as a bonus, defining subtopics for this structure is a cinch. In presenting both sides of an issue or question, divide the topic into three parts: an explanation of the issue or question, the arguments for, and the arguments against. Each of these subtopics, of course, may be subdivided. The explanation of the issue or question may include a history, a discussion of significant laws or court cases, a description of social conditions, and other factors. The arguments for and against subdivide into, well, arguments — each sub-subtopic being one reason for or against the issue you're evaluating or the question you're considering. A pro-and-con paper may take a stand, or it may simply present the merits and problems of both sides, letting the reader decide.

Don't confuse arguments with evidence, the facts you supply to support an argument. Each argument in a pro-and-con paper contains a paragraph (or lots more, depending upon the length of the paper) of evidence. Check out the section, "Sorting Notes: Placing the Right Idea in the Right Basket," later in this chapter, to learn how to distinguish the two.

Interest groups — various viewpoints on one issue

When you read through your notes, you may notice that some of the experts you quote don't agree with each other. Or, you may see statements like "X is good for the Googrubs but disastrous for the Glubgoos." Or, you may feel as if you're looking at one event through a series of different lenses. If you're in any of these situations, chances are you have an interest-group paper.

Interest groups are all those people who have a stake in the outcome of an event or who have a particular point of view on an issue. The topic of the paper is examined from all those points of view, and each point of view is one subtopic. For example, say you're writing about the fall of the Republican government during the Spanish Civil War. Interest groups include the republicans, the monarchists, the anarchists, the church, the army, and the peasantry. Each of those groups is one subtopic. Or, perhaps you're writing about the meaning of the lighthouse in Virginia Woolf's masterpiece, *To the Lighthouse*. Interest groups here may be views from various schools of literary criticism — feminism, deconstruction, and so forth. In either case, your paper looks at one idea through all those different lenses. For examples in each subject area, as well as business, of possible interest-group topics, see Chapter 12.

I'm using the word *group,* but keep in mind that a *group* is not necessarily made up of people. If you're writing about global warming, your subtopics may include the effect of global warming on agriculture, commerce, health, wildlife, and so on. Each of those subtopics describes a different reaction to the same thing — hot winters and super hot summers. So each of those subtopics is an "interest group" in your paper.

Hypothesis, test, results — "I wonder. . . ." and proof

If you've ever been in a science lab, you know that the scientist creates a *hypothesis* — a statement to be tested and judged true or untrue. (Actually, the statement may be proved untrue but never the opposite. The tester says only that the test results "support" the hypothesis.) Outside the science lab, you may find yourself creating a hypothesis as you review your notes. Perhaps you've got a ton of information on music and culture in the late 1960s and early 1980s. (Okay, you picked up some of it firsthand while dancing the night away, but it's still information.) You create an educated guess: The music of the two time periods had a similar impact on American culture. Then you go back through your notes, maybe checking a few more sources, and test your hypothesis. You find a great deal of material in support of your hypothesis and some that weakens your case. Soon you've formulated the results of your inquiry, deciding that your hypothesis is at least partly correct.

The subtopics in this sort of paper are as follows:

- ✔ An explanation of the hypothesis
- ✔ The standards you used to judge the accuracy of the hypothesis
- ✔ Information supporting the hypothesis, grouped logically
- ✔ Any information that may disprove or weaken the hypothesis, again organized into subgroups
- ✔ Your conclusion about the accuracy of the hypothesis

Defining most of the subtopics of a hypothesis paper is easy, but the information for and against may give you some trouble. The problem is that you must create logical categories within each subtopic — sub-subtopics. In the next section, "Sorting Notes: Placing the Right Idea in the Right Basket," I explain how to untangle ideas. This technique may be applied to information supporting or weakening a hypothesis.

Sorting Notes: Placing the Right Idea in the Right Basket

Whoever cautioned against putting all the eggs in one basket was right, maybe not for groceries but definitely for research papers. Earlier in this chapter, in the section entitled "Mining Research Notes for Subtopics," I explain how to define the subtopics for your research paper. After you have the subtopics — the baskets that gather similar bits of information into one spot — you have to sort your notes and place the right idea or fact into the right basket.

Sometimes the task of sorting is a no-brainer. If one subtopic in your paper on holidays is Halloween, every note about trick-or-treating goes in that category. But sometimes separating the fruit of your research labor is as tough as untangling a plate of cooked spaghetti. Each strand of information seems stuck to all the others.

Here's a technique to help you distinguish material for one subtopic from the material for another:

✔ If you've taken notes on index cards, lay the "problem cards" — the ones you're having trouble sorting — on a table. If you've taken notes in a computer file or notebook, write the confusing notes on index cards, one sentence per card.

✔ Sort the cards into piles, one pile for each subtopic.

✔ As you sort, check to see whether two or more cards say *exactly* the same thing in different words. If so, you probably don't need both cards. Put one of the duplicate cards aside. Later, when you're actually writing the paper, flip through the "duplicate" pile to see whether you've omitted something.

✔ Is one card similar to, but not exactly the same as, another? Perhaps that card represents a subtopic, or even a sub-subtopic, of the card it resembles.

✔ Sometimes a fact or idea relates equally to two subtopics. Sounds like a problem, but actually this situation may be an advantage. Place the idea at the end of your discussion of one subtopic. When you begin the next subtopic, use the idea as a transition. This technique works best if the fact or idea is of some importance, not just a detail. See Chapter 16 for more information on transitions.

If you're writing a pro-and-con or interest-group paper, you have to deal with both arguments and evidence. An *argument* is a reason you support or oppose the issue. *Evidence* is the proof that backs up your argument. For example, an argument in favor of gun control laws is the fact that the courts have often upheld the right of the state to regulate firearms. Evidence supporting that argument is made up of the cases themselves — their verdicts and the judges' opinions. In creating subtopics and sorting information, don't confuse arguments and evidence.

If you're lucky, all your notes fall nicely into one "basket" (subtopic) or another. If you're normal (that is, not so lucky), a few ideas refuse to go into any basket. Don't despair. Spend a moment reconsidering your subtopics. Should you add another? Redefine one subtopic slightly to accommodate more ideas? If not, leave the ideas aside for the moment. You have another chance to classify your information when you make an outline and still another opportunity when you sit down to write the rough draft. Odds are everything will become clear during one of those tasks. In Chapter 14, I explain how to make an outline. Part V discusses the writing process in detail.

Chapter 14

The Battle Plan: Constructing an Outline

*W*hen I was in grade school (When? The earth was still cooling!), the only thing I learned about outlines was that I had to place the Roman numerals and capital letters a certain number of spaces away from the left-hand margin. Outlining at that point in my life was a chore I did only to satisfy the teacher. But as a writer I've found that an outline is not just a set of indented sentences or an annoying homework assignment. An outline is a battle plan for writing.

These days I seldom worry about indentations and the proper spot for a capital letter when I construct an outline. If the outline doesn't look pretty, I can work through the ugliness. But I can't work without the outline, and I craft it carefully because the outline takes me where I want to go — to a logically organized piece of writing.

In this chapter I explain how an outline helps you in the writing process. I show you two common systems for outlining, and I explain the numbering and indentations, just in case your Authority Figure cares about the niceties and wants you to submit an outline along with the finished paper. I also show you two sample outlines — one, fittingly enough, on the advantages of outlines, and another on the nonexistent literary masterpiece, *Dental Dreams*.

Drawing Up a Battle Plan: Why Outlines Are Necessary

After giving up such unimportant pastimes as eating, sleeping, and watching television in favor of research, thesis statements, and subtopics, you may think that you're as ready as you'll ever be to pick up the pen or turn on the computer and write. Wrong. First take a few moments (okay, an hour or so, but not a huge amount of time) to construct an outline. Why? Because an outline will improve your paper. (For the lowdown on how to do research, check out Part II For information on thesis statements, see Chapter 11. For more about subtopics, read Chapter 13.)

Take a look at Figure 14-1 for an explanation of how an outline helps your paper, written, appropriately enough, in outline form.

How Outlines Help: An Outline on Outlines

I) Logic
   A) Subtopics in order
   B) Transitions clarified
   C) Omissions discovered
II) Evidence
   A) All relevant facts accounted for
   B) Irrelevant facts revealed and omitted
III) Elimination of distraction
   A) No hunting for stray evidence
     1) Outline tells you what's going where
     2) Label locates evidence in your notes
   B) No need to think about logical thread
   C) Concentrate on one idea at a time

Figure 14-1:
The structure of an outline.

Figure 14-1's "outline on outlines" describes in only a few words why an outline is important, but I'll expand on a couple of points. Subtopics are the baskets you use to sort information. In an outline, you line up the subtopics, putting them in order. Once you've got an outline, you should be able to see the logical path that the reader will travel from the first paragraph (the *thesis*) through the proof and on to the last paragraph (the *conclusion*). The outline reveals gaps or off-topic elements.

The outline stage is a great time to check transitions. Is one idea logically linked to the idea before or after it? You don't have to write the transitional words at this stage, but you should be able to identify the relationship — *why* one idea follows another. If you can't, consider changing the order.

Outlining also gives you a chance to identify ideas that *don't* fit the chain of logic you're creating. Be ruthless: If you can't find a good spot for something, put it aside. Later, go back over the whole outline to see whether you need that piece of information. Recheck once you've got a rough draft. But if something still doesn't fit, forget about it!

The biggest advantage of outlining is the boost to your concentration. You can't design an airplane while you're actually flying it, and you shouldn't decide *what* you're saying while you are in the midst of figuring out *how* to say it. If you have the blueprint for the paper before you sit down to write, all you have to think about when you're in the chair is the writing itself.

Indenting by the Rules: How to Format an Outline

All you really need in your outline is a list of the ideas and facts you'll include in your paper, arranged in order. You don't have to obsess about spacing and labeling, unless your personal Authority Figure cares. (Always check!) If the outline is just for you, make it as informal as you wish. But before you decide, consider this fact: The indentations and labels of a formal outline give you a diagram of the paper, and the diagram actually helps you identify logical connections. Everything in an outline with the same indentation and the same type of number or letter is of equal importance.

One school of outlining goes for the minimum — a few words to remind you what you're writing about. That sort of outline is called a *topic outline.* (Figure 14-1 is a topic outline.) Another type of outlining is written in complete sentences, and, shockingly enough, it's called a *sentence outline.* (Figure 14-2 is a sentence outline.) Which one should you use? Unless your Authority Figure has a preference, go with the system that feels right. A topic outline is fine when you know your subject cold. A word or two is enough to remind you of everything you want to say. A sentence outline helps to clarify the details of what you're writing. It also helps to check the flow of logic. If you read the sentences in the outline, you should "hear" a paragraph that makes sense. Also, if you're dreading the moment when you actually have to sit down and write the paper, go with a sentence outline. The more you have on paper, the easier the writing will be.

Before you write your own outline, decode one to see how the format works. Check out Figure 14-2, the outline for an English paper on *Dental Dreams,* an imaginary novel by Lucius Peaworthy. The thesis of the paper is that the life of Boblet, a character in *Dental Dreams,* is symbolized by the tubes of toothpaste he buys and discards. He's one of those obsessive characters who's always brushing and flossing, in between breaking up and reuniting with the love of his life, Grima, running for president, being impeached, and attending an exorcism. (Peaworthy's publisher insisted that he go after the *X-Files* market share.) The raw material includes the novel, critical essays on Peaworthy's work, Peaworthy's letters and diary, and the paper writer's own interpretation. The conclusion? Personal-product symbolism is increasingly important in contemporary fiction.

I) Introduction
  A) Quotation from novel: "Boblet contemplated the wonder before him - aisles of goods, tuna fish cans piled hundreds of feet in the air, paper plates and window cleaners, baked beans and personal hygiene accessories. He was in heaven. He was home." (p. 24)
  B) Thesis statement: The life of Boblet, a character in Lucius Peaworthy's novel Dental Dreams, is symbolized by the tubes of toothpaste he buys and discards.
II) Toothpaste can't be put back into the tube, and Boblet can't correct mistakes.
  A) Quotation from Boblet's father Ishmael: "You want to go back, don't you? Well let me tell you something, something I learned the hard way. There is no way back, and the sooner you accept that fact, the better off you'll be." (p. 40)
  B) Boblet tries to correct mistakes and fails.
    1) Boblet's attempt to reconcile with his ex-wife fails.
    2) Boblet staples his thumb to the carpet and can't pull it out.
    3) Boblet writes a letter of retraction to editor of newspaper, who rejects it.
    4) The press is hostile to Boblet's apology because he attempts to "redefine the meaning of 'is'" (p.188)
III) Toothpaste spurts from the tube in unplanned directions, and Boblet's life takes unexpected turns.
  A) Boblet receives an emergency brain transplant.
  B) Boblet's long-lost brother shows up on eve of Boblet's impeachment.
  C) Boblet's DNA mutates.
  D) Quotation from Peaworthy about novel: "I thought I was writing the story of a slacker, but Boblet kept telling me that his story was completely different. When I started writing, I didn't plan to bring in anything at all about an exorcism, but it soon became obvious that I had to write that climactic scene. Boblet never knows how his life will turn out, and neither did I."
    (Book #3, p. 330)
IV) Toothpaste is messy, as is Boblet's relationship with Grima.
  A) Quotation from Baer (critic): "The gooiness of the paste mirrors Boblet's constant marriage and divorce to Grima." (Book #8, p. 12)
  B) Toothpaste leaks over love letter from Grima.
    1) Quotation from Peaworthy about love-letter scene: "The pathos of that moment when Grima tells him that she loves him and, therefore, must order his assassination! And the stain of the toothpaste, mixed with the blood...life's mundane and sublime together." (Book #3, p. 450)
    2) Quotation from critic Baer: "As surely as Boblet drops toothpaste globs on the floor, he insults his Grima even as he tries to compliment her."
    (Book #8, p. 26)
    3) The fact that Boblet breaks up and reunites with Grima 15 times indicates a messy relationship.

Figure 14-2:
An example
of a
sentence
outline.

V) Toothpaste is scented to cover unpleasantness; Boblet tries to cover up unpleasantness in his life.
   A) Boblet holds a press conference to "spin" his reputation.
      1) Boblet says that the answer about the starlet's appearance in the nude hinges on the meaning of "is."
      2) Boblet distributes perfumed favors for press: "On each chair was an envelope. 'I ask the American public to forgive me,' it read. A whiff of lilac rose to Grima's nose as she picked up her envelope." (p. 687)
   B) Boblet attends the exorcism.
      1) Boblet calls it "the ceremony."
      2) Airbrushes the video to hide head twirling.
VI) Toothpaste is associated with important moments in Boblet's life.
   A) He buys a new brand whenever he reunites with Grima.
      1) Quotation from novel: "Mint? Whitener? Boblet picked up one box after another. Surely one would have the answer, surely one would change...everything." (p. 99)
      2) Boblet discards each brand whenever he breaks up with Grima.
         a) He throws out the first tube when Grima weeps.
         b) Quotation from novel: "The rolled plastic sat on the bottom of the wastebasket, discarded like his hopes for a better life." (p. 32)
         c) He changes brands after the failed reconciliation attempt.
         d) Quotation from critic, L. Stanfo: "Boblet's pathetic nature exhibits itself most prominently when he stares sadly at the used tube of dental paste in the trash can, traces of the product still smeared on his lips, an ineffective substitute for Grima's kiss." (Book #4, p. 16)
   B) Boblet uses toothpaste at important moments.
      1) He is brushing his teeth when he first glimpses Grima.
      2) Quotation about toothpaste during exorcism: "His head whirled, 360° - his teeth were falling out, and he had brushed them so carefully that day!" (p. 78)
      3) Just before the press conference he brushes with mint-flavored paste.
      4) He drips toothpaste on Grima's letter.
      5) Quotation from Baer (critic): "Just as Proust had his Madeleine, Peaworthy has his toothpaste." (Book #8, p. 55)
VII) Conclusion: Personal-product symbolism is increasingly important in contemporary fiction.

Figure 14-1 is a good model of proper outline format. Figure 14-2 follows most, but not all, the strict rules for outlining. Many English textbooks state firmly that you're not supposed to label the introduction and conclusion or include the text of quotations and page numbers in the outline. But I think labels are helpful because they remind you of the task at hand — introducing or concluding the arguments of your paper. I like including the text of quotations and the page numbers because I don't want to pause to find the quotation in my notes. But be aware that these elements aren't part of the official English-teacher way to outline. If your personal Paper Assigner wants the super correct (but in my opinion less useful) version, omit the "introduction" and "conclusion" labels, the text of the quotations, and the page numbers.

If you've been careful in your note taking, all your research is identified by source and page number. (Chapter 8 explains how to do so efficiently.) If you wish, include those identifications in your outline. The identifications point you to the right spot in your notes so you won't waste time looking for something, and they help you cite sources correctly. But remember: Identification numbers are for you, not for your Authority Figure. Remove them from the outline you show the Paper Assigner, and follow the standard system of citation in the finished paper. (Chapter 18 explains citations.)

Now for an analysis of the *Dental Dreams* outline in Figure 14-2. In the *Dental Dreams* outline, the major sections of the paper, all labeled with Roman numerals and flush with the left-hand margin, are as follows:

- ✔ **Introduction**

- ✔ **First subtopic:** Toothpaste can't be put back into the tube, and Boblet can't correct mistakes.

- ✔ **Second subtopic:** Toothpaste spurts from the tube in unplanned directions, and Boblet's life takes unexpected turns.

- ✔ **Third subtopic:** Toothpaste is messy, as is Boblet's relationship with Grima.

- ✔ **Fourth subtopic:** Toothpaste is scented to cover unpleasantness; Boblet tries to cover up the unpleasantness in his life.

- ✔ **Fifth subtopic:** Toothpaste is associated with key moments in Boblet's life.

- ✔ **Conclusion**

Shortcut to success

The outline of a paper is a lot shorter than the paper itself, and you can use this fact to your advantage. If you're unsure about the content of your paper or if you just want a little extra advice, ask the Paper Assigner to read your outline and tell you if you're on the right track. Many Paper Assigners are too busy to comment on a full draft, but most are able to squeeze out some time to skim an outline. You need to include enough information to convey the main points of the paper, so it's probably a good idea to submit a sentence outline, rather than a topic outline. Once you've received the official comments, alter the outline, secure in the knowledge that you're on the right track.

Each of the subtopics in the previous list may be divided into smaller pieces, which I refer to as sub-subtopics. Think of these smaller pieces as divisions of the subtopic or as the supporting points you'll use to prove the truth of the statement the subtopic makes. Either way, indent five spaces and label the sections with capital letters. For example, the second subtopic in the *Dental Dreams* outline is divided into four sub-subtopics:

- ✔ **First sub-subtopic:** Boblet receives an emergency brain transplant. (This episode, by the way, represents Peaworthy's attempt to sell the book to soap-opera fans.)

- ✔ **Second sub-subtopic:** Boblet's long-lost brother shows up on the eve of Boblet's impeachment. (Same marketing strategy.)

- ✔ **Third sub-subtopic:** Boblet's DNA mutates. (Gotta get those sci-fi fans to buy the book!)

- ✔ **Fourth sub-subtopic:** Quotation from the author about the novel.

You can subdivide the categories of the outline as often as needed. Each time you subdivide, the numbering system changes and the indentation increases by five spaces. For example, category IIB — Boblet tries to correct mistakes and fails — is divided into four parts, each of which is labeled with an ordinary Arabic numeral. The most common system of numbering for both topic and sentence outlines uses the following labels in this order, with these indentations:

I) Roman numeral (flush with left-hand margin)

A) Capital letter (five spaces from left-hand margin)

1) Arabic numeral (ten spaces from left-hand margin)

a) Lowercase letter (15 spaces from left-hand margin)

The numerals and letters of an outline may be followed by a parenthesis, as you see here, or a period. Either method is acceptable.

Here's another numbering system, which relies on decimal points:

1. First subtopic (flush with left-hand margin)

    1.1 Supporting point for first subtopic (five spaces from left-hand margin)

    1.2 Another supporting point for first subtopic (five spaces from left-hand margin)

2. Second subtopic (flush with left-hand margin)

    2.1 Supporting point for second subtopic (five spaces from left-hand margin)

    2.1.1 Supporting point for 2.1 (ten spaces from left-hand margin)

2.1.2 Another supporting point for 2.1 (ten spaces from left-hand margin)

2.1.3 Another supporting point for 2.1 (ten spaces from left-hand margin)

2.2 Another supporting point for the second subtopic (five spaces from left-hand margin)

2.3 Another supporting point for the second subtopic (five spaces from left-hand margin)

3. Third subtopic (flush with left-hand margin)

Notice that the three main points (you can have as many as you want) are ordinary numbers. Every time you divide a main point into smaller categories, add a decimal place and number the points in order.

You can't divide something into only one part. Every time you indent in order to divide a topic or a subtopic into smaller parts, make sure you have at least two points!

Picky English-teacher rule: The first word in each outline point is capitalized. The topics in a topic outline do not end with a period, though of course the sentences in a sentence outline do.

Computer word-processing programs often have an outline function that makes formatting easy. In Microsoft Word, for example, you may click on "Format" and select "Bullets and Numbering." Then click on the "Outline Numbered" tab and choose the format that appeals to you. The "customize" function allows you to assign Roman numerals, capital letters, or other labels to each level of the outline. Every time you press "enter," the program stays on the same level (subtopic, sub-subtopic, etc.) unless you want to change the level. On the toolbar two miniature outlines with arrows allow you to move to a higher or lower level of the outline. Click as often as needed until the correct label and indentation appear.

Have you tucked everything into the outline, labeled, indented, and ready to roll? Great. Time for the last step: Place the title of the outline (which is the same as the title of the paper) on the top line. *Now* you're done. (For tips on titles, check out Chapter 11.)

Turning Notes into an Outline: A Practical Guide

You've got a bushel of notes and a dandy set of subtopics. (See Chapters 8 and 9 for tips on note taking and Chapter 13 for instructions on defining subtopics.) You've selected Door Number Two (topic outline, standard format). Now all you have to figure out is how to squeeze all that information into the outline.

Don't panic and abandon your research paper and hopes for a diploma (or a raise) in favor of a career in beachcombing. Outlining isn't as hard as you may think. Here's the technique, explained for each of the major note-taking systems:

Index cards

If you've taken notes on index cards, outlining is easy:

1. **Sort the cards into piles, one for each subtopic.**

2. **Give each subtopic a title and a Roman numeral on the outline.** If you create a topic outline (see preceding section on outline format for more information), write the title on the appropriate line of your outline. If you create a sentence outline, turn the title into a sentence and then write it on the outline.

3. **Examine each subtopic pile separately.** Figure out what categories it contains. Sort the cards from each pile into those categories. Give each category a title, and place it on the outline. At this level of sorting, use capital letters.

4. **Take a moment to read the cards in each of the new, smaller piles.** Can you divide the pile into even smaller bundles? Keep sorting, labeling, and separating, filling in the outline as you go.

5. **Put any leftover cards in a "discard" pile.** You may never use that information, but check the discard pile when your rough draft is completed. You may find a place for some of the information at that point in the process.

Computer files

Here's how to create an outline from computerized notes:

1. **Make each subtopic a field and sort the notes by that field if your notes are in a database program.** (See Chapter 8 for more information.) If your notes are in a word-processing file, cut and paste until everything for one subtopic is grouped together.

2. **Give each subtopic a title and a Roman numeral and enter it on the outline, in the same way described in the preceding section, "Index cards."**

3. **Look at all the notes belonging to one subtopic.** Sort them into smaller categories, giving each new category a title and placing it in the outline, labeled with a capital letter.

4. **Keep sorting into more and more focused subdivisions, entering each on the outline at the appropriate level.** (For more information on format, see "Indenting by the Rules: How to Format an Outline," earlier in this chapter.)

Notebook

If you've taken notes in a notebook, you can still sort them. Here's how:

1. **Get some colored markers or crayons, one for each subtopic.** Put a slash next to each item in your notes, using the same color for all the notes belonging to the same subtopic.

2. **Give the subtopic a title and a Roman numeral.** Enter it on your outline as described in the preceding "Index cards" section.

3. **Flip through your notebook again, rereading all the notes slashed with one color.** Subdivide them into categories. Put a second slash to the right of the first, color-coding the new categories. Enter the new categories on your outline as described in the preceding "Index card" section.

4. **Read the double-slashed notes again, sorting and adding a third, color-coded slash (or eventually, even more) until everything is divided, labeled, and entered on the outline.**

Salt to taste: When to change the outline

When you're writing, keep the outline next to the computer (or next to your pen). Think of the outline as the recipe for the project you're trying to "cook up." The basic recipe is good (otherwise you wouldn't be cooking it) but you may need to add a little salt or pepper during the cooking process as you taste the results of your labor. Follow the outline faithfully, but add or subtract bits "to taste" while you write. Here's why: Every step in writing a research paper involves thinking. You *reflect* when you choose the sources, *ponder* when you narrow from subject to topic to thesis, and *contemplate* every note you take. But writing is a form of thinking, also. It's entirely possible that you'll see something differently when you're finally ready to express it in polished prose. New idea = outline change.

If your notes are in a word-processed computer file and you hate cutting and pasting, print out your notes and follow the instructions in this section. Color-coded slashes work just fine for any written notes. Or, print out your notes and use scissors to slice them into pieces, which you may sort with the technique described in the preceding "Index cards" section. Just be sure that each little piece of paper has the number of the source and the page number on it. (See Chapter 8 for more information on numbering sources.)

Checking the Logical Path

Once your outline is ready, review it one more time, asking these questions:

✔ Does the title of the outline reflect the contents of the paper?

✔ Does the outline begin with a good introduction to your topic?

✔ Do the subtopics represent the major points of your argument or survey?

✔ If your paper has a thesis, do the subtopics support the thesis?

✔ Are the subtopics in logical order?

✔ Can you identify the transitions between one subtopic and another?

✔ Have you included all the relevant points within each subtopic (the sub-subtopics)?

✔ Can you identify any gaps in the logical thread?

✔ Do any points lead you off-topic?

✔ Does the outline end with an appropriate conclusion?

When you can answer "yes" to all of these questions, the outline is finished — and you deserve a break before undertaking the Next Big Step: Writing the paper. (Part V tells you how.)

Part V
Turn on the Computer, Fill the Fountain Pen: It's Time to Write

The 5th Wave   By Rich Tennant

"I know your paper is on infomercials, but I still wouldn't use transitions like, 'But wait, that's not all...' and 'Act now and I'll include extra information on my topic!'"

In this part . . .

You've turned off the phone, signed off the Internet, and told your friends to stop throwing pebbles at your window (or over your cubicle wall). The reason for the isolation? It's time to write. If you're like many people, it's also time for a mini-nervous breakdown.

Calm down. Writing a research paper is easy, once you've prepared for the task by collecting information and organizing it. (If you haven't, go back and read Parts II and III on how to find research material and take notes and Part IV on how to define subtopics and create an outline.) In this part, I discuss the writing itself, tackling each part of the research paper — introduction, body, and conclusion — and the annoying but crucial stuff like citing sources. I tell you how to polish the final draft and how to overcome writer's block.

So cheer up! Now that you've arrived at the writing, you've almost finished the job.

Chapter 15

Allow Me to Introduce Myself: Writing an Effective Introduction

I'm wading through a stack of research papers on Shakespeare's *Julius Caesar*. One paper starts off with a sentence about government in ancient Rome. *Fine*, I think, *the writer's talking about old guys in togas.* Then the writer moves to present-day presidential campaigns. *Okay*, I think, *he's comparing Shakespeare's view of ancient Rome to modern politics.* But then the writer throws in a sentence about violence. *Hmm*, I mutter, *he wants to relate violence to government — but to the government of ancient Rome, modern America, or Shakespearean England?* At this point only one thought is running through my mind: *What's this paper about, anyway?*

When you write an introduction, you don't want to leave the reader guessing. A confused reader may toss your paper without finishing it. After putting a zillion hours into a research paper, you don't want it to hit the trash bin.

Never fear. In this chapter I explain what that all-important first paragraph or section known as the introduction must contain and show you how to avoid the most common pitfalls of introductions: vagueness, boredom, and disorganization. I also guide you through the special requirements of science research papers and business plans.

Setting Your Reader on the Right Path: What an Introduction Accomplishes

Want me to visit? Invite me politely. Give me a map with the destination clearly marked. A travel video would be nice, too, especially one showing ecstatic tourists drinking margaritas.

The introduction to a research paper invites readers to visit your topic. You have to be polite (that is, write with formal and correct English) and provide a route to the destination (the thesis statement or topic sentence). To entice the reluctant, overworked, or uninterested reader, you should also supply the research-paper equivalent of a travel video (a fascinating anecdote, an intriguing quotation, or a fact that relates the topic to something the reader cares about).

The introduction serves as a quick orientation for the reader. How quick? If the paper is short, the introduction is probably a single paragraph. If the paper is long, the introduction may be a multiparagraph section. You decide how much you need; the length is less important than the content. A good introduction answers these questions and causes these responses:

> **Question:** What's this paper about?
>
> **Response:** Now I know what I'm reading.
>
> **Question for a paper with a thesis:** What is the author trying to prove?
>
> **Response:** I'm ready to consider your arguments.
>
> **Question for a paper without a thesis:** What ground will the paper cover?
>
> **Response:** I understand the scope of your research.
>
> **Question:** Why should I read this paper instead of delinting my raincoat or cooking up a batch of alfalfa cookies?
>
> **Response:** I actually read the paper instead of chucking it.

For more information on thesis statements, see Chapter 11. For information on papers without a thesis, check out Chapter 1 (definitions and characteristics) and Chapter 11 (how to write a topic sentence).

Depending upon your Authority Figure's preferences, your introduction may also contain a statement about your own connection to the topic (why you felt a pressing need to explore the links between boy bands and classical Chinese opera, for example).

Most but not all introductions also briefly state the subtopics you'll cover. For instructions on defining subtopics, read Chapter 13.

Science and social science research papers — those reporting the results of an experiment you performed — follow a strict, specialized format. So do business plans. See "Writing Introductions for Science and Business Research Papers" later in this chapter for guidelines on how to introduce these papers.

What does an introduction accomplish? It sets your readers on the right path, making them ready, willing, and able to follow you through the twists and turns of information to the conclusion of your research paper.

Creating and Placing the Essential Elements of the Introduction

If you're baking a cake, you need to assemble the ingredients: flour, eggs, chocolate, milk, and so forth. Then you have to place those ingredients in the correct spot. (Hint: Don't put the raw egg on top of the sprinkles.) If you're writing an introduction, you need to assemble the ingredients also: the topic, the thesis statement or topic sentence, the "hook" that lures the reader into the paper, and the subtopics. Then you need to situate these "ingredients" so that they have maximum impact. The following sections serve up the recipe, with examples.

As someone who spends far too many hours reading research papers, I believe that the writing in these papers can be interesting as well as informative, and that's the style I've employed for the examples in this section. However, some Authority Figures disagree; they favor a writing style that they call "academic" and I call "dry as a year-old watermelon." If your personal Authority Figure smiles only once a year, strip your writing to the essentials and use big words wherever possible (but only if you're sure that you're using them correctly).

The topic

Am I reading about Milton's *Paradise Lost* or *National Lampoon's Vacation*? Is this paper about giraffes, pickles, or jazz? The title of the paper narrows the wide world of topics, helping the reader focus on the particular topic you've written about. But the title isn't enough. The introduction needs to state the topic as well. If you're writing about picnics in Antarctica, be sure that at least one sentence contains the phrase "picnics in Antarctica."

The topic may be mentioned directly in the thesis statement or topic sentence. Or, the topic may be mentioned in another sentence.

For music or art papers, be sure to name the work (musical piece or artwork) and the artist. If you're writing about a work of literature, be sure that your introduction contains the title and author. Don't label these elements; slip them into the sentence casually. For example:

> **Bad statement:** The book is called *Pistachio Ice Cream and Potato Chips.* The author is Melanie Butterfat.
>
> **Why it's bad:** Okay, it's not *bad,* but it *is* clunky and rather obvious.
>
> **Better statement:** The main character in Melanie Butterfat's novel, *Pistachio Ice Cream and Potato Chips,* is nutritionally challenged.
>
> **Why it's better:** The title and author are inserted into a statement about the book. The reader gets the information along with another fact about the work.

Thesis statement

Somewhere in the introduction you need to tuck in a *thesis statement* — a declaration of the point you will prove in the paper. Chapter 11 goes into every picky little detail on how to create a good thesis statement. Here I'll just explain where to put it. Briefly, you have three choices: beginning, middle, and end.

In the sample introductions in this section, I've underlined the thesis statement so that you can identify it immediately. Don't underline the thesis statement in your paper unless the Paper Assigner specifically asks you to do so.

Thesis statement at the beginning

If the first sentence in your introduction is the thesis statement, the reader knows immediately where you're going. The rest of the introduction explains how you're going to get there and why the trip is worthwhile. First-sentence placement is forceful; you're leading with a punch to the jaw. The downside is that the rest of the paragraph or section may seem anticlimactic. The reader knows what's going on, so why read the rest? The reader may be tempted to cut to the chase and skip to the body of the paper.

The best way to keep readers with you is to catch their attention with a story, a quotation, or an interesting fact. See "The Hook" later in this section for more information.

Here's a single paragraph introduction, suitable for a short paper on flea fitness that no sane person would ever write. (You've now learned something about *me*.) The paragraph leads off with the thesis statement.

> <u>Physical training for fleas greatly increases the bugs' lifespan.</u> Once considered a fad for flea owners with too much disposable income, tiny exercise cycles and resistance machines have proved to be valuable weapons in the fight against insect heart disease. Tests on competitive marathon flyers show that these bugs have better circulation than their couch-potato relatives. Even something as simple as flea push-ups three times a week provides health benefits. But for some observers, health is a side issue. "I can't tell you how proud I am to see scrawny little bugs turn into sleek, conditioned athletes," comments Chester A. Arachnid, flea enthusiast and former circus trainer.

Notice that the thesis statement is followed by sentences about exercise machines, flying, and nonmechanical exercises — the three subtopics of the paper. The introduction ends with a quotation, always an interest-getter.

Thesis statement in the middle

If you plop the thesis statement in the middle of the introduction, you have a chance to lead with an eye-catching quotation or an intriguing little story or description. Next is the thesis statement, followed by the subtopics you'll cover in the paper. Placing a thesis statement in the middle of the introduction works well as long as you avoid one pitfall: Don't let your statement get lost inside the introduction. If the reader can't identify the thesis, its primary purpose — to let the reader know what you're going to prove — is defeated.

Here's the flea-fitness introduction from the preceding section "Thesis statement at the beginning" reworked so that the thesis statement is in the middle.

> "I can't tell you how proud I am to see scrawny little bugs turn into sleek, conditioned athletes," comments Chester A. Arachnid, flea enthusiast and former circus trainer, as his tiny charges pump iron and fly laps around Arachnid's indoor air track. Arachnid's not just enjoying the spectacle, he's caring for his pets' health. <u>Physical training for fleas greatly increases the bugs' lifespan.</u> Once considered a fad for flea owners with too much disposable income, tiny exercise cycles and resistance machines have now proved valuable weapons in the fight against insect heart disease. Tests on competitive marathon flyers show that these bugs have better circulation than their couch-potato relatives. Even something as simple as flea push-ups three times a week provides health benefits.

The quotation and the description of Chester A. Arachnid's training regimen starts the introduction off with a bang. The last three sentences set up the subtopics.

Thesis statement at the end

My personal favorite, this arrangement pulls the reader in with an interesting hook (quotation, story, description) and then hits the thesis statement at the end of the paragraph or section. Between the hook and the statement are the subtopics.

Here's the flea introduction, rearranged:

> "I can't tell you how proud I am to see scrawny little bugs turn into sleek, conditioned athletes," comments Chester A. Arachnid, flea enthusiast and former circus trainer, as his tiny charges pump iron and fly laps around Arachnid's indoor air track. Arachnid's not just enjoying the spectacle; he's caring for his pets' health. Once considered a fad for flea owners with too much disposable income, tiny exercise cycles and resistance machines have now proved valuable weapons in the fight against insect heart disease. Tests on competitive marathon flyers show that these bugs have better circulation than their couch-potato relatives. Even something as simple as flea push-ups three times a week provides health benefits. <u>Physical training for fleas greatly increases the bugs' lifespan.</u>

The introduction ends with a punch, sending the reader on to the body of the paper with a clear message. Ending the introduction with the thesis statement allows you to lead with your best stuff — something that catches the reader's eye and shouts *read me*. One possible pitfall: If the introduction is very long, you may lose your reader before he or she gets to the point.

Topic sentence

Not all papers have thesis statements. General surveys or reports still need introductions, which contain topic sentences.

The term *topic sentence* is often used to refer to the sentence in each paragraph that carries the main idea. Here I'm using the term to refer to the sentence that communicates the main idea of the entire paper.

Like thesis statements, topic sentences may appear at the beginning, middle, or end of the introduction. (For examples of all three, see the preceding section on thesis statements.) Just to show you one topic-sentence introduction, here's a variation on the flea theme I used as examples in the thesis-statement section.

To be completely clear, I've underlined the topic sentence. Don't underline the topic sentence in your paper unless your Authority Figure specifically tells you to do so.

Until the late twentieth century, the streets of the world were filled with gifted teachers coaxing fleas to fly on miniature trapezes or to shoot out of tiny cannons. But the Flea Anti-Cruelty Act of 1970 changed all that. Overnight, thousands of flea-circus enthusiasts were out of luck as flea academies shut down and flea circuses went bankrupt. The techniques for training performing insects have since been forgotten by all but a few black-market instructors. <u>Flea training, once a thriving profession, is now a lost art.</u>

The introduction tells the reader what to expect — a description of the golden age of flea-circus training, something about the techniques of training, an explanation of the law that outlawed the practice, and information about today's illegal flea trainers. The last sentence about "lost art" informs the reader that the paper will cover two time periods.

The hook

The local cable system carries 104 channels, and the satellite dish provides a few thousand more. The instant messaging notice is blinking. How, with choices like these, can you catch your reader's attention? With a hook to snag the reader before he or she moves on to bigger and better things.

I know what you're thinking. It's bad enough that the Authority Figure has ruined your life by giving you a massive research project. Now you're supposed to "hook" him or her into reading it? Yes. The reality is that the Authority Figure — the person, by the way, who will evaluate your work — is probably up to the eyeballs in unread research papers. In that situation, which paper would you prefer? The one that looks interesting or the one that shouts *wake me up when this one's over*?

Some Paper Evaluators — those who spend summer vacation in Death Valley and winter break in Glacier National Park — like to suffer, and boredom appeals to them. If you're writing for this sort of Authority Figure, skip the hook. Simply present the facts as intelligibly as you can, employing your most advanced vocabulary and most formal tone.

Hooks come in a million varieties, including the tried and true versions that are covered in the following sections.

Anecdote or example

Writing about global warming? Don't start off with boring statistics. Tell me that the future headquarters for summer baseball will be northern Alaska because everywhere else will be too hot. Or tell me that skiing will be possible only on indoor, air-conditioned slopes. Is your paper about sharks? Begin with the story about the shark that attacked a kid wading in shallow water. Does your paper discuss the antiwar protests of the Vietnam era? Discuss the hippies chanting outside the Pentagon, trying to levitate the building.

Anecdotes — little stories — grab attention. So do examples, as long as they're interesting. Include a good anecdote or example and you're halfway to your goal of a good introduction.

Be sure to connect the opening anecdote or example to the rest of the introduction with a strong transition. For more on transitions, see Chapter 16.

Description

Writing about a war? Describe a battle, including the shells bursting in air and the flag that was still there. Is your topic animal rights? Take me to a laboratory and describe the conditions. Art history paper? Start by making me *see* the work you're analyzing.

Descriptions should be accurate (your research helps here) and vivid (now you need your writing skills). Go for a "you are there" effect.

The transition between the description and the thesis/topic should be easy to write, assuming you've chosen the right thing to describe. The transition expresses the relationship between the description and the thesis or topic. If you can't express that relationship, you've probably chosen the wrong description.

Quotation

The urge to eavesdrop on other people's conversations indicates the appeal of quotations. Plus, they're easy to find. No matter what you're writing about, chances are someone famous said something interesting about it. Look through your notes for relevant quotations or consult *Bartlett's* or another reference work. (Chapters 5 and 6 provide more information on reference sources.)

The quotation may be the first or last sentence in your introduction or it may be inserted into the middle. (Check out the preceding section on thesis statements for examples of quotations placed at various spots.)

You may also plop a quotation alone in the center of the page, preceding the first paragraph by a double blank space. The quotation sets the tone for the introduction and for the entire paper, but it is not part of the text. For example:

> *Eyes are red,*
>
> *Spirits are blue,*
>
> *Revenge is sweet,*
>
> *So dead are you.*
>
> —Oscar Mull

Oscar Mull's immortal words capture perfectly the tone of cynicism and despair expressed in his epic poem, *The War Against Littering*. Blah blah blah blah . . . [The paper continues.]

If you're writing about a literary work, you may begin by quoting a relevant passage from the text. The passage should be dramatic enough to grab the reader's attention. It should also relate to the ideas you're considering in the paper.

Be sure to cite the source for all quoted material, unless you're quoting something that is so well known that it has passed into the realm of common knowledge — quotations such as "war is hell" and Homer Simpson's "do-oh." (If you can quote it by heart, it's probably common knowledge.) For more information on citations, see Chapter 18.

Question

Have you ever read a paper that began with a question? Have you figured out that the author of the paper wants to engage you in the topic by provoking an answer? Have you also figured out that I'm employing the question technique right now? Are you annoyed yet?

The preceding paragraph illustrates the appeal (and the turn-off) of questions. Your reader, addressed directly, becomes involved immediately because he or she needs to supply an answer. However, if the question is bogus, not really leading the reader into something worthwhile, you lose. The reader dumps the paper faster than I hang up on phone advertisements, and believe me, that's *fast*.

Once you begin with a question, answer it or show the importance of the question. Be sure that the thesis/topic of the paper relates to the question you posed.

Relate to reader

Most of *Research Papers For Dummies* is written in what we grammarians call *second person*. That is, I'm talking directly to *you* about *your* work. Second person tends to draw the reader into the paper. It reminds me (the writer) that what I'm saying is not just abstract information floating on the airwaves. It places you (the reader) squarely in the center of my consciousness. If it works, it makes the reader see how the material relates to his or her concerns.

Some Paper Assigners don't allow *first person* (the grammarian's term for *I* and *me*) or second person (the grammarian's term for *you*). You may have to stick with *third person* (talking *about* the subject impersonally). Ask!

An important announcement

In this sidebar I explain *announcing*, making sure that you understand what announcing is. I will also discuss when you can and cannot use this technique in your paper.

Okay, here goes. Reread the first sentence of this sidebar. Notice how it *announces* what this sidebar is about and what the sidebar will cover? That technique is called announcing or sign-posting. Here's another example:

> In this paper I will compare the nutritional value of bubblegum to that of artificial cheese.

You can also announce the topic and thesis of your paper without using personal references (*I* or *we*), as in this example:

> This paper examines the leisure activities of fruit flies.

One important note: Paper Evaluators either love announcing or hate it. In my experience, no Authority Figure is neutral. Find out before you write which category your Paper Assigner falls into.

Subtopics

In Chapter 13 I discuss how to define subtopics in more detail than anyone would ever want. Earlier in this section (when I explain where to put the thesis statement or topic sentence) I tell you how to work subtopics into the introduction. But before you close the book and go ice fishing, you should consider one more subtopic of the issue of subtopics: how to express them in the introduction.

You've got two options: sentences or words/phrases. If you choose sentences, each subtopic is communicated to the reader in — you'll never guess — a sentence. In the section, "Thesis statement," the introductions about physical training for fleas mention three subtopics, each expressed in a complete sentence. Following is one of those introductions. The subtopics are underlined and numbered.

Don't underline or number the subtopics in your paper unless the Authority Figure who assigned the paper specifically requests that you do so.

> Physical training for fleas greatly increases the bugs' lifespan. Once considered a fad for flea owners with too much disposable income, (1) <u>tiny exercise cycles and resistance machines have now proved valuable weapons in the fight against insect heart disease</u>. (2) <u>Tests on competitive marathon flyers show that these bugs have better circulation than their couch-potato relatives</u>. (3) <u>Even something as simple as flea push-ups three times a week provides health benefits</u>. But for some observers, health is a side issue. "I can't tell you how proud I am to see scrawny little bugs turn into sleek, conditioned athletes," comments Chester A. Arachnid, flea enthusiast and former circus trainer.

The full paper contains a section on flea fitness machines, marathon flying, and exercise routines. If you choose to state the subtopics as words or phrases, the introduction changes. Here's the new version, with the subtopics underlined and numbered:

Physical training for fleas greatly increases the bugs' lifespan. (1) <u>Fitness machines</u>, (2) <u>marathon flying</u>, and (3) <u>simple exercise routines</u> provide health benefits to these insects. But for some observers, health is a side issue. "I can't tell you how proud I am to see scrawny little bugs turn into sleek, conditioned athletes," comments Chester A. Arachnid, flea enthusiast and former circus trainer.

Which is better? The word/phrase version is shorter and gives the information quickly and efficiently. The sentence version is more interesting. Bottom line: You decide.

Not all introductions include the subtopics. When writing for rigid Authority Figures with definite ideas about format, ask about their preferences.

Having trouble naming your subtopics for a word/phrase introduction? Reread your outline. Chances are you'll find words or phrases there. If not, imagine that you are creating a title for each subsection of the paper. Use those titles to name your subtopics.

Steering Clear of Vague Introductions

Which introduction would you rather read?

Introduction #1:

In every human being's life a certain number of unpleasant experiences occur. Some of these experiences are helpful, and others are not. One of the most common unpleasant experiences is the paper cut. Paper cuts cause several bad effects, including pain. They also have other bad consequences, such as the possibility of infection. Langley Lee Lang, as well as several other scientists, has discovered a few simple precautions with which everyone can avoid paper cuts.

Introduction #2:

A swift shuffle through a pack of papers, and suddenly a line of blood appears — a paper cut. Paper cuts hurt, and they open the body to infection. A few simple precautions decrease the frequency of paper cuts, according to Langley Lee Lang and other scientists.

I'm betting that you chose the second introduction. It's more vivid (you see *a line of blood appears*) and it's shorter. Most important, it doesn't have any vague, general statements like this one: *In every human being's life a certain number of unpleasant experiences occur. Some of these experiences are helpful, and others are not.* The second introduction is very specific. Instead of *bad consequences* it states that *paper cuts hurt, and they open the body to infection.*

In writing an introduction, think of general statements as salt and specific statements as steak. What ratio would you like for supper? Lots of steak and just a pinch of salt, right? (For the vegetarians out there, think of salt and your favorite chips.) Don't waste the reader's time with vague statements! Check out these before-and-after pairs:

> **Vague statement:** The _____ (fill in the blank with your topic) has both advantages and disadvantages.
>
> **Why you should avoid it:** *Everything* has both advantages and disadvantages, except perhaps bubonic plague.
>
> **Better statement:** Choosing a CEO by means of an essay contest may yield someone with no business experience but good creative writing skills.
>
> **Vague statement:** Many authors have considered universal themes such as life, love, death, and friendship.
>
> **Why you should avoid it:** Cut to the chase. Which author and theme are you writing about?
>
> **Better statement:** Marmeduke Duckworth's novel, *Plato and Mr. Potato,* explores the friendship between an ancient Greek philosopher and a child's toy.

Bottom line: Avoid sentences that could appear in any one of 20 different research papers. Go for sentences with details.

Details, yes. Evidence, no. Remember that the introduction comes *before* you make your case (argue for your thesis). The evidence that you use to prove your thesis belongs in the body of the paper, not in the introduction. For more information on the difference between evidence and arguments, see Chapter 14. For guidelines on how to write the body of the paper, see Chapter 16.

Most people who read papers for a living (teachers, professors, supervisors) have assembled *detectors* that immediately buzz when the paper writer begins to (a) flatter, (b) pad, or (c) lie. Don't include any of these sentences in your introduction, because if the buzzer goes off, the evaluation of the paper takes a nose dive:

> **Bad sentence:** *Blah blah* is a magnificent example of a masterpiece.
>
> **Why it's bad:** You may actually like *blah blah*, whatever it is (literary work, musical composition, history text, marketing plan), but the sentence doesn't convey any personal reaction at all. In fact, the sentence is a great candidate for the Golden Shovel Award. (I'll let you guess what's being shoveled.)

New sentence: *Blah blah* seems confusing at first glance, but the author's circular structure perfectly suits the theme of the cycles of life.

Bad sentences: The process of photosynthesis enables plants to convert sunlight to energy. Energy, when it is derived from photosynthesis, is very useful to plants. Plants need energy, and they get it from photosynthesis.

Why they're bad: Yawn. All three sentences say the same thing. The writer has amnesia or a lot of pages to fill up.

How to fix it: Cut the repetitive sentences (the second and the third). The first sentence does the job.

Bad sentence: Mesnikogg's analysis leads to an entirely new theory of gravity.

Why it's bad: Okay, it may not be bad, as long as Mesnikogg really did lay the groundwork for an entirely new theory of gravity. But if you intend to show that Mesnikogg proved that gravity keeps everybody from floating into space, you're in trouble.

How to fix it: Don't lie. Say something real about Mesnikogg's analysis.

Writing Introductions for Science and Business Research Papers

If you're wearing a pinstriped or germ-proofed suit, this section's for you. Come to think of it, most of the scientists I know wear jeans and sneakers. Okay, whatever you're wearing, if you're writing a science research paper or a business plan, read on.

These two types of papers follow rules that are stricter than the meanest teacher. Their introductions share some of the same characteristics of the general introductions I've discussed elsewhere in this chapter, but each veers away into its own little universe.

If you're writing a research paper about someone else's research, your introduction follows the general guidelines described earlier in this chapter. If your paper reports the results of an experiment that you performed, the introduction has these characteristics:

✔ The introduction is like a funnel: It begins with broad, general ideas and narrows down to specifics, ending with the hypothesis of your experiment — the idea that you tested.

✔ The general ideas include a description of the problem in its widest terms. For example: *Elevator phobia afflicts an estimated 500,000 people worldwide.*

✔ The introduction makes a statement about the relevance of the issue you're studying: *The 50 percent increase in the number of skyscrapers over the last ten years makes the issue of elevator phobia more pressing.*

✔ Science and social science writing should be concise. Don't waste words on a "hook." Draw the readers in by making them understand the importance of what you've studied.

✔ The introduction also includes a survey of other research done on the topic. For example: Elevator phobia most often begins after childhood trauma (Babcock 1968) or after an elevator accident (Dropler 2000).

All references to the work of other scientists must be cited properly. Science and social science papers generally follow the guidelines of the American Psychological Association. In the preceding example, the citations are in APA style. For more information on how to cite sources, see Chapter 18.

✔ The introduction may also explain why you chose to study this particular topic. Even if you worked alone, use *we* instead of *I*.

✔ The introduction ends with the hypothesis that the study or experiment tested.

✔ Some journals require a statement about the results of the experiment in the introduction; don't include one unless you're sure that the Paper Evaluator wants you to do so.

Chapter 12 contains more information on how to form a hypothesis and how to format a science research paper.

A business plan is a research paper you present to potential investors when you're looking for bucks (or euros or some other legal tender). The introduction to a business plan is called an *executive summary*. The executive summary is a stripped-down version of the whole paper. A good executive summary answers these questions:

✔ Who are you? Describe the company or the potential company. Provide information on your background and the qualifications of the principal executives.

✔ Why is your new or expanded company needed? Explain what problem your business will solve or what need it will fulfill.

✔ How will your company solve the problem or fill the need you've identified? Be specific here. Show the investor how your company will differ from the competition.

✔ Who will benefit? Discuss the market for the goods and services you'll provide.

✔ What time frame and how much money are you talking about? Explain how quickly your new factory will be ready for production or when the services will be available. Also talk about when you'll need each level of financing — the amounts and dates.

The tone of a business plan should be, well, business-like. A business plan is not the place for informality, humor, sarcasm, or slang. Nor should it be wordy. The writing in the business plan should reflect the way you will accomplish your task: with efficiency and without waste. For more information on the format of business plans, see Chapter 1.

Help! I can't write the introduction

The introduction is the first part of the research paper, and therefore it's probably the first thing you sit down to write. So you sharpen your pencils or fire up those electrons (or whatever it is that makes computers work) and . . . freeze. Not a single word comes into your mind. Does this sound familiar? If so, don't despair. The introduction may *not* be the best place to begin the work of writing. Because it sets the tone for the entire paper, the introduction sometimes turns out best when it is written *after* you've finished the body and maybe even the conclusion. If you have trouble getting started, check your outline. Do you have a good first sentence for any particular section? If so, write that section first. For more tips on overcoming writer's block, check out Chapter 20.

Chapter 16

The Body of Evidence

. . . .

In This Chapter

▶ Writing the body of the paper

▶ Tackling each subtopic in turn

▶ Sticking to the topic

▶ Creating logical transitions

▶ Using evidence, quotations, and visual aids effectively

▶ Forming a concession and reply

. . . .

*I*n detective stories the *body* is the murder victim, the most hated guy in town. In Research-Paper World, the *body* is the large mid-section of the paper, the place to display the information you've collected. As you tackle the body of your research paper, you may feel that the detective-story definition of *body* is more appropriate, with the murder victim being your sanity.

In this chapter I explain how to break the task of writing the body of the research paper into manageable parts. I show you how to tie the parts together with logical transitions and discuss how to stay focused on the topic. I explain how to present evidence and how to use quotations effectively. I also throw in a couple of writer's tricks: one picture is worth a thousand words (visual aids) and concession and reply (answering your critics in advance).

Putting Meat on the Bones: Writing the Body of the Paper

By the time you sit down to write, you should have a working outline — the skeleton of your paper. The outline lists the subtopics that make up the body of the research paper. In this section I explain how to write the first draft of each of these subtopics. First I tackle method, and then I give you some style pointers. (Chapter 14 tells you how to create an outline. For tips on defining subtopics, see Chapter 13. Chapter 19 describes how to polish the first draft and create a final product.)

Method

No magic method gets the words out of your head and onto the page. But some techniques do make writing the body of the paper less painful. The details:

✔ Before you write, look over your outline and concentrate on the subtopics. Does one particular subtopic seem easier (or less threatening) than the rest? If so, start with that subtopic. Don't feel obliged to write the paper in order, though you may certainly do so if that method appeals to you. Later, when all the subtopics are written, put them in order.

✔ Read through all the notes for one subtopic before beginning to write. Keep the notes in a handy spot so that you can refer to them as you work.

✔ With a good outline and properly labeled notes (Chapter 8 gives you the lowdown on note taking), you won't spend a lot of time hunting for the next fact or quotation you need for a particular paragraph. But if something escapes you, don't get hung up in a major search. Leave a space for the fact or quotation and insert a quick note to yourself. Keep writing, and fill in the blanks later. Just don't forget to delete the note before handing in the paper. You'd be surprised how many people submit papers with sentences like this one: _Poe's "The Gold Bug" is a famous story written in [LOOK UP DATE]._

✔ Once you incorporate a note into the paper, put a single slash across the note card. Resist the temptation to express your paper-writing annoyance by obliterating the note. You may need to go back later to recheck your information.

✔ Every time you select a fact, quotation, or idea from your notes, consider the issue of citation. Do you need to credit the source? If the answer is yes, take the time to insert the source identification number. Don't agonize over citation format while you're in the midst of writing. At the end of each work session, go back and create proper citations. Taking care of documentation at this stage makes writing the final draft a lot less time-consuming. (Chapter 8 explains an efficient system for keeping track of sources. Chapter 10 tells what must be documented and Chapter 18 provides the proper format for citations.)

✔ Don't try to write a perfect paragraph or section at this stage of the process. Just pour thoughts onto the page or screen. Later, when an entire section or draft is completed, you'll have time to revise. This rule is so important that I'll say it again: Don't try to write and edit at the same time. Write first; edit later.

✔ As you write, a brilliant sentence or idea may occur to you. If it belongs in the paragraph you're working on, write it down. If it doesn't belong in the paragraph you're working on, write it down anyway — in a separate computer file or on a sheet of paper. If you know where you want to put the information, make a note to yourself: "For last paragraph of fire hazard subtopic," for example. Every once in a while, review these "outtakes" and place them in the proper subtopic.

✔ After you've written one subtopic, repeat the procedure for another subtopic. Look at the outline and choose another section that sparks a reaction in your mind. Write the subtopics in any order you wish, until you've completed all of them.

✔ No matter how wonderful your outline, don't be afraid to change it as you write the paper. Of course, it's not a good idea to decide — after six weeks of research and two days of outlining — that *the real estate market* is a better topic than *the poetry of William Carlos Williams*. But small adjustments are inevitable. If an additional argument occurs to you, go right ahead and insert it into the appropriate section. If a section seems disorganized, play with the order of ideas until it makes sense.

If the Authority Figure who will evaluate your paper has read and approved the outline, *ask* before you institute a change, unless the difference is truly minimal. Also, if you have to hand in an outline along with the paper, be sure that the outline reflects the finished product. Correct the outline as you write.

✔ Once the subtopics are finished, put them in order and read through them one more time. Adjust first and last sentences so that each sub-topic flows smoothly into the next. ("Connecting the Dots" later in this chapter explains how to link one subtopic to another.)

Style

Asked to name the most difficult aspect of writing, one famous author replied, "Getting the words right." This section about "getting the words right" explains how to achieve the proper tone and diction in your paper.

Tone is an English-teacher's term for the attitude that your writing reflects, such as formal, informal, humorous, or don't-take-that-tone-with-me-young-man. *Diction* (another English-teacher term) refers to word choice. Tone and diction are related, of course, because the words you place on the paper help to express an attitude.

The tone of a research paper should be formal, unless you're writing for Professor Groovy (see Chapter 2) and he wants you to "become one with the topic" and "express your inner self." In that case, informal is a good bet. Formal diction is also your best choice; a research paper is no place for slang. Go for the word that expresses what you want to say, but remember that clarity is your goal. You want the reader to get the message, not take a vocabulary course.

A paper with formal tone and diction, I must point out, is not as stuffy as a nose in hay fever season. If you're a student or have ever been one, you can probably point to a textbook that you truly hated because every sentence was yards long and contained at least a dozen words that no one in the real world ever uses. And, I admit, a certain number of academics seem to love that sort of writing. But out of a love for language and a respect for the art of writing, please reject stuffiness. To illustrate what I mean:

> **Bad, stuffy sentence:** According to Snuffledrup's landmark study, the interpersonal exchanges arising from transient encounters in a site devoted to hedonism and profit rarely effect a true "I-Thou" nexus of communication.

> **Formal, nonstuffy, good sentence:** According to Snuffledrup's landmark study, brief conversations in bars rarely result in meaningful communication.

See the difference? As you write, try to sound like yourself — but your best, dressed-up-for-company self. Don't kid around, but take pity on the poor Paper Evaluators: Don't put them to sleep!

The tone of business writing is always formal. (Ponder for a moment the meaning of *business-like* and you'll get the idea.) But don't try to impress your boss by using vocabulary that's beyond your reach. First, you may use the wrong word. Most dictionaries tell you the definition, but not the feelings attached to a word (the *connotation,* as we English teachers put it). For example, the dictionary defines both *skinny* and *slender* as *low in weight.* But one is a compliment and the other isn't. Second, if you don't know the meaning of a word without help from the dictionary, the boss probably doesn't either. Do you really want your boss to walk around feeling inadequate? To put it another way, an Authority Figure who has to look up words in the dictionary while reading your research paper is *not* a happy camper. Also, be careful with *jargon.* Jargon is the specialized language that flourishes in the workplace. Jargon from my own workplace includes *prog,* short for the "Academic Progress Reports" that we all write to report a student's lack of progress, as in *I'm going to prog him if he's late one more time.* Jargon is fine for conversation, but not always for research papers. If the report is going out of the office — perhaps to potential investors or clients — choose words that actually reside in the dictionary, not in your cubicle, unless you're sure that the intended audience will understand you. If the report will stay in the office and you're sure that the jargon is widely accepted, go ahead and use it.

Defining Paragraphs and Writing Topic Sentences

In the body of a research paper, as in any other piece of writing, the building blocks are paragraphs. Each paragraph should have one main idea. Suppose you're writing a paper about the wedding traditions of the Stiffsnobs, an ethnic group I created for the purpose of this example. (Don't look for them in your anthropology text.) One subtopic deals with clothing. In a short paper, one paragraph may contain everything about the Stiffsnob wedding wardrobe — the bride's lucky red-and-white-striped socks, the groom's green hat and veil, the maid of honor's ankle bracelet, and so on. In a longer paper, one paragraph may be devoted entirely to the bride, one to the groom, one to the maid of honor, and so forth.

The main idea of each paragraph is expressed in a *topic sentence,* which may be placed at the beginning, middle, or end of the paragraph — in other words, anywhere. Here are two examples of topic sentences in the Stiffsnob wedding-tradition paper. The first example is for a short paper in which all the clothing information occurs in the same paragraph. The second example is for a long paper in which the clothing information is spread over a number of paragraphs. Notice how the topic sentence fits the paragraph.

Example #1:

> <u>As in most cultures, the Stiffsnobs follow rigid rules in selecting clothes for a wedding</u>. The bride, who traditionally shaves the left half of her head, wears a special blue velvet half-cap on the unshaven right side. In keeping with the Mollyglub legend, most brides wear red-and-white-striped socks, which are considered lucky. Recent studies suggest an increase in the number of Stiffsnob brides who purchase Western-oriented, white, cowgirl dresses (Bloom 1997), but a substantial number continue to wear a folded purple tablecloth pinned in strategic spots. The groom's costume is, if anything, more elaborate than the bride's. Clad from head to toe in green netting, the groom must shave his wife's initials on his head and wear a conical green hat. The grooms from the Western provinces wear boots (Arkwright 1998), while those from the East favor clogs (Ollivi 2001). The groom's parents wear yellow tent like robes, and the bride's parents cover their simple white bodystockings with purple shawls. The best man and maid of honor both display chunky, silver ankle bracelets, cunningly revealed by short Capri pants.

Example #2:

> <u>As in most cultures, a Stiffsnob bride follows rigid rules in selecting and donning clothes for her wedding</u>. The bride, who traditionally shaves the left half of her head, wears a special blue velvet half-cap on the unshaven right side. In keeping with the Mollyglub legend, most brides wear red-and-white-striped socks, which are considered lucky. Recent studies suggest an increase in the number of Stiffsnob brides who purchase Western-oriented, white, cowgirl dresses (Bloom 1997), but a substantial number continue to wear a folded purple tablecloth pinned in strategic spots. The pins are donated by female relatives of the groom, each of whom ceremoniously inserts the pin into the garment while chanting, "He should have married a doctor" (Arkwright 1998). Not to be outdone, the bride's relatives gather flowers for the traditional bouquet, which they present to the bride with the statement, "You could have done better" (Ollivi 2002).

To make identification easier, I've underlined the topic sentence in the sample paragraphs. Don't underline any sentences in your research paper unless the Paper Assigner asks you to do so.

The term *topic sentence* may also refer to a sentence that states the main idea of an entire paper. (Chapter 11 gives more detail on that sort of topic sentence.) In this section I'm using the term to refer to the main-idea sentence of each paragraph.

How long should a paragraph be? Long enough to do the job. Just be sure that all the information in the paragraph relates to one main idea. If the paragraph is extremely long (over a page), check it. Can you break it into two smaller sections, each with a different main idea? For example, suppose the preceding sample paragraph on Stiffsnob brides were much longer. It might be broken into a paragraph on clothing, a paragraph on jewelry or accessories, and another on nasty relative's comments. If the paragraph is extremely short (only two or three sentences, perhaps) consider combining it with another paragraph and changing the topic sentence to include the new, expanded main idea.

Business writers may find that a number of shorter paragraphs, each a half-page in length, serve them well. Busy readers (and business executives certainly fit that definition) often skip long, dense pages of prose.

Staying on Topic: The Tuna Fish Defense

In a highly unscientific survey, I have discovered that most people like tuna fish and chocolate cake. So why not just throw both in a bowl, mix them up, and have the combo for lunch?

Tuna fish mixed in with chocolate cake — how disgusting can you get! Yet this sort of mixture pops up in research papers all the time. The writer has a bunch of thoughts that are quite interesting, even valuable. Most of the thoughts may be just what you need (chocolate cake) and relate well to the paragraph you're writing. But one great idea (tuna fish) doesn't belong; in fact, it seems to relate to a completely different section or even another paper entirely. Unfortunately, instead of presenting each thought in the proper place, too many writers plop both of them in one paragraph — the research-paper equivalent of Tuna-Chocolate Surprise.

As an example of a misplaced statement, here's an altered version of the paragraph about the fictional Stiffsnobs from the preceding section, "Defining Paragraphs and Writing Topic Sentences." Consider the entire paragraph as a delicious slice of chocolate cake — with one glob of tuna fish in it. Can you spot the tuna?

> As in most cultures, a Stiffsnob bride follows rigid rules in selecting and donning clothes for her wedding. The bride, who traditionally shaves the left half of her head, wears a special blue velvet half-cap on the unshaven right side. In keeping with the Mollyglub legend, most brides wear red-and-white-striped socks, which are considered lucky. Red-and-white socks are produced in local factories or imported from abroad. Recent studies suggest an increase in the number of Stiffsnob brides who purchase Western-oriented, white, cowgirl dresses (Bloom 1997), but a substantial number continue to wear a folded purple tablecloth pinned in strategic spots. The pins are donated by female relatives of the groom, each of whom ceremoniously inserts the pin into the garment while chanting, "He should have married a doctor" (Arkwright 1998). Not to be outdone, the bride's relatives gather flowers for the traditional bouquet, which they present to the bride with the statement, "You could have done better" (Ollivi 2001).

The "tuna fish" is sentence four, which informs the reader that red-and-white socks are produced locally or imported. Nice to know, but you're not discussing where clothing is manufactured; you're discussing what the bride wears and the ceremonial insults that take place as she's getting dressed. Verdict: Dump sentence four. Add a section about clothing origins or save it for another occasion, perhaps a study of the economics of sock manufacture.

To avoid adding "tuna fish" to your writing, be sure that you know what each paragraph is about. Mentally underline the topic sentence of each paragraph, or do it physically if you're working on a word processor, but be sure to delete the underlining in the final version. (If you're not sure how to identify or write a topic sentence, check out the preceding section, "Defining Paragraphs and Writing Topic Sentences.") Now ask yourself whether *every* sentence in the paragraph relates to the topic sentence. If so, fine. If not — throw the tuna back in the ocean.

Connecting the Dots: Moving from One Subtopic to Another

Time for a new subtopic in this chapter. How do you know? A subhead — "Connecting the Dots: Moving from One Subtopic to Another" — tells you so. A subhead is one way to "connect the dots" for the reader. It announces that one subtopic is finished and another is about to begin. Another way to "connect the dots" is with a *transition* — a word or phrase that links ideas.

Subheads

Subheads help to organize your writing. Think of them as the label tabs on a set of file folders; each label explains what's inside. If your research paper is rather long (ten+ pages), you may use subheads to introduce each subtopic. However, the Authority Figure currently ruining your life with impossible research assignments may not want subheads. *Ask* if you're not sure about the preferred style.

Don't write subheads in a fancy font like the ones in this book. The font that you've chosen for the text of your paper is best. As a general rule, subheads are centered on a separate line, sometimes with an extra blank space between the subhead and the first line of the text. Unless your Authority Figure has a sense of humor (and you're *absolutely sure* that your jokes will be appreciated), don't write the kind of clever subheads you find in *For Dummies* books (she said modestly). Stick to the facts and make sure the subhead conveys the content of the section.

Science or social science research papers that report the results of original experiments *always* have subheads identifying each section — "Methods and Materials," "Results," "Discussion," and so forth. Some Authority Figures want you to center the subhead and others prefer that you place the subhead flush with the left-hand margin. Ask!

Transitions

A short or medium-length paper generally doesn't need subheads. Instead, to keep the paper flowing nicely move from one subtopic to another with transitional words or phrases. Think of a transition as a little hook that connects the last sentence in one paragraph or section to the first sentence of the next paragraph or section. Good transitions make your writing smooth and clarify the chain of logic you've created.

It's possible to place a transition at the end of a subtopic, but you're more likely to place one in the first sentence of a new paragraph or section. To choose a transition, define the relationship between the ideas in each paragraph or section. Here are some possible relationships, followed by the words that express them and a few sample sentences (Note: I haven't supplied citations for any of these sample sentences. In an actual research paper, you may need to cite sources. Chapter 10 tells you when to credit a source, and Chapter 18 tells you how to do so.):

- ✔ **Relationship:** Additional idea
    - **Transitions:** Also, moreover, in addition to, besides, furthermore, likewise, not the only, not only

- **Sample sentence #1:** *In addition to* the new taxes, Prime Minister Angustia *also* proposed a mandatory period of community service. (This sentence links a section about new taxes to a section about mandatory community service.)

- **Sample sentence #2:** *Besides* melon balls, photographer Deegee Dee is *also* known for portraits of large eggplants. (This sentence links two paragraphs about truly bizarre art.)

✔ **Relationship:** Contrasting idea

- **Transitions:** On the other hand, in contrast to, however, despite, in spite of, nevertheless, nonetheless, otherwise, unlike

- **Sample sentence #1:** *On the other hand,* Angustia asked that his own family be exempt from community service because of "their previous service to the nation." (This sentence links a section about Angustia's proposal to a section describing the favors he wanted for his family.)

- **Sample sentence #2:** *However,* the balloon's propulsion system did not work as well as Bayer had hoped. (This sentence links a section about how great the new propulsion system was supposed to be to a paragraph describing Bayer's extremely rapid, involuntary descent.)

✔ **Relationship:** Comparison

- **Transitions:** Than, equally, as/as, similarly, similar to, like

- **Sample sentence #1:** *Similar* to Blithering's theory of intelligence is Ot's concept of intuition. (This sentence links sections about two theories of intelligence.)

- **Sample sentence #2:** Blithering's theory is *as* ridiculous *as* Ot's. (This also links sections about two theories of intelligence.)

✔ **Relationship:** Cause/effect

- **Transitions:** Therefore, because, hence, thus, so, accordingly, consequently, as a result

- **Sample sentence #1:** *Because* the film has no humans, the audience was unable to relate to the characters. (This sentence links a section describing the animation of a filmstrip entitled "Vegetable Pals" with a section describing the reasons the film grossed $2.42.)

- **Sample sentence #2:** *Thus,* the senate did not ratify the peace treaty. (This one links a section describing the treaty's problems with a section about the legislative response.)

✔ **Relationship:** Time

- **Transitions:** Previously, after, before, since, still, yet, up until, then, later, before, earlier, finally, in the end

- **Sample sentence #1:** No bunnies hopped *after* the Easter eggs were confiscated. (This one links a paragraph about the seizure of Easter eggs with a paragraph about postseizure bunny reaction.)

- **Sample sentence #2:** *In the end,* the Union of Holiday Workers intervened. (This sentence links a paragraph about postseizure bunny reaction to a paragraph about a holiday-character strike.)

✔ **Relationship:** Example

- **Transitions:** For example, for instance, illustrating, showing

- **Sample sentence #1:** Goblins, *for example,* refused to haunt. (This sentence begins a paragraph illustrating several reactions to the holiday-character strike.)

- **Sample sentence #2:** *Illustrating* the dismay of the holiday-deprived public was the Valentine's Day rally. (This one begins a paragraph about the rally, one of several paragraphs about the reaction of the public to the holiday-character strike.)

A common grammar error is to stick two sentences together with the transition *however, therefore, consequently,* or *nevertheless.* These transitional words are *not* conjunctions. (That's grammarspeak for words that may legally join two sentences.) If one of these words is the only glue holding two complete thoughts together, add a semicolon. For example:

Complete thought #1: His eyebrows look like lima beans.

Complete thought #2: His hair resembles shredded cabbage.

Illegal joining: His eyebrows look like lima beans, however his hair resembles shredded cabbage.

Corrected sentence: His eyebrows look like lima beans; however, his hair resembles shredded cabbage.

One popular but clumsy transition is what I call "knee bone connected to the thigh bone" in honor of an old song that lists all the bones and their connections. In this sort of transition, the writer restates the chain of logic of the entire paper at the beginning of each new subtopic. Bad idea! Here's an example, drawn from a paper about teenage drinking. The thesis is that setting a legal drinking age is counterproductive. The subtopics follow this line of reasoning:

A legal drinking age affects adolescents.

Adolescents test limits.

When faced with a limit on drinking, adolescents will only drink more.

Setting a legal drinking age is counterproductive.

Check out the beginning of the third subtopic, which has a "knee bone connected to the thigh bone" transition sentence:

Because the legal drinking age really targets adolescents and because adolescents tend to test any limits imposed on them, when faced with a legal drinking age, adolescents will only drink more.

What's wrong with this transition sentence? Everything. It's not a hook; it's a summary of the paper thus far, all squeezed into one sentence. Transitions suggest to the reader how the subtopics are connected. They shouldn't present a miniature outline of the paper.

Presenting Evidence and Relating It to a Thesis

How do you present evidence? According to television, you whip out a stained handkerchief and wave it at the jury while saying, "Ladies and Gentlemen, this handkerchief is the *real* murder weapon!" The judge gasps, the accused murderer cries, and some quiet guy in the corner of the courtroom is hauled off to jail. Neat, huh? Presenting evidence in research papers is not quite so dramatic but just as important, because the evidence proves that the thesis is true. The formula is simple: No evidence = no proof, and no proof = no paper. And no paper = no passing grade or no key to the executive washroom.

If your paper is a general survey without a thesis, the "evidence" is simply the information you've gathered. Your goal in this sort of paper is to present what you've learned in a logical way. You don't have to worry about persuading the reader that a particular idea is correct. (For more information on papers without theses, see Chapter 11.)

Getting down to specifics . . .

Which passage is better?

The crowd went wild after the election. Everyone was very excited when the news was announced. Some people rioted, and a number of arrests were made.

As Flumflug's victory was announced, the supporters in Grand Great Hotel began to scream. One press report stated that "overeager campaigners" snatched tablecloths from the banquet tables and "whirled them in the air, dishes and all" (Sgrub 23). In about an hour, the police moved in. Captain B.F. Peerce reported that 434 people were arrested, most for "drunk and disorderly" conduct or for "illegal use of lighting fixtures" (Ebenexer 89).

The first one, right? Just kidding. The second one is much better because the writer chose the specific over the general. In writing the body of the paper, you should too!

The evidence is grouped by subtopic and is generally summed up by a topic sentence. ("Defining Paragraphs and Writing Topic Sentences" earlier in this chapter contains examples and explanations.) When you present evidence, you have to navigate between two traps. The first trap is failure to relate the evidence to the argument you're making. The second trap is overexplanation of the relationship between the evidence and your thesis. Somewhere in the middle is the perfect presentation. Here are some sample passages illustrating the traps and possible corrections. Both passages are from a paper titled "Ghosts in Modern Drama" with this thesis: Ghosts in the plays of Bridie Oplyx always represent a desire for revenge. (Don't expect to see this one on Broadway, because I made it up.) **Note:** I haven't cited sources here, but you should.

✔ **Problem:** Passage not related to thesis.

- **Passage:** The appearance of Hedwig's ghost in Act II coincides with Heathe's speech about muffins. "I choked on a muffin," explains Heathe as the ghost places phantom baked goods into the oven.

- **Analysis:** The thesis is about revenge, but the passage doesn't refer to revenge at all. The reader can't connect the evidence to the thesis.

✔ **Problem:** Passage related too obviously to the thesis.

- **Passage:** Another example of the ghost's representing the desire for revenge is the appearance of Hedwig's ghost in Act II, which coincides with Heathe's speech about muffins. "I choked on a muffin," explains Heathe as the ghost places phantom baked goods into the oven. Heathe hates the cook who baked the muffin that choked Heathe during the election campaign. Heathe's greatest desire is to get revenge on the cook, as critic Dwayne D. Duane points out. So the appearance of the ghost at this moment shows that the ghost represents Heathe's desire for revenge.

- **Analysis:** Nothing like hitting the reader over the head with the point! This passage presents the evidence and then labels it _twice_. The writer obviously doesn't trust the reader's intelligence and goes into overdrive.

- **Possible correction:** The appearance of Hedwig's ghost in Act II coincides with Heathe's speech about muffins. "I choked on a muffin," explains Heathe as the ghost places phantom baked goods into the oven. Heathe's choking incident is the crucial factor in his loss of the election. As critic Dwayne D. Duane points out, Heathe blames this loss for all the troubles in his life (the war, his mother's illness, his head cold). The ghost's cooking symbolizes Heathe's desire to have the muffin cook fired and later, executed.

- **Why this passage is better:** The word _revenge_ isn't in the passage, but the last two sentences make it clear that Heathe has a grudge against the cook and wants to hurt him. Both these factors add up to _revenge_, which the last sentence links to the appearance of the ghost. The evidence isn't labeled clumsily, but the reader gets the point.

Inserting Quotations

Quotations are the research-paper equivalent of no-limit credit cards — they can get you a lot of stuff you'd *really* like to have (credibility, immediacy, interest), but they can also get you into trouble *fast* if you don't use them properly. In this section I talk about when and how to insert a quotation into the body of your paper.

Quotations are the actual words of another person that you copied from a book, recording, or live interview. If you place those words in the paper, you're quoting, and you need to acknowledge that fact by placing quotation marks or by giving another signal to the reader that the words are not your own. You also need to credit the source. If you don't acknowledge that the words came from somewhere other your own brain, you're heading toward a failing grade (or the want ads). Chapter 18 shows you how to cite sources properly.

When to insert a quotation

As you leaf through your research notes, you probably notice a lot of quotations — some helpful, some not. How do you tell the difference? And how many quotations do you need? How long should a quotation be? And where should you put them? Here's a guide:

✔ Look for quotations that express interpretations or opinions, not just facts. For example, suppose your paper is about the possibility of life on Mars. You have a quotation from a NASA scientist who analyzed data from the Mars Lander. Don't bother quoting the scientist if all she does is relay some facts (such as how much the lander cost and how long it took to reach the planet). If you need those facts, simply place them in one of your own sentences, citing the source. But if the scientist weighed in on the little-green-men question, go for a direct quotation.

✔ Insert a quotation if it adds a special edge — information that doesn't come alive in any other way. Say you're writing a history paper on the Great Hopscotch Rebellion of 1652 (which took place only in my imagination). You've got an eyewitness account from a champion hopscotch player who was the first to refuse to pay the chalk tax. If the player's words are dramatic and interesting and relate to one of your subtopics, you may want to insert the quotation in your paper. For example, suppose you're making the point that the rebellion began nonviolently. If all you have from the hopscotch champ is a simple "I did not want to pay the tax," don't bother quoting. But suppose the champ said "I told the tax taker that I was loath to pay yon tax, but I did deny his urge to fight, asking only to be allowed my hop." Now that's a quotation you can use!

✔ Use quotations of an author's views if you're comparing or commenting on those views. For example, suppose your point is that Flibber T. Gibbet's analysis of Greco-Roman mud wrestling is hopelessly biased.

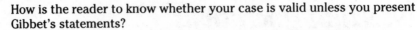

How is the reader to know whether your case is valid unless you present Gibbet's statements?

✔ Insert quotations to show attitudes, emotions, motivations, symbolism, and writing technique if you're writing about a work of literature. Don't quote an event in a novel or play if your only point is that the event happened. In that case, just use your own words to explain the event. But if you're interpreting the text, the words should be in your paper.

✔ Ask yourself whether you need the entire quotation or just a part of it. For example, suppose you're writing about visual imagery in a particular poem. Just quote the images you're discussing, not the entire line or stanza the images appear in. Show the reader that words are missing by inserting three dots (. . .) or four, if a period at the end of a sentence is missing.

✔ Refrain from using quotations in a business report, unless you're giving examples of consumer reaction.

Quotations are great, but don't overuse them. The Paper Evaluator wants to know that you've done the research, but he or she also expects to see some of *your* writing. A string of quotations, however wonderful they are, is *not* a paper; it's a string of quotations. Insert quotations according to the guidelines in this section and analyze or connect each to the point you're making. If you can't connect the quotation, or if the quotation doesn't fall into one of the categories I've outlined, you're probably better off with your own words.

How to insert a quotation

Finding the right quotation and the right spot to place it is only part of the job; you also have to figure out how to insert the quotation smoothly into the text. Here's how:

✔ If the quotation is short, insert it into the text of your paper. If the quotation is longer than three lines, you may block it. A *blocked* quotation is alone in the center of the page, separated from the text above and below it by extra blank space. It is usually double-indented (with a wider margin on each side) and single-spaced.

✔ Regardless of whether the quotation is inserted in the text or blocked, don't just plop it in the paper without some sort of analysis or explanation. (One exception to this rule is an *introductory quotation*. Check out Chapter 15 for an example and explanation of an introductory quotation.)

  • **Quotation plopped into text:** Plotclev's last novel was not a success. "The book business isn't what it used to be" (Zzyx 359). The publisher printed only 450 copies and sold 2.

- **Why it's bad:** Who said the quoted words? Why are they in the paragraph? As the passage is now, the reader has to guess.

- **Quotation with analysis before:** Plotclev's last novel was not a success, and he attributed the failure to the publisher, not to the writing, commenting, "The book business isn't what it used to be" (Zzyx 359). The publisher printed only 450 copies and sold 2.

- **Quotation with analysis after:** Plotclev's last novel was not a success. "The book business isn't what it used to be," commented Plotclev in an effort to explain its failure (Zzyx 359). The publisher printed only 450 copies and sold 2.

- **Why the last two examples are better:** Now you know who spoke (Plotclev) and why the quotation is there (to show that Plotclev did not lose confidence in his writing).

✔ Don't analyze the quotation before *and* after unless you have something new to say. Repetition is a waste of the reader's time.

✔ If you have two quotations that prove the same point and want to use both, place a few of your own words in between them. Don't just string one after another. Check out these examples:

- **Bad use of quotations:** Plotclev hated all critics: "You are incompetent and a disgrace to the nation." "Everyone knows that you are overdue for retirement."

- **Better use of quotations:** Plotclev called the literary critic of the *Moscow Times* "incompetent and a disgrace to the nation" and said that the critic was "overdue for retirement."

✔ Don't label the quotation with phrases such as these: *This quotation shows that.... An example of Plotclev's confidence is.... In this quotation I've proved that....* If the quotation is linked logically to your argument, the reader grasps the point. A label is unnecessary and tiresome.

✔ You may translate a quotation from another language into English, assuming that English is the language of the entire paper. However, don't "translate" any quotations from old-fashioned English into your own modern words, even if you're really proud of yourself for decoding a comment from Queen Elizabeth I. Just make your point in the analysis and let the reader figure out what the quotation means. However, if the quotation contains a truly strange word, you may place its meaning in brackets inside the quotation.

✔ The footnote, endnote, or parenthetical note tells the reader where the quotation comes from, but you may also identify the speaker or author of the quotation in the text. If you do so, provide labels (historian, art critic, eyewitness) for names that are likely to be unfamiliar. However, don't say something like "Famous writer William Shakespeare once said...." Assume that the Paper Evaluator knows anything that falls into the category of common knowledge.

One Picture Is Worth . . .

They say that one picture is worth a thousand words. In my case, one picture was worth an afternoon of shopping. I was writing about Stonehenge, the ancient and mysterious set of giant stones located in England. After I had spent eight or nine hours torturing sentences in an attempt to describe the circular ruins, my editor called with a simple suggestion. "How about we insert an illustration?" she said. Brilliant! I dumped the paragraph describing the stones and wrote a short lead sentence. Then I went to Bloomingdale's.

Illustrations — photos, drawings, graphs, charts, and other visual aids — may add a winning edge to your research paper. Visuals present information that can't be communicated any other way, or they present information as a quick summary of material in your text.

If you're writing an art research paper, it should include a photocopy (color, if possible) of the work of art you're discussing. Call each photocopy or illustration a "Figure" (always capitalized) and number the illustrations. When you refer to the work in the text of your paper, include a reference to the figure number, as follows: *Munchkin's sculpture of* Toto *(Kansas City, Metro Art Museum, Figure 8) is. . . .* Most teachers prefer that you place the illustration near the text, but some want all the visuals at the end of the paper. Ask! Under the illustration place a caption.

For their own reasons that they never explain to anyone else, scientists divide visual aids into two categories: Tables and Figures. *Tables* present data in columns. *Figures* include all other types of visual aids, including maps, graphs, photos, drawings, and diagrams. In the body of your science paper, separately number all the Tables consecutively (Table 1, Table 2, Table 3, and so on) and all the Figures consecutively (Figure 1, Figure 2, Figure 3, and so on). Figures and Tables (always capitalized) should be placed near the text that refers to them, and all the visual aids should be discussed *somewhere* in the text. Don't repeat the information in the Table or Figure; interpret it. As an example, check out Figure 16-1 — a fictional survey on everybody's favorite green vegetable.

Table 12: Dislike for Brussels Sprouts by Age of First Eating		
Age of First Eating	Dislike Somewhat	Dislike More Than Nuclear War
0 -2	20%	80%
3-5	30%	70%
6-9	55%	45%
10+	75%	25%

Figure 16-1: A sample table.

Source: *Myxpz School Survey, 2001.*

Notice that the title in Figure 16-1 clearly explains what information the Table contains. All the columns are labeled, and the source of the information is given. Tables are labeled above, and Figures below, the data.

Now here's how a reference in the text should look:

> Surveys show that the later children are exposed to Brussels sprouts the less intense their dislike of that vegetable (Table 12).

Now take a look at Figure 16-2 for an example of, well, a Figure!

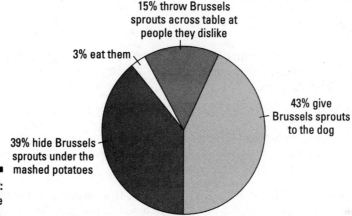

15% throw Brussels sprouts across table at people they dislike

3% eat them

43% give Brussels sprouts to the dog

39% hide Brussels sprouts under the mashed potatoes

Figure 16-2: A sample figure.

Figure 12: Reactions to Servings of Brussels Sprouts

Bosses usually love visual aids; they get a lot of information very quickly and (I suspect) they like the way a research paper looks when little graphs and charts are sprinkled around it. However, don't waste time and paper presenting information in visual form if one sentence will do the job just as well.

Answering Objections in Advance: Concession and Reply

Concession and reply is a writer's trick, but you probably learned the oral version when you were quite young, maybe in the cradle. Here's the oral version in action:

> Young Person: I'd really like to go to the movies tonight. Now I know you're going to say that I can't because it's a school night and I failed

every course but recess last semester, but this trip is different. The film is about car chases, and seeing it will really help me with my science homework because cars follow the laws of physics. Yes, I know you're worried about my homework, but I did all my homework already.

Old Person: You've convinced me. I'll drive you there.

Okay, maybe that last line is a bit unrealistic, but you get the idea. Young Person has figured out *in advance* what Old Person's objection will be (homework) and answered it. The research-paper concession and reply is similar. As you prove the thesis, consider the arguments that may be used against you and explain why those arguments do not invalidate your thesis. Here are a couple of concession-and-reply passages:

Example #1:

True, the murder rate has risen 4 percent in the last year, but most of that increase came from the Banana Peel Killer. If his crimes are removed from the statistics, the overall trend is still downward.

Example #2:

Algernon does stand up whenever a lady enters the room, but apart from this minor courtesy, his behavior is uniformly disrespectful to the female characters.

In the first example, the thesis of the paper is that crime is decreasing. The murder rate is an exception. Rather than ignoring that little detail, the writer attempts to account for it by explaining that the 4 percent increase really stems from one spectacular crime. In the second example, the thesis deals with Algernon's attitude towards women. The writer wants to be sure that Algernon's superficial courtesy does not make the reader ignore his truly piggish behavior.

Chapter 17

And in Conclusion . . .

Toward the end of most speeches, the audience stares with glazed eyes and daydreams about the coffee cart in the lobby. Suddenly, one phrase perks everybody up: *And in conclusion* . . . . You can almost see the rebirth of hope as one thought flickers across the room: *We may get out of here before the next millennium after all!*

Of course, your research paper will be so informative and so interesting that the Paper Evaluator reading it will gasp with dismay as the last pages near. Nevertheless, the phrase *in conclusion* still draws special attention. And even without that phrase, the conclusion of your paper has a strong impact because it's the last thing the Paper Evaluator reads.

In this chapter I show you the difference between a conclusion and a summary and tell you which one to write. (Hint: The chapter's not titled "And in Summary . . .".) I explain how the conclusion relates to the rest of the paper and provide a couple of useful models. Chances are at least one of the models will be appropriate for your particular research paper. I also show you how to conclude a paper that doesn't have a thesis and a paper that reports the results of your own original science research.

Summarizing versus Concluding: How to Tell the Difference

Think of your paper as a plant. You start the paper with a thesis — the root. You outline a bunch of subtopics — the branches. You provide a lot of great evidence — the leaves. Now it's time for the plant to flower — the conclusion. A flower is a natural outgrowth of the plant, but a flower is also different: The rest of the plant is green (or brown and shriveled, in the case of the plants on my windowsill), but the flowers are pink or red or whatever. I'll stop beating this comparison to death because I'm sure by now you get the point. The conclusion grows naturally from the thesis and body of the paper, but it's not exactly the same as the preceding sections. The conclusion's a bit showy, the place for your best thinking and writing. A good conclusion shows that you've done what you set out to do — prove your thesis. But it also goes a little further by revealing the implications or significance of the information in the paper.

For the definition of thesis, see Chapter 3. For more information on writing a thesis statement, check out Chapter 11. To learn how to write a conclusion for a paper without a thesis, read "Concluding a Survey Paper," later in this chapter.

Papers reporting the results of your own science or social science experiments follow a special format. Check out "Concluding Science Research Papers" in this chapter for more information.

Business executives don't like surprises. The conclusions you've reached in the course of your research belong at the *beginning* of a business report, in a section entitled "Executive Summary." An *executive summary* is a paragraph that summarizes everything in the paper. In writing an executive summary, pretend that each word costs a thousand dollars. Shorter is better! On the other hand, don't leave out anything important. The information on conclusions in this chapter does *not* apply to business writing.

As long as I'm explaining what a conclusion *is*, I should spend a moment explaining what it *isn't*. A conclusion is *not* the introduction all over again, written in slightly different words. Nor is it a simple restatement of the thesis and subtopics. That's a *summary* — the paper in miniature. Many conclusions contain a bit of summary because they bring the reader back to the thesis and declare it proved. Some conclusions also mention the most important subtopics. However, conclusions always move beyond the range of the paper, taking the ideas to the next logical step.

Should you end your paper with a conclusion or a summary? Back to the comparison I used a couple of paragraphs ago: Would you like to see a flower sitting on top of a plant, or a hairy little ball of roots and branches? Personally, I opt for the flower (the conclusion), not the ball of roots and branches (summary). I think I've got a lot of company. True, you may have an Authority Figure who's a root-and-branches fan. If the person who assigned the paper asks for a summary, write a summary. But if you haven't been told otherwise, assume that you should write a flower, er, a conclusion.

Packing the Essentials: What the Conclusion Must Contain

Going on a trip? Don't forget the airline tickets, passport, and toothbrush — the essentials. Writing a conclusion? Don't forget a reference to the thesis and an expanded idea — also known as the essentials. If you like (and if your Paper Evaluator likes), throw in a dramatic punch and a shortened version of the main points of the paper. Presto! A conclusion.

General survey papers without thesis statements follow a different pattern. See "Concluding a Survey Paper" in this chapter for a guide to writing conclusions for nonthesis papers.

How long should your conclusion be? Long enough to accomplish the task. Include the essentials and, if you wish, a dramatic element. As a general rule, a short paper needs only a paragraph. A longer paper may have two or more concluding paragraphs, and a thesis or dissertation (Chapter 1 describes these papers) may need a concluding chapter.

The following sections show how to cook up a grand finale for a thesis-based research paper.

Thesis reference

The *thesis* is the idea you set out to prove all those pages and sleepless nights ago. Now that you've proved it, you've earned the right to a pat on the back, and the conclusion is the spot to do so. Somewhere in the conclusion, state that you've made your case and the thesis is correct. Don't be too obvious, as in these examples:

- ✔ **Thesis statement (from the introduction):** The character of King Archibald is based on a native of Philadelphia.

  - **Poor reference to the thesis statement (from the conclusion):** I have proved that the real King Archibald was a native of Philadelphia.

  - **What's wrong:** Don't say "I have proved." Be more subtle!

  - **Better version:** Because Ken Smithler loved comics, it is not surprising that he based his main character, King Archibald, on the famous cartoonist Archibald A. Smith of Philadelphia.

- ✔ **Thesis statement (from the introduction):** All Martians are born with a capacity for language.

- **Poor reference to the thesis statement (from the conclusion):** So we see that all Martians are born with a capacity for language.

- **What's wrong:** I've read this sentence before. How about a bit of variety? (Yes, I know there *are* no Martians, but work with me here.)

- **Better version:** As Gewald P. Dinger states, "The capacity for language, clearly hard-wired into the brain, distinguishes Martians from Venusians and Jupitarians."

✔ **Thesis statement (from the introduction):** No one was a clear winner of the American presidential election of 2000.

- **Poor reference to the thesis statement (from the conclusion):** In my opinion, neither Al Gore nor George W. Bush was a clear winner of the American presidential election of 2000.

- **What's wrong:** Why label this statement as your opinion? Since you chose the thesis statement, the reader knows that you think it is true. If you've done a good job, the evidence in your paper proves the thesis. Don't weaken the conclusion by labeling it as an opinion.

- **Better version:** Because the winner of the American presidential election of 2000 was "None of the Above," voting reform is essential.

Slide the thesis reference into a sentence that has another point to make. Because the sentence has at least one other idea in it, the reader won't feel a sense of deja vu; yet you make your point: *My thesis is right!*

Expanded idea

The conclusion should open the door to the world beyond your paper. I'm not talking about a *beam-me-up-Scotty* transport to a whole new universe. The conclusion is *not* the spot to begin another paper, nor is it the right place for evidence. So don't state any ideas that require huge amounts of proof. Instead, let the conclusion offer a glimpse of something bigger than what you've already tackled. You may provide this glimpse in any of several different ways. Read on!

What's it all about, Alfie?

I've taken the title of a famous film to describe the sort of conclusion that discusses the significance of your research. Okay, nobody's pretending that your paper is going to change the course of world events. But pushing the boundary of ignorance a little further away *matters*. Why? Answer that question in relation to your research paper. For example, suppose you've proved that animal subjects appear more frequently than human beings in the art of a particular society. Why is that information important? Your conclusion may focus on the idea that art reflects a particular society's attitude towards nature. Maybe your paper shows that a certain aardvark is an endangered species. The conclusion discusses the implications of a food chain without aardvarks in it.

No rest for the weary

Think of this type of conclusion as the *more-work-to-be-done* model. The more-work-to-be-done conclusion sets out an agenda for future action. Suppose your paper traces the effect of a government policy or law. It explains how things have improved or describes the setbacks. In the conclusion you tell the reader what else has to happen in order to improve conditions, fully implement the goals, and reach a perfect world. The more-work-to-be-done conclusion also explains which aspects of your topic remain unknown and sets out a blue-print for future researchers.

In writing a more-work-to-be-done conclusion, take care not to belittle your own research. If you tell the Authority Figure that your research into the habits of honey bees is only preliminary and that *more must be done* to achieve a basic level of knowledge about the little stingers, you're essentially discounting the value of your paper. Is that really the message you want to give your Authority Figure?

Getting glasses

Has your research led you to believe that everything you once thought about the topic is now different — as different as a nearsighted person's view of the world after getting glasses? If so, your conclusion may include an explanation of how your vision (of the topic) has changed. If your research is truly original and thorough, you can also go out on a limb and conclude that what historians or scientists or literary critics or some other sort of expert once believed about your topic is off the mark in light of your discovery or analysis. But beware: it's one thing to tell the expert reading your paper that you've learned something and quite another thing to tell the expert that the World of Experts should learn from *you*.

The big picture

After analyzing one work of art or literature in your paper, you may conclude by expanding your analysis to a larger arena. How does the art or literary piece fit into the artist's or writer's entire body of work? How does the piece you describe match or defy the trends of the time period? The advantage of a big-picture conclusion is that you get a chance to spread your wings and soar over a large chunk of territory. The danger is that you'll spread yourself too thin and try to cover material that is better suited to an entire paper. Also, be sure that you actually understand the territory you're soaring over. If you want to use the conclusion to consider Marmaduke Gilfrond's third novel in light of the other 43 works he produced before his death at the age of 112, be sure that you know enough about the other 43 works to speak knowledgeably.

The big-picture conclusion should contain some specifics, as in *Gilfrond's third novel,* Hay in the Attic, *is the only one of his works to present a pitchfork as a symbol of life's choices.* Don't make a general, meaningless statement in a big-picture conclusion, as in *Gilfrond's third novel,* Hay in the Attic, *is the best of his works.*

To I or not to I, that is the question

Should your conclusion be written in what grammarians call the *first person singular* (I, me, my) or *first person plural* (we, us, our)? The answer is a definite *maybe*. Some Paper Assigners prefer the personal approach, but others specify *third person* (that's the grammatical term for talking *about* the subject without any of the first-person pronouns). Many historians, for example, write in first person plural, also known as *the royal we.* So a history paper may state that *we find no evidence of hula hoops in the colonial era,* even if only one person is the author. Some science papers also follow this pattern, as in *we blew up the test tube* rather than *the test tube was blown up.* Your best bet? Check with your Authority Figure before you write.

Puzzle piece

This type of conclusion is similar to big picture, which I describe in the preceding paragraph. I chose the title "Puzzle piece" because of the way two pieces of a jigsaw puzzle snap together. A puzzle-piece conclusion relates the material in your paper to just one other aspect of the same topic. For example, say you've studied the development of abstract thinking in young children. Your conclusion may offer a glimpse of how the development of thought relates to emotional development. Or, suppose you've studied one aspect of a work of art or literature — perhaps point of view in a novel. Relate point of view to character development.

Social notes

The conclusion may relate a particular work of art or literature to the conditions in the society that the work depicts or the society that produced it. For example, if you're writing about Africans in Shakespeare's *Othello,* you may make reference to the way Africans were viewed in England during Shakespeare's lifetime. Or, you may compare the way Africans are viewed in the play to the way that Africans were viewed by the seventeenth-century residents of Venice, the setting of the play.

In writing a social-notes conclusion, be sure that any statements you make about the society are accurate. Also, don't make sweeping, controversial generalizations about the society you're mentioning. Sweeping, controversial generalizations must be supported by evidence, and the conclusion is no place for an entirely new argument. (If you want to make that argument, write another paper.)

Alternate universe

You've proved what happened and why. Now imagine an alternate universe. Supposed *it* — whatever *it* your paper is about — had never happened. What would be different about the course of history, the current situation, contemporary trends, and so on? The answer provides a quick look at another reality and forms the basis of your conclusion. For example, suppose Britain had quelled the American rebellion. What would change?

I recommend

An I-recommend conclusion calls for changes. If you're truly appalled by what you've found in your research and want the situation to change, an I-recommend conclusion is for you. Similarly, if you're truly delighted by what you've found in your research and want measures taken to ensure that nothing changes, write an I-recommend conclusion.

Critic's corner

Here's where you get to evaluate the ideas, objects, or situations you've described. Imagine, for instance, that you've proved a certain point about a philosopher's work. In the conclusion, say whether or not you agree with that point. (A quick, true story: A student of mine, having finished a rough draft of a philosophy paper, was having trouble with the conclusion. I recommended that he say whether he agreed with the philosophy he had analyzed. "I don't have any opinion," he replied. "It's not real. It's philosophy.")

Another variation of critic's corner may be your reaction to a creative work. Just be sure that you go beyond statements such as *I like it* and *only a little less annoying than root canal.* Say something a bit more profound, as in *I was moved by the character of Lizzie, who faces an army of floor cleaners and successfully defends her territory. The character of Timon, on the other hand, seems unreal. His attack with dental floss lacks plausibility.*

Critic's corner comes with a huge warning sticker: Some Paper Assigners love it, and some hate it. So before you attempt a personal conclusion of any sort, check with the Authority Figure who will read your paper.

Dramatic last punch

Okay, I admit that some Authority Figures don't see drama as an essential. But it doesn't hurt to have a little zing in the last paragraph of your research paper. Try a quotation — a particularly vivid or appropriate comment that refers to your thesis or to the "expanded idea" I explain in the preceding section. An anecdote or description may work also, if it illustrates the main idea of the paper. For a paper on water pollution, for example, you may tell the reader about the time a river in Ohio caught fire. (Really. This one I didn't make up!) Perhaps an example will pep up your conclusion. If you're writing about lawsuits and personal injury, for instance, you can't go wrong by mentioning the person who sued for hot-coffee burns. (I didn't make this one up either. Truth is stranger than even my imagination.)

One particularly effective "last punch" relates to the introduction. Say you're writing about the treatment of Native American tribes by the United States government. The "hook" in the introduction (see Chapter 15 for more about hooks) catches the reader's attention by describing the forced removal of a tribe from its ancestral lands. Tell part of the story in the introduction and finish it in the conclusion.

If you interrupt a story, placing half of the story in the introduction and half in the conclusion, don't switch gears abruptly without alerting the reader. Use italics or a different font to signal that the story is separate from the rest of the text. Take care to include strong transitions between the text and the story. This sort of splitting works best in a short or medium-length paper; in a very long paper the reader may lose track of the story's opening.

Subtopics

Not every conclusion includes the subtopics, and my personal preference is to leave them out. However, some Paper Assigners prefer that you cite the most important points of your argument in the conclusion. If you do mention the subtopics, don't repeat the wording you used elsewhere in the paper. For example, if you write *legal reasons* in the introduction, mention *law* in the conclusion. Also, don't discuss the subtopics in detail. The reader got the idea in the body of the paper; the conclusion is simply a reminder.

Getting It Together: How to Combine the Essential Elements of a Conclusion

After you've gathered the elements of a good conclusion (see preceding section, "Packing the Essentials: What the Conclusion Must Contain"), you have to mix them up to achieve maximum effectiveness. Time for some samples! This section contains three conclusions suitable for short papers. Conclusions for longer papers may follow the same pattern, but each element (thesis reference, expanded idea, dramatic last punch) expands to reflect the greater complexity and detail of the paper. For each sample short-paper conclusion I provide the thesis and information on the contents of the paper. I also analyze the conclusion so you can see what's where.

Writing a paper without a thesis? The next section, "Concluding a Survey Paper," gives directions on writing a conclusion for a nonthesis paper.

None of the information in these conclusions is true, at least as far as I know, and the people and literature I refer to don't exist. The style is correct, but don't rely on these "facts."

Case #1: The Nearsighted Porpoise

Here are the facts and the conclusion:

- ✔ **Thesis:** Nearsighted porpoises are responsible for most of the collisions between marine animals and oil tankers.

- ✔ **What's in the paper:** Survey of data on porpoise eyesight and oil shipping, maps of shipping lanes and porpoise habitat, information on tanker-marine animal collisions.

- ✔ **Conclusion:** The oil industry often runs touching television commercials proclaiming its concern for wildlife, but the tragic plight of nearsighted porpoises is not yet part of the industry's agenda, according to a spokesperson for Big Petro, Inc. "We can't worry about every little flipper," commented Arlene Agro.[23] But as we have seen, collisions between tankers and marine life cost the industry over a billion dollars a year, and nearsighted porpoises account for the bulk of the problem. If only for economic reasons, the oil industry should finance a study of porpoise eyesight immediately. Installing audio alarms on every tanker and painting the hulls day-glo orange are immediate, cost-effective steps towards safer seas that will benefit both human and marine life.

- ✔ **Analysis of the conclusion:** The first sentence adds a note of interest, as does the quote from the soon-to-be-fired Arlene Agro. The thesis is restated in sentence three. The conclusion ends with three recommendations for future action — a study of porpoise eyesight, audio alarms, and fluorescent paint.

Case #2: Poetry of Antarctica

Check out the content and conclusion for this paper:

- ✔ **Thesis:** The harsh conditions in Antarctica are mirrored in the poetry of the region.

- ✔ **What's in the paper:** Description of harsh conditions (cold, killer penguins, lack of food, storms, icebergs), analysis of major poetic works, critical views showing relationship between poetry and conditions

- ✔ **Conclusion:** As Ronald Alplem comments, "The Antarctican winter is present in the poems of Oliver Crankcase and Maybella Morric as surely as it was present in the icebergs on which they lived" (Alplem 55). Perhaps poets always interact somewhat with their environment, but in the case of Crankcase and Morric, the involvement was purposeful, born of the deep love they felt for their continent and their passionate hatred of cold weather. The imagery, theme, and diction of their work reflect the temperature, killer penguins, starvation, and icebergs of their homeland. The poems discussed in this paper are, as Swonmonk says, "the Big Chill as it really is" (Swonmonk 9).

✔ **Analysis of the conclusion:** The second sentence restates the thesis, using different words, and adds a new idea — that the poets *purposely* used the environment in their poetry. The two quotations add interest and also reinforce the thesis. The chief subtopics — imagery, theme, and diction — are mentioned.

Case #3: Mxpox versus Dindin: An Important Supreme Court Decision

Here are the data from the paper and its conclusion:

✔ **Thesis:** *Mxpox versus Dindin* effectively destroyed the market for personal hygiene devices.

✔ **What's in the paper:** The paper begins with a description of the scene during the Supreme Court oral arguments and then goes into the background of the case, lower court decisions, arguments for and against at the Supreme Court level, the decision itself, and the consequences for the personal hygiene market.

✔ **Conclusion:** Holding aloft the automatic eyebrow plucker that she says ruined her life, Jordana Mxpox exited the Supreme Court building on January 25, 2001. Through another door stepped Alexander Dindin, CEO of Eyebrows, Inc., whose personal-products empire crumbled in the months following the decision. The ruling for the plaintiff in *Mxpox versus Dindin* hit the company hard. Its stock dropped ten points almost immediately, and by June, Eyebrows, Inc. was out of business. Dindin filed for bankruptcy soon after. Although Justice Robe wrote in the majority opinion that "manufacturers of safe personal-hygiene devices have nothing to fear,"[3] the fact is that no company has been willing to touch America's eyebrows since the fall of Dindin's company. *What's next?,* the American consumer may well ask. Popcorn poppers that leave a stray kernel unpopped, hair dryers that miss a damp tress — are they the next targets of a legal system that seeks a completely risk-free society?

✔ **Analysis of the conclusion:** The first two sentences take the reader back to the introduction, which described the Supreme Court hearing. The thesis is restated and affirmed in the sentence containing a quotation from Justice Robe. The last sentence expands into a larger arena, mentioning the implications of the decision for other manufacturers.

Concluding a Survey Paper

Many research papers, especially those written in middle school or early high school, don't have a thesis statement. These papers aren't attempting to make a case for one particular idea. Instead, they're *surveys* — general roundups of information on one topic. Like all research papers, survey papers begin with an introduction, present information in a body, and end with a conclusion. The conclusion of a survey paper doesn't state that the thesis is proved, but it does contain many of the other elements that I describe earlier in this chapter.

Here's what you need to cook up a conclusion for a survey paper: a reference to the topic, a restatement of the main idea of the paper (but not in the same words you used in the introduction), and a dramatic punch to make a lasting impression on the reader. Some survey-paper conclusions mention the most important subtopics. The best survey-paper conclusions also expand the topic in many of the same ways as a thesis-paper, such as:

- ✔ **One for the road:** Surveys, by definition, give examples. The conclusion may provide one more, particularly good example, *one for the road,* as they definitely *don't* say in bartending school. For example, imagine that you've written about the music of Argentina. A look at a great tango, one you didn't mention in the body of the paper, may send your reader away with a rose clenched in his or her teeth.

- ✔ **Crystal ball:** Based on the material you've collected, what does the future hold in relation to your topic? For instance, after describing the history of the bagel, consider the next step: Parmesan bagels? Bagels with cream cheese baked inside? Anchovy-pineapple bagels? I'll stop before you decide never to eat again, but you get the point. Forecast.

- ✔ **Personally speaking and critic's corner:** Why did you pick this topic? Now that you've completed your research, what do you think about it? What is your evaluation of the art, literature, or music you've studied? For more discussion of these expanded ideas, check out the "Critic's corner" section, earlier in this chapter.

Concluding Science Research Papers

I'm sure that scientists have all kinds of fun in the lab, booby-trapping Bunsen burners and telling jokes about gravity and the like. But in their research papers, the motto is quite serious: *Give me the facts and don't waste my time!* To accomplish this goal, science research papers follow a fairly rigid format. In this chapter I deal with the *discussion* and *conclusions* sections, the names scientists give to the two sections that are the rough equivalent of the conclusion of other types of research papers. (For more information on all parts of a science research paper, turn back to Chapter 12.)

The research papers I'm talking about in this section report the results of original science or social science experiments. The experiments involved may be lab-oriented or may be the result of observation in the field. If your paper doesn't report the results of original research and simply explores scientific issues, ignore this section. Your research paper should follow the rules expressed elsewhere in this chapter.

Briefly, the introduction of a science research paper presents the problem to be studied and a *hypothesis,* an educated guess that the experiment will test. The body of the paper explains how the experiment was performed and presents the results of the experiment without interpreting them. The interpretive part of a science research paper contains two main elements: a *discussion* and the *conclusions*.

Some Paper Assigners, especially in middle school or early high school, ask that you create two separate sections for the discussion and conclusions. Other Paper Assigners want all the information tucked into one section entitled "Discussion." Ask about the preferred format before you write.

In the discussion, interpret the data of the experiment, pointing out patterns and what you think they mean. For example, you might mention that older rats had a tendency to ignore the cheese and go for the cafe latte, suggesting that the rats' tastes become more sophisticated as they age. If your experiment had any flaws that may affect the data (as in *some rats may not have been hungry* or *I accidentally dropped the cheese in dishwashing liquid*), mention these flaws in the discussion. The discussion section is a good spot to expand your thoughts about the experiment, putting your work into a larger context. How does your experiment relate to other experiments done on the same issue? What are the implications of your findings?

Think of the *conclusions* section as the postgame wrap up. Mention what your experiment accomplished — whether or not the data supports or disproves the hypothesis, important discoveries, and significant trends. The conclusions section is the final verdict, so to speak. It is not the place for lots of data, but it *is* the spot for specific reasons. In other words, don't rewrite the chart that matches the circumference of the balloon with the temperature of the air inside. Instead, state that *the balloon expanded 3 centimeters for each degree increase in temperature, supporting the hypothesis that hot air occupies a greater volume.* In your conclusions you may also suggest areas for further investigation.

Don't use the conclusion to comment on how much you liked or disliked performing the experiment. Keep your emotions to yourself! One science teacher told me that whenever she reads "I had fun doing this experiment," she is sorely tempted to write "That's nice, but I really don't care."

Chapter 18

The Picky Stuff: Citing Sources

● ●

In This Chapter

▶ Choosing the correct citation format for each subject area

▶ Citing sources properly in the text of the paper

▶ Crediting electronic sources

▶ Creating a bibliography or source list

● ●

Nothing is pickier and more trivial than the rules on formatting *citations* — the little identification tags that identify the sources of the information, ideas, or quotations in a research paper. Granted, giving credit to the people whose brain-products you've consumed while researching the paper is crucial. But where to put the comma? And how to decide when you need parentheses or a colon? Give me a break. As they say in New York City, *like I care.*

Unfortunately, everyone writing a research paper has to care. Why? Because Paper Evaluators care. Also, if you're thinking of publishing your own brain-product someday, the editors will care. So take a deep breath and prepare to plunge into the world of footnotes, endnotes, parenthetical notes, and source lists. First I explain the general principles of citation, and then I help you navigate the ins and outs of the three major systems — APA, MLA, and Chicago.

Giving Credit Where Credit Is Due: Documenting Sources

Author Junius Q. Iceman's vivid analysis of banana splits, which you mention on page 2 of your research paper, must be credited to Iceman. Otherwise you're guilty of plagiarism, also known as the theft of ideas and a giant no-no in Research Paper World. (Chapter 10 tells you everything you always wanted to know about plagiarism, beginning with how to avoid it.) So how do you credit Iceman? And where? Read on.

The whole world of citations rests on two principles:

- ✔ The material in the paper that comes from something other than your own brain should be clearly identified in the text or in a footnote or endnote.

- ✔ A short identification in the text or in a note should lead the reader to a more complete description of the source, one that contains every fact needed to locate the original.

The identification in the text is done with parentheses, tucked into the sentence right after the material you're citing. Footnotes and endnotes depend on little raised numbers placed just after the material you're citing. These raised numbers alert the reader to a citation in a footnote at the bottom — or foot — of the page, or to an endnote at the end of the paper. Regardless of whether you use footnotes, endnotes, or parenthetical notes, complete descriptions of all the sources you cite must also appear in a source list at the end of the paper. The source list used to be (and sometimes still is) called a *bibliography,* a term derived from the Greek word for *book.* These days researchers usually tap into electronic sources, so the term *bibliography* has morphed into the more neutral *list of sources, reference list,* or *works cited.*

The two principles of citation I've just explained are universal; every field of study accepts them. Sadly, not much else about citations is universal. Citations have *styles,* which are described in *manuals of style* — 4,560-page books with small print. I explain manuals of style and take you through the basics of each system later in this chapter.

If you're not sure how to cite a source, ask your Paper Evaluator. But no matter how confused you are, cite the source in some form or another. In academic terms, putting the comma in the wrong place in the citation is a skinned knee, but omitting a citation is a broken leg — or worse. Similarly, if you're not sure whether or not you need to cite a particular idea, *cite it.* Better to annoy your Authority Figure with too many citations than to risk plagiarism.

Save time and trouble! Every time you cite a source in the text, prepare the reference-list entry. If you're working on a word processor, keep two files active: the text file and the reference-list file. Toggle between them as you type.

Citations in the text

In the text, the citation may be made with a raised number, which leads the reader to a footnote or endnote, or the citation may be in parentheses.

Footnotes and endnotes

Footnotes and endnotes may be used to comment on something in the text — the typed equivalent of an offhand remark. In this section I don't deal with that sort of note. I refer only to footnote and endnote citations of sources.

Footnotes and endnotes are not as popular as they used to be; two of the major style systems — the APA and the MLA — have dumped them in favor of parenthetical notes. If your Paper Assigner wants them, number footnotes and endnotes consecutively. Place the number at the end of the sentence unless you have more than one source in a sentence, in which case the number should follow the material you're citing. Check out this example:

> Junius Q. Iceman's theory states that banana splits taste better if the banana is peeled before insertion in the bowl.[4]

The little "4" alerts the reader that the previous statement is not from the paper-writer's brain. To find out who wrote about Iceman's theory, the reader checks note #4 either at the bottom of the page if it's a footnote or at the end of the paper if it's an endnote.

When citing sources, don't mix and match footnotes and endnotes; use one or the other throughout the paper. If you're working on a typewriter, endnotes are easier because you don't have to worry about squeezing in the notes at the bottom of the page. (A word processor does the squeezing automatically.)

If you've got some spare cash and *a lot* of notes, you may want to invest in a special computer program that formats your notes automatically. You select the style and fill in a form with the source information. A few mouse clicks later you have a perfect note.

The footnote or endnote provides basic information about the source: author, title, publisher, and so on. The first note for a particular source has all the information, and later notes give just enough to identify which source you're talking about. Here are two sample notes indicating that the banana-split theory comes from page 12 of that immortal masterpiece, *I Scream for Ice Cream* by Leo O. Fishped. These notes are suitable for endnote placement. One is for a first reference, and the other for a later reference:

First reference:

> 4. Leo O. Fishped, <u>I Scream for Ice Cream</u> (New York: Cowpat Press, 2001), 12.

Later reference:

> 7. Fishped 12.

About a thousand years ago when I was in high school, later references to a source contained little Latin abbreviations — *Ibid.* and *op.cit.* or *loc. cit. Ibid.* referred to the last complete citation; *op.cit.* and *loc. cit.* to earlier citations. The Big Three citation systems no longer recommend these Latin terms, though Chicago allows *Ibid.* You may run across them during the research phase of your project, but you probably shouldn't use them in your own writing.

Parenthetical citation

In a *parenthetical citation,* the source is credited in parenthesis, as in these examples:

> Junius Q. Iceman's theory is that banana splits taste terrible if the peel is not removed (Fishped 12).

> According to Fishped, Junius Q. Iceman favors removing the peel from the banana before inserting it in the banana split (12).

As with footnotes and endnotes, the information in parenthesis tells the reader that the opinion about the banana may be found on page 12 of something written by someone named Fishped. To find out more, the reader consults the list of sources. Notice that the first example of a parenthetical citation puts Fishped's name in parenthesis because the name isn't in the text. In the second example, Fishped is mentioned in the text, so only the page number is in the parenthesis. Science citations add the date. (The "APA style" section later in this chapter gives the details.)

Source list

Identifying the source with footnotes, endnotes, or parenthetical citations is only part of your job as a research paper writer. You also need to supply a list of sources at the end of the paper. The source list is usually in alphabetical order according to the last name of the author or, if the author is unknown, according to the first important word in the title. (Ignore *a, an, the.*) In the preceding banana-split example, the source should be listed under "F" for "Fishped." After seeing the footnote, endnote, or parenthetical note, the reader may turn to the back of the paper and find out when and where the information was printed (or posted, in the case of Web sites).

One system of sources, generally used only for scientific papers, assigns a code number to each source. The works-cited list is arranged in numerical order. The reader matches the code number in the text to the works-cited list.

Here's a sample source-list entry for the Fishped book, written in MLA style. (For information on other styles, see "Meeting the Major Players in the Citation Game" later in this chapter.)

> Fishped, Leo O. <u>I Scream for Ice Cream</u>. New York: Cowpat Press, 2001.

The title in the preceding example is underlined. If you prefer, you may also italicize the title. Each entry in a source list is typed with a *hanging indent.* Every line after the first is indented five spaces.

Meeting the Major Players in the Citation Game

Playground turf wars *(This is our treehouse and you can't play in it!)* are nothing compared to the turf wars over citations. Each academic field seems to delight in stating that *we do it this way, not like those other guys.* Some of the rules actually make sense. Science, for example, tends to follow the American Psychological Association format, which places the date close to the beginning of the citation. Because science is frequently date-sensitive, this practice is justified. However, most of the rules fall into the category of *because we said so and we're in charge.* Considering the fact that you're *not* in charge, your only option is to grit your teeth and put the comma where they want it.

Three style systems dominate the academic and publishing world. Each system is explained in a *manual of style* (containing nothing about hemlines). Most humanities papers follow the format specified by the Modern Language Association (MLA) or the University of Chicago, which entered the citation game about a century ago. The Chicago system is described in *The Chicago Manual of Style* (CMS). Science and social science papers frequently rely on the format preferred by the American Psychological Association (APA).

In this section I take you through the basics of the Big Three, showing you how to cite the most common printed and electronic sources in the text and in the source list. Most paper writers will find everything they need here. However, you *won't* find what you need if you're citing from a translated edition of a privately printed article excerpted in an anthology with five editors, two of whom have the same last name. For complicated situations like that, you'll have to go directly to a manual of style or to one of the Web sites associated with these systems:

- ✔ **APA:** American Psychological Association. *Publication Manual of the American Psychological Association.* 4th ed. Washington, DC: American Psychological Association, 1994. `www.apa.org/journals/faq.html`

- ✔ **MLA:** Gibaldi, Joseph, and Walter S. Achert, eds. *MLA Handbook for Writers of Research Papers.* 4th ed. New York: Modern Language Association, 1995. `www.mla.org` (Click on "Frequently Asked Questions.")

- ✔ **CMS:** University of Chicago Press. *The Chicago Manual of Style.* 14th ed. Chicago: University of Chicago Press, 1993. `http://www.press.uchicago.edu/Misc/Chicago/cmosfaq.html#1`

A number of other fields also publish manuals of style, which describe the tiny variations that enable their members to say *we do it this way.* As always, check with the Paper Assigner about the preferred format. Here are a few of the specialized manuals:

✔ **Biology:** Council of Biology Editors. *Scientific Style and Format,* 6th ed. New York: Cambridge University Press, 1994.

✔ **Chemistry:** American Chemical Society. *ACS Style Guide,* 2nd ed. Washington, DC: ACS, 1997.

✔ **Education:** National Education Association. *NEA Style Manual for Writers and Editors,* Rev. ed. Washington, DC: NEA, 1974.

✔ **Law:** *The Bluebook: A Uniform System of Citation.* Cambridge: Harvard Law Rev. Assn., 2000.

✔ **Mathematics:** American Mathematical Society. *A Manual for Authors of Mathematical Papers,* Rev. ed. Providence, RI: AMA, 1990.

✔ **Music:** Holoman, D. Kern. *Writing about Music.* Berkeley: University of California Press, 1988.

✔ **Political Science:** Kelly, Jean P. et al., eds. *Style Manual for Political Science,* Rev. ed. Washington, DC: American Political Science Association, 1985.

Now for the details on the Big Three.

APA style

The American Psychological Association (APA) guidelines apply, not surprisingly, to psychology papers. Also, and this may be a surprise, the guidelines may apply to science papers that have nothing at all to do with whether or not you had a happy childhood. If you're writing in any of the sciences, including the social sciences, your very own Authority Figure may demand that you follow APA style.

Citations in the text

For citations in the text, APA favors parenthetical notes that include the author and the date of publication. If you're referring to a particular section of a source, not to the entire thing, you should also include the page number(s) or another locator (screen or paragraph number for electronic sources, for example). For works with unknown authors, a portion of the title identifies the source.

The information has to appear *somewhere* in the sentence, either in the text or in the parenthesis. Here are examples of citations in the text. **Note:** The bracketed material is *not* part of the example and would *not* appear in your research paper.

McMcuin (2000) described the Cabbage Complex as acquired behavior. [refers to an entire work]

The Cabbage Complex is an example of acquired behavior (McMcuin, 2000). [refers to an entire work]

According to one psychologist, "The Cabbage Complex is acquired behavior. No one is born with a fear of cabbage. You have to be taught to hate the vegetable" (McMcuin, 2000, conclusion section, ¶ 3.). [refers to a portion of a document with numbered paragraphs but no page numbers, common in electronic sources]

Fear of cabbage is an acquired trait (Cabbage, 1998, p. 3). [refers to a source — book, magazine article, encyclopedia article, and so on — with a title containing the word *cabbage,* author unknown]

McMcuin concluded in his 2000 study that the Cabbage Complex is "acquired behavior. No one is born with a fear of cabbage. You have to be taught to hate the vegetable" (p. 3.). [refers to a particular page — author and date are in the sentence, so only the page is in parenthesis]

Celery appears in dreams as a symbol of imperial power (A.G. Freud, personal communication, October 4, 1999). [personal interview]

Agpok and Gluescap (2000) noted that carrots tended to provoke responses with expansive arm movements. [refers to an entire work with two authors]

Cite all the authors (up to five) the first time you mention the source. In later citations, use the first author's name followed by "et al." (an abbreviation meaning *and others*) as in this example:

Metternick et al. (1998) found that carrot consumption rises during times of stress.

To cite a work with six or more authors in the text of your paper, give only the principal author's surname, even for the first citation. (The principal author is the first name listed on the paper.) Follow the author's name by "et al."

The reference list

APA calls the source list a *reference list.* The reference list should be at the end of the paper, double-spaced and in alphabetical order. Each entry has a hanging indent of five spaces. Every source you cite in the text should be matched to a reference-list entry, except for personal communications (interviews you conducted yourself, e-mails or letters from the source to you). Personal communications are not included in the reference list because the reader generally can't access these private sources.

Here's a selection of reference list entries covering the situations you're likely to encounter as you write your paper. To help you understand what you're seeing, I've added comments in brackets. The bracketed material should *not* appear in your reference list. Longer comments on APA reference-list style appear next to tip or warning icons. Because these are just examples, I haven't placed the entries in alphabetical order, but your reference list should be alphabetized.

The APA doesn't follow the usual English-teacher rules on capitalization. In titles, all proper nouns are capitalized, but all other words aren't, except for the first word of the title and the subtitle.

> McMcuin, R. (2000). *The cabbage complex: Are you born with it?* (3rd ed.) Washington, DC: Vegetaria Press. [a book with one author, third edition.]
>
> Agpok, A. and Gluescap, Q. (2000). *The vegetable-speech connection.* Baltimore, MD: Kohlrabi and Sons. [book with two authors]
>
> McMcuin, R. (2000). The cabbage complex: Are you born with it? *Vegetaria Weekly, 54,* 334-335. [article in a periodical — periodical name and volume number italicized or underlined]
>
> Agpok, A. and Gluescap, Q. (2000). The vegetable-speech connection. *Vegetarium, 54* (5), 23-55. [article in a periodical — volume and issue number given; issue number in parentheses]

Many scientific periodicals number the pages consecutively for an entire year. If the February issue ends on page 99, the March issue begins on page 100. A few periodicals begin each issue with page 1. In that case, give the *issue number* as well as the volume number. (Check the cover for the issue number. It should follow the volume number.)

List all the authors' last names and first initials, up to six authors. Everyone unfortunate enough to be seventh or later on the list is represented by "et al."

> The carrot as an indicator of stress level. (1998, August), *Vegetarium, 3,* 18. [article in a periodical, no author given]
>
> Our friend the carrot. (2001, January 8). *The New York Thymes,* p. B2. [newspaper article, no author given]
>
> Claptrap, H. (1997). Vegetables as a measure of well-being. In G.H. Kett (Ed.), *Food glorious Freud* (pp. 34-55). New York: Vegetaria. [article or essay in a collection]

In the preceding example, the word "In" tells the reader that the title of the book is *Food glorious Freud,* edited by G. H. Kett. The author and title of the article or essay are H. Claptrap and "Vegetables as a measure of well-being."

> Snappy, L. (1999). *Beans and behavior* (F. Lima, Trans.). New York: Vegetaria. (Original work published 1512) [translation]
>
> Foofaroo, X. (2002). Lima beans. In *The encyclopedia worldiana* (Vol. 5, pp. 456-460). Atlanta: Bean Press. [encyclopedia article]
>
> Tomato, R. (2003). *Eating red vegetables.* In J. Beet (Series Ed.), *Vegetables of the world: Vol. 3. The non-green veggies.* Seattle: Vitamin Press. [multivolume work]

Audio-visual sources — films, CDs, television broadcasts, and so on — are identified in the source list *in brackets.* In the following three examples, the brackets are part of the entry and *should be* included in your reference list.

> Loldilol, Q. (Executive Producer). (2002, January 7). *The vegetable report* [Television broadcast]. Atlanta: Turning News.

> Doremi, F. (2000). Brussels sprouts, my love. [Recorded by Soladi Do]. On *Edible music* [CD]. Tampa: Alfalfa Records.

> Gidget, G. (Producer), & Gadget, H. (Director). (1990). *The cabbage that ate San Francisco* [Motion picture]. United States: Parachute *Pictures.*

Electronic sources include URLs (the Internet address of the source) and the date you retrieved the information. (In the follow examples the bracketed information is *not* part of the entry.)

> Correlation between vegetable consumption and national prosperity. (2002, January 6). Retrieved January 8, 2002, from http://www. vegetarium.gov.html [article with no author's name obtained from a Web site]

> Kohlrabi, H. (2002). Correlation between vegetable consumption and National prosperity. *Vegetarium, 3,* 18. Retrieved January 8, 2002, from Eating Database. [article from electronic database]

> United States Vegetable Commission. (n.d.) *Guidelines for sensible vegetable consumption.* Retrieved February 1, 2002, from http://www. usvc.gov/ rept [undated article from government Web site — n.d. = no date]

Don't put a period after a Web address, and don't hyphenate one that runs past the end of a line. Just divide the address at a period or a slash.

MLA style

If you're writing in the humanities, your Authority Figure will probably specify that your citations follow the Modern Language Association (MLA) format. In contrast to the science guidelines I describe earlier in this chapter, the MLA de-emphasizes the date, perhaps because a book on ancient Greek literature written in 1839 may be just as relevant as one written in 2002. The MLA refers to the source list as a *list of works cited.* The source list typically contains only those works actually cited in the paper, not every work consulted during the research process.

Citations in the text

In the text, the MLA specifies parenthetical notes instead of footnotes or end-notes. The system is the same for all types of sources — books, periodicals, pamphlets, audio-visual, and so on. The author(s), if known, and the page numbers should be given in your own text or in parenthesis. If you're referring to an entire work, mention the work in the text and skip the parenthetical citation. If you're citing two or more works by the same author, include the author's name and an identifying word from the title, underlined or italicized (for a book) or in quotation marks (for an article or essay). For works with unknown authors, use only an identifying word from the title, underlined or italicized (for a book) or in quotation marks (for an article or essay). For a chapter or an essay in a collection, cite the author of the part you're referring to, not the editor of the entire collection. Don't place any commas in the parenthesis, and don't bother with the date unless you need it to distinguish between two works with the same title and author (perhaps a yearly report). Every citation in the text must be matched with an entry in the works-cited list at the end of the paper.

Here are some sample citations, with a few short comments in brackets. The brackets are *not* part of the citation and should *not* appear in your paper:

> Globdub's *Domination* contains many practical tips on establishing a worldwide empire. [referring to an entire work, no parenthetical note]

> Globdub based his theory of world domination on the actions of the Martian invaders (190-193). [author's name in text, pages in parenthesis]

> One theory of world domination was based on the actions of Martian invaders (G. Globdub 190-193). [author's name with distinguishing initial, in a paper with sources from two authors named Globdub, pages in parenthesis]

Notice that the parenthesis is placed *before* the period because the parenthetical information is part of the sentence.

> The play may be interpreted as a series of developmental milestones (Blahblah and Chatter 45). [work by two authors]

> However hard the task, the playwright shows that learning to tie one's shoes is always a noteworthy accomplishment (Blathersby, Nincom, and Poop 8). [multiple authors]

> Riding a bike, on the other hand, is presented as an easy task (Contusion et al. 12). [multiple authors]

If you're citing a work by two authors, place *and* between their names. For more than two authors, place commas between the names and separate the last two with *and*. If the source has more than three authors, you may cite only the first author and follow the name with the abbreviation *et al.* (Latin for *and others*). If you use *et al.* in the text, use it in the works-cited list also.

> The artistic drape of the toga is typical of the artist's style (Renaissance 99). [book with unknown author, title contains the word *renaissance*]

> Bears flock to Hollywood hoping to become stars ("Bears" 88-102). [article with unknown author, title contains the word *bears*]

The Hamster Society of America (HSA) recommends that you avoid stepping on your pet (HSA, screens 5-6). [Web site with no page numbers and no identified author]

To cite an electronic source in the text, include the name of the author (if known) in the text or in parenthesis, followed by any available location information. Electronic sources often don't have page numbers, but sometimes the screens or paragraphs are numbered. If there's no way to pinpoint the location, identify the work in your own text and don't put anything in parenthesis. Be sure to include all the information you have about the source in the works-cited list at the end of the paper.

List of works cited

All sources should be identified completely in the list of works cited. The entries should be arranged in alphabetical order according to the last name of the author (if known) or the first word in the title (if the author is unknown). (Ignore *a, an,* and *the*.) Notice that every line after the first is indented five spaces.

These sample entries are followed by brackets with some comments. Don't include the brackets or comments in your paper. Also, your list should be in alphabetical order.

> Globdub, Gregor. <u>The Martian Strategy: What We Can Learn About World Domination from Our Little Green Friends</u>. New York: Greenton Press, 2003. [book with one author, title may be italicized or underlined]

> Globdub, Gregor. "The Martians." <u>Case Studies in World Domination</u>. Ed. John Finchwick. New York: Greenton, 2003. 55-90. [chapter or essay in a collection]

> Globdub, Gregor. "What We Can Learn About World Domination from Our Little Green Friends." <u>Dictators' Gazette</u> 33 (2003): 34-35. [article in a periodical, periodical title underlined or italicized, volume number given]

Most scholarly periodicals number pages consecutively throughout the year. If the last page of the January issue is 111, the first page of the February issue is 112. If the periodical you're citing does *not* follow this system and instead begins each issue with page 1, you must also supply the *number* of the issue. (Check the cover or title page for the volume number and the number of the issue.) In the preceding example, the volume number (33) may be followed by the issue number (2) and then the year, in this format: 33.2 (2003).

> Glove, Filbert, and Maurice Mitt. <u>Bears Don't Care.</u> Rev. ed. New York: Winterwear Press, 1981. [book, two authors, revised edition]

> Glove, Filbert, and Maurice Mitt. "Bears Don't Care." <u>Animal Performance</u> 28 Feb. 1999: 88-102. [article, two authors, periodical as a date instead of a volume number]

Glove, Filbert, Maurice Mitt, Benjamin Bootie, and Sally Shoe. <u>Bears Don't Care, But Ocelots Do.</u> New York: Winterwear Press, 1981. [book, multiple authors]

Glove, Filbert, et al. <u>Bears Don't Care, But Ocelots Do.</u> New York: Winterwear Press, 1981. [book, multiple authors]

Notice that the first entry in the preceding set of examples is a *revised edition,* indicated by the abbreviation after the title. For any edition other than the first, state the edition name or number after the title.

<u>Bears Don't Care, But Ocelots Do.</u> New York: Winterwear Press, 1981. [book with no identified author]

"Bears Don't Care." <u>Animal Performance</u> 28 Feb. 1999: 88-102. [article with no identified author]

Baer, Amanda. "Lemurs Are Shy." <u>Animal Ins and Outs</u>. Ed. Felicia Fox. Boston: Fauna, 2001. 7-18. [essay or chapter in an edited collection]

"Lemurs." <u>The Encyclopedia Faunalia</u>. 2nd ed. 2001. [encyclopedia article]

Treat an encyclopedia entry as if it were an article in a periodical. Some encyclopedia entries are signed; if so, cite the author and page in the text in the usual MLA style. If the entry is not signed, cite a word from the article title in the text. Alphabetize the entry according to the author's last name (if known) or the title of the article. Don't worry about the editor of the entire encyclopedia. Most encyclopedias are reprinted many times, so the edition number and date are especially important. With an encyclopedia, you don't normally list the city and publishing company.

"Parakeets." <u>Household Pets and Astrology.</u> Narr. George Bush. Dir. Nancy Reagan. Turning Network. 10 January 2002. [television broadcast]

Mervin, Xander. <u>The Music of Antarctica.</u> PGI Records, 1999. [recording]

<u>Taxidermy Driver.</u> Dir. Arthur Jones. Perf. Tom Cruz, Robert Neero, Hannibal Elephant. Warned Bros., 1932. [film]

"Fake Photo Backgrounds." <u>Fotofair Online.</u> 2002. Foto International. 4 June 2002 `<http://fotofair.com/fake/background.html>`. [online article, no author given, URL and retrieval date identified]

The electronic address — the URL — should appear on one line if at all possible. If you need more than one line, don't hyphenate. Break the URL at a slash mark.

<u>Hamster Lovers' Home Page</u>. Hamster Society of America, 15 June 2002 <http://www.hamfan.org/faq/>. [Web page, retrieval date identified]

Santa Claus. Telephone interview. 24 December 2000. [personal interview]

Tooth Fairy. Re: Molar rates. E-mail to the author. 1 January 2002. [e-mail communication to author]

Chicago Manual of Style

The Chicago Manual of Style describes the APA and MLA systems. It also goes into detail on the footnote/endnote system of citation, which the other two manuals discourage. So if your Authority Figure likes those little elevated numbers, *Chicago*'s the system for you. All the sources you use in your paper are listed in a *bibliography* or *reference list* (*Chicago*'s preferred terms) at the end of the paper.

Footnotes and endnotes, first reference

The form for footnotes and endnote citations is the same; only the placement is different. Don't combine footnote and endnote citations in one paper. The first citation for a particular source is complete, and later citations to the same work are shortened. (See the next section for a more complete explanation.) Footnotes are preceded by a raised number corresponding to the number in the text. Endnotes are preceded by a number on the same level as the text, followed by a period. The first line of each note is usually indented five spaces from the left-hand margin. (Chicago also allows nonindented notes.) All notes are single-spaced.

Footnotes and endnotes are much easier with a word processor, which numbers them automatically. Also, the software figures out how much text to put on a page so that the footnotes fit — a truly horrendous task on a typewriter. If you're working with a typewriter, try to convince the Paper Assigner to accept endnotes. If you're stuck with footnotes, beg or borrow a computer if at all possible.

Here are some examples of footnotes, all for the first reference. I've included some comments in brackets. (**Note:** Don't include bracketed comments in your paper. They're just for your information.) If these were endnotes, the number 7 would be on the line, not above it, and followed by a period.

[7]Eggbert Babbers, *The Ice Age* (San Antonio: Warg, 1958), 88. [book, title may be italicized or underlined]

[7]Eggbert Babbers and Madeline Paris, *The Sleet Age* (San Antonio: Warg, 1958), 88. [book, two authors]

[7]Eggbert Babbers, Madeline Paris, and Winnie Pooh, *The Ice Cream Age* (San Antonio: Warg, 1958), 88–95. [book, three authors, multiple pages]

[7]Babs Witherspoon et al. *The Cake Age* (San Antonio: Warg, 1958), 88. [book with more than three authors, indicated by "et al."]

[7]Egalia Babbles, The Coffeecake Age, ed. Madeline Paris (San Antonio: Warg, n.d.), 88. [book with both an author and an editor, no date]

[7]Ellen Bebbleflock, *The Latte and Bagel Age,* 3rd ed. (San Antonio: Warg, 1958), 88. [book, not the first edition]

[7]Thomasina Calloway, *The Age of Overpriced Coffee,* A Short History of the Universe, vol. 3 (San Antonio: Warg, 1958), 88. [book in a series — volume 3, title of the volume italicized or underlined, title of the series in normal font]

[7]Eggbert Babbers, "The Martini Age," *History Today* 33 (1932): 44–45. [article in a periodical, periodical title italicized or underlined, volume and year given]

[7]Ernestine Gabbers, "The Gin and Tonic Age," *History Today* 33 (October 1932): 44–45. [article in a periodical, volume number and date given]

[7]Otto Blabs, "The Tell-All Age," *History Today* 30 September 1932, 44–45. [magazine article, no volume number, date supplied]

[7]"The Tell-All Age," *Hanover Times,* 30 September 1948, 4. [newspaper article, no author given]

[7]*Encyclopedia of Useless Information,* 33rd ed., s.v. "Martini." [encyclopedia article, abbreviation "s.v." — *under the word,* that is, the word that you looked up to find this article.]

[7] "The Martini in History," in *Slopkoff's Survey of Potable Beverages* [database online] (New York: Hangman Press, 1999, accessed 4 September 1999); available from Mxyx Information Services, San Francisco, Calif., p. 5 of 6. [article retrieved from an online database. The article title is enclosed in quotation marks and the "publication" title is italicized or underlined. The retrieval date is given.]

[7]Therese Blas, "The Martini Age," *Bartender's Today* 33: L54-67, 20 October 1998 [journal online]; available from `http://www.bar.org/journal`; accessed 4 September 1999. [article from an online journal, periodical title italicized or underlined, volume, line numbers, and date given, as well as date retrieved]

In the preceding two examples, the brackets enclosing the words "database online" and "journal online" are part of the note and *should* be included.

[7]Eggover Easy, *History of the Cholesterol Scare,* audiotapes of lecture presented at meeting of the Poultry Society, Newton, New York, December, 2001 (Chicago: University of Chicago Press, 2002). [audiotape, lecturer, title, date, and publisher given]

[7]*Eggs Benedict* (Philadelphia: Society for Nutritional Education, 1999), filmstrip. [filmstrip]

Footnote or endnote, later references

The first note is like a hamburger with everything on it — onions, chili, bacon, cheese, whatever. The second note is the plain beef patty — no frills, just enough to let you know what you ate. In the previous section I gave you examples of first-reference notes. Now for the second helpings. Here are the rules:

- ✔ If you cite the same source twice in a row, you may use the Latin abbreviation *Ibid.,* which means "in the same place." If you're on the same page, *Ibid.* alone does the job. If you're in the same source but on a different page, put a comma and the page number on which you found the information after *Ibid.*

   You may have heard of other Latin abbreviations, such as *op. cit.* and *loc. cit.* These are out of style (or at any rate, out of style manuals) and shouldn't be used. Stick to *Ibid.* and dump the rest of the Latin.

- ✔ If you're not referring to the same source twice in a row, use a shortened form of the earlier note. Include only the author's last name and the page number, separated by a comma. If two of your sources were written by people with the same last name, add a first initial. If you have two sources from the same author, add the title, as follows: Gallstone, *Joy of Eating,* 44.

- ✔ For works with unknown authors, give the title and page(s).

- ✔ If the title is very long, shorten it. For example, you may shorten *A Short Treatise on the Joy of Eating in Everyday Life* to *Joy of Eating.*

Bibliography or reference list

The bibliography or reference list is the list of nearly all the sources you used in preparing your research paper. (You don't have to list newspapers or well-known reference works so long as the footnote or endnote is complete.) Alphabetize the entries in the reference list according to the last name of the author. If a source has no known author, alphabetize according to the first significant word in the title, ignoring *a, an,* and *the.* Each entry has a hanging indent: The first line is flush with the left-hand margin and all the other lines are indented three spaces. *Chicago* style calls for single-spaced entries.

The reference list includes all of the information that appears in the note, but the format is slightly different:

- ✔ The author's last name appears first, followed by a comma and the first name (Woods, Geraldine).

- ✔ For works with more than one author, the first author's name is written with the surname first, and the other authors' names are written in first-name-last-name order (Woods, Geraldine and Morton Mellon).

- ✔ In a reference list, most parts of the entry are separated by periods.

- ✔ Unless your source is a chapter or a section of a larger work (such as an article in a collection), don't include page numbers in the reference list.

- ✔ If the reference list contains two works by the same author, include the author's name in the first entry, as well as the title and the usual publication information. In subsequent entries, put an underlined blank where the author's name would normally be and then complete the entry with the title and publication information.

Here's a shortened reference list, showing a variety of sources, with my comments in brackets. **Note:** Don't include brackets in your reference list.

Argbug, Appleton. *The Floss on the Mill.* Philadelphia: Quaint Press, 1988. [book, one author]

_____. *Flossing Fantasies, 5th ed.* New York: Dental Deeds, 2002. [book, also by Argbug, edition other than the first]

Callwell, Connie, ed. *An Introduction to Hygiene.* Vol. 8, *The Health Compendium,* by Zillia Zenk. Boston: Hufflin Mifftown, 1999. [one book in a multivolume work, with the editor and title of the entire set listed first, followed by the particular volume you used]

Dalloway, Clarissa. "My Favorite Walks in London." *Party Time* 14 (June, 1929): 45-88. [article in a periodical, volume number and date supplied]

Ramsay, Missy, and Lily Briscoe. "Seaside Holidays." *London Monthly,* 15 August 1911, 49-68. [article in a periodical, two authors, volume number, date, and pages given]

Splittcaiarn, Angus. Interview by author, 18 December 1975, New York, tape recording. [personal interview]

Tulip, Tiptoe. *Horticulture and Dance* (Stanford, Alaska: Department of Cultural Affairs, 1999. Database online. Available from ARTLINE, ED 3829. [online article]

Unblook, Renata. "Concerto for Hundreds of Tubas." Cademil 18917, 2001. Cassette. [musical recording, with publisher and catalog number]

Victory at Ocean. Produced and directed by Mary Derpich. 15 min. Persich Pictures. 16 mm. [film]

Victory over Ocean. Boston: Hufflin Mifftown, 1999. [book, no author given]

Chapter 19

It's a Breeze: The Final Draft

In This Chapter

▶ Polishing the rough draft

▶ Formatting the final draft

▶ Checking grammar and style

*O*ne last word. That's it! You're done. You toss the research paper in your backpack, eager to dump the thing on the professional torturer who assigned it ages ago. Then you pause. Does that pile of paper — your first complete draft — represent your best work? Or is it a diamond in the rough, waiting for polish?

Rough diamond, right? So with a weary sigh you prepare to give the research paper one more chunk of your time and energy — the last effort, but an important one. In this chapter I explain the ins and outs of the final draft, telling you how to turn a dull stone into a brilliant gem. Specifically, I show you how to smooth sharp edges from your style, fix grammar errors, and take care of the small details that turn a good rough draft into a great final product.

Polishing Is Not Just for Shoes

Moving from a rough to a final draft is actually the easiest stage of the research-paper project. Here's an overview of the process:

✔ Unless the deadline is staring you in the face, put the rough draft aside and take a break. When you pick it up again, you'll see it with fresh eyes.

✔ Read through the complete draft, checking content. Does the chain of logic make sense? Is the transition from one section to another clear? If something seems out of place, missing, or otherwise incorrect, make a note. Then correct the content as necessary. (Chapter 14 discusses the logical thread of the paper, and Chapter 16 explains transitions.)

✔ Reread the draft, this time checking style. Is the writing smooth? Do the sentences vary in length and pattern, or is the writing monotonous? Have you been wordy or repetitive? Patch up the prose as needed. (For details, check out the next section, "Styling Your Sentences.")

✔ One more time: Read the draft with a pen in hand, checking for misspelled words and grammar errors. (Need help? "Fixing Grammar Gremlins" later in this chapter explains how to correct the most common mistakes.)

✔ Recheck the citations (see Chapter 18 for the whole story) to ensure that you've credited the appropriate sources and that the citation format is accurate.

✔ Retype or print out the final draft. Add a title page, outline, and table of contents (if your Paper Assigner wants them). Attach the list of sources to the end of the paper. Insert illustrations as needed. Check the page numbers. (For more information on format, see "Putting It All Together," later in this chapter.)

✔ Make a copy, in case the original is lost, and hand in the original. Now go out and celebrate a job well done.

Styling Your Sentences

Constructing a basic sentence is simple: Combine a subject (the person or thing you're talking about) and a verb (the word or words expressing the subject's action or state of being). Be sure each sentence contains at least one stand-alone, complete thought.

You don't need to know grammatical terms to create a sentence. You do need to keep in mind some elements of style, such as variety and clarity, to go beyond the basics. Here's a guide to sentence style:

✔ Don't write choppy sentences. Choppy sentences are short. Choppy sentences often repeat words. Choppy sentences sound juvenile. They also sound like karate hits. Read these sentences. Do you hear the problem? Avoid choppy sentences.

✔ Sentences with a lot of commas may also sound choppy. To correct this problem, take out all unnecessary commas. You say you have no extras? Maybe so, but in 99 percent of the research papers I read, I delete at least five commas *per page*. So check! If all the commas are necessary and the sentence still sounds choppy, reword.

✔ In the golden age of novels — the age of Charles Dickens, when readers had few other alternatives for amusement and obviously also had a great capacity to pay attention to one particular idea, even when it was expressed in a sentence that challenged the breath capacity of an opera singer — megasentences were acceptable and even admirable; but now enormously lengthy sentences are considered annoyingly complicated and somewhat affected, so prudent writers avoid them. (Having trouble decoding the preceding Sentence-on-Steroids? Here's the main idea: Once upon a time long sentences were okay. Now they're not, so don't write them.)

✔ Two last points on sentence length: Your best bet is variety. A mix of long and short sentences holds the reader's attention better than sentences of all one length. Once in a great while an extreme is okay — a very short sentence for an important idea that you want to deliver like a punch to the gut or a very long sentence for a complex concept that you want to express as a unit.

✔ As I write this sentence, my pet parakeets are flying around my head, hoping I'll get up and play with them. As they fly, I ignore them. As you read this paragraph, one thought flies through your mind. All these sentences start with *as*. But the English language presents a choice of a half million words and a huge variety of grammatical elements. In constructing your sentences, take advantage of that variety. Play around a bit, and if necessary, yank yourself out of any ruts you've fallen into.

✔ Reading your work aloud is a good way to check for sentence length and variety and other qualities. It's also a good way to scare co-workers and friends. (*She's over there talking to herself! Should we call 911?*) Put on some loud music or lock yourself in the bathroom. Then read. Good writing *sounds* good. If you stumble over a particular sentence, consider revising it.

✔ Don't stop to check your work while you're actually writing. Wait until you've finished for the day or until you've completed an entire section or draft. If you pause too often to edit, you may lose your train of thought.

✔ Would you like to sit through a 40-minute meeting or a 20-minute meeting, assuming you accomplish the same amount in each? I'm betting that you chose the second option. Remember that preference when you sit down to write. Avoid wordiness and repetition, as in the following examples:

Wordy: At this present point in time . . .

Better: Now

Wordy: A tall 6'7" basketball player

Better: A 6'7" basketball player

Wordy: In my opinion, I think the main character is deranged.

Better: The main character is deranged. (Of course that's what you think. Why else would you write the sentence?)

Wordy: The commissioner built many highways, expressways, and roads.

Better: The commissioner built many roads. (*Highways* and *expressways* are roads; don't repeat.)

Fixing Grammar Gremlins

Don't get nervous; this section is not about labeling every part of the sentence with terms no sane person ever cared about. Instead, I mention some picky points that often stump paper writers. I group similar topics together, so if you know pronouns are your downfall, skip directly to that section and find what you need. For more information on the always-intriguing English language, check out *English Grammar For Dummies* by yours truly (Wiley Publishing).

Verbs

Verbs are words that express action or state of being. Verbs have *tense,* the ability to express time, and *number,* as in singular or plural. Many verb problems flow from these two qualities.

Tense

Tense problems can make you, well, tense. Here's how to solve them:

- ✔ In writing about literature or another sort of artwork, use present tense:

  Wrong: Hamlet killed his uncle.

  Right: Hamlet kills his uncle.

- ✔ To express two actions in the past, one occurring before the other, use *had* for the earlier action:

  Wrong: Marquod had joined the army and is still a member today.

  Why it's wrong: Only one action is in the past, so *had* is unnecessary.

  Right: Marquod joined the army and is still a member today.

  Also right: Marquod didn't find out about the 50-mile march until after he had joined the army.

  Why it's also right: Two actions take place in the past (first — joining the army; second — finding out about the march).

- ✔ To express an idea with links to both past and present, use *has* or *have:*

  Wrong: Marquod was a member of the army for ten years and will retire soon.

  Right: Marquod has been a member of the army for ten years and will retire soon.

Number

Singular subjects take singular verbs *(Agnes has),* and plural subjects take plural verbs *(clowns have).* You probably match most subject-verb pairs correctly simply because they sound right, but a few special cases may perplex you.

- Some expressions — _as well as, in addition to,_ and _along with_ — seem to add people or things to the subject. And if you add, you expect to have more than one and thus a plural. Sorry! Grammar is not as logical as math. Ignore those expressions and match the verb to the subject:

  The elephant, in addition to the rhinoceros, was angling for a peanut. (_elephant_ = singular subject; _was angling_ = singular verb)

- _Either/or_ and _neither/nor_ join two subjects. Match the verb to the nearest subject:

  Either Mary or her quite contrary enemies have sabotaged the garden. (_have sabotaged_ = plural verb; _enemies_ = closest subject)

- _Either_ and _neither,_ without their partners (_or, nor_) are always singular:

  Neither of the ray guns is set to stun. (_is_ = singular verb)

- _Each_ and _every,_ no matter what they precede, always take singular verbs:

  Every marshmallow and chocolate sprinkle in that sundae is poisoned! (_is_ = singular verb)

Other verb errors

Two more verb issues pop up frequently in research papers:

- In general, verbs should be _active_ instead of _passive._ In a sentence with an active verb, the subject does the action: _I broke the window._ In a sentence with a passive verb, the subject receives the action: _The window was broken by me._ Passive is acceptable if you don't know who did the action: _He was murdered yesterday._ It is also acceptable if you don't want to say who did the action: _The last doughnut was eaten._

- If you pair one subject with two verbs, don't put a comma between the verbs:

  Wrong: Robbie robbed, and then at the last minute repented.

  Right: Robbie robbed and then at the last minute repented.

Pronouns

Pronouns (_I, you, her, it, our, theirs,_ and so on) take the place of nouns. They're useful little guys, but they cause more problems than any other part of speech, especially in terms of number (the difference between _I_ and _we_) and case (the difference between _I, me,_ and _my_).

Number

Do you need a singular or a plural pronoun? Here the lowdown on pronoun number:

- ✔ Some pronouns are singular (*I, me, he, him, she, her, neither,* and so on) and some are plural (*we, us, their, both, them, ours,* and so on). Some may be either singular or plural depending upon the word they're replacing (*who, whom, that, which,* and so on). Singular and plural don't mix in the grammar world. Singular nouns match singular pronouns and singular verbs. Plural nouns match plural pronouns and plural verbs. Some examples:

  Neither of my uncles takes syrup on his sardines. (*neither, takes, his* = singular)

  The government is issuing new ID cards to its employees. (*government, is, its* = singular)

  Both of the boys have requested extra money from their parents. (*both, have, their* = plural)

  Few writers understand their role in promoting good grammar. (*few, understand, their* = plural)

- ✔ The "ones" (*everyone, someone, no one, anyone*), the "things" (*everything, something, nothing, anything*), and the "bodies" (*everybody, somebody, nobody, anybody*) are all singular. Be sure to match them with singular verbs *and* singular pronouns. If you're like most people, choosing the correct verb is automatic, but choosing the pronoun isn't. Here's an example:

  Wrong: Everyone is supposed to clean their room.

  Why it's wrong: *Everyone* is singular, and *their* is plural. The singular verb *(is)* is okay.

  Right: Everyone is supposed to clean his or her room.

  Also right but sexist: Everyone is supposed to clean his room.

  Why it's right: Very traditional grammarians (guess whether they are more likely to be male than female) have always taught that the masculine word (*his,* for example) may represent both male and female.

- ✔ Pronouns expressing quantity (*any, most, all, some, none*) may be either singular or plural. To decide, check out the most important word in the phrase following one of these pronouns (the object of the preposition, for all you grammar buffs). If the word is singular, the pronoun is singular. If the word is plural, the pronoun is plural. Some examples:

  Some of the money is counterfeit. (*some* is singular because it refers to *money,* which is singular)

  Some of the dollar bills are counterfeit. (*some* is plural because it refers to *bills,* a plural word)

✔ *Who, which,* and *that* are other pronouns that may be either singular or plural. In matching a verb to one of these pronouns, decide which noun the pronoun is replacing. Then match the verb to that noun, singular with singular, plural with plural. Some examples:

Every student who cuts three times will be executed. (*Who* replaces *student,* a singular noun, so the verb, *cuts,* must also be singular.)

The memos that are sitting on the desk should be filed in the wastebasket. (*That* replaces *memos,* a plural noun, so the verb, *are sitting,* must also be plural.)

✔ Companies and organizations — even those that end with the letter *s* — are singular and are matched with singular verbs and pronouns (*Sears is selling its merchandise, AT&T has phones in its attic,* and so on).

Case

Pronouns have *case* — subject, object, and possessive forms. The subject of the sentence is who or what you're talking about. Subject pronouns include *I, he, she, we, they, who,* and *whoever.* Objects answer the questions *whom?* or *what?* after verbs. In the sentence *I broke the window, window* is the object. Objects also follow *prepositions,* relationship words such as *to, above, by, for,* and *about.* Pronouns that may be objects include *me, him, her, us, them, whom, whomever.* A few pronouns may be either subjects or objects (*you, it, some, either, both,* and so on). Possessive pronouns (*my, his, her, our, ours, its,* and so on) show ownership.

✔ Pronouns expressing ownership (*my, his, her, their, our, its,* and so on) never have apostrophes. An apostrophe is a little hook-shaped punctuation mark that shows ownership when it's attached to a noun *(Billy's banana).* Apostrophes may also mark the spot in contractions where letters are missing (*don't, isn't, he's,* and so on).

✔ Don't send a subject pronoun to do an object's job, and vice versa. Your "ear for good English" probably detects the correct pronoun most of the time. Problems often arise with compounds, two or more words doing the same job in the sentence. To choose the correct pronoun, check each part of the compound separately:

Wrong: The umpire scolded Joe DiMaggio and I quite unnecessarily.

Check: The umpire scolded Joe DiMaggio. (OK so far.) The umpire scolded I. (Uh oh — should be *me.*)

Right: The umpire scolded Joe DiMaggio and me.

✔ To decide between *who* and *whom* (a dilemma grammarians dreamed up just to annoy you), keep in mind that *who* is for subjects and *whom* is for objects. Check every verb in the sentence, making sure that it is paired with a subject. Chances are *who* will turn out to be one of the subjects. If all the verbs have other subjects, you probably need *whom* for an object.

✔ Before you decide on the correct pronoun, untangle questions or sentences with unusual word order. The appropriate pronoun should be more obvious in the untangled version, as in the following example:

Original sentence: Who/whom shall I say is calling?

Untangled: I shall say who/whom is calling.

Correct sentence: Who shall I say is calling? (*Who* = subject of *is calling*)

Strict grammarians know that *who* and other subject pronouns may also function as *predicate nominatives,* a fancy term referring to words that complete the meaning of the subject. You'll seldom need pronouns as predicate nominatives in your research paper, so I ignore them here.

✔ In the grammar world, object pronouns have more clout than possessive pronouns. To choose between the two, figure out what you are trying to emphasize, as in these examples:

Wrong: The citizens objected to him drinking.

Why it's wrong: The citizens objected to the drinking, not to the person. The object pronoun *him* puts too much emphasis on the person.

Right: The citizens objected to his drinking.

Why it's right: The possessive pronoun *his* describes *drinking.* The emphasis is on *drinking,* where it belongs.

The preceding rule works for nouns also; *John* is more emphatic than *John's.* Hence

Wrong: The citizens loved John drinking.

Right: The citizens loved John's drinking.

Other pronoun errors

Pronouns may trip you up in other ways:

✔ Make sure that all your pronouns refer clearly to one noun:

Wrong: In the paper it says that grammar is dumb.

Why it's wrong: The pronoun *it* refers to nothing.

Right: According to an article in the paper, grammar is dumb.

Also right: Lucian Verbal reports in today's paper that grammar is dumb.

Okay, I know that all you smart readers have pointed out one exception to the preceding rule. You may say *It is raining* and similar sentences without error, even though *it* refers to nothing. However, don't replace the name of an author or publication with *it,* as in the preceding example.

✔ Make sure all your pronouns refer to only one noun:

Wrong: Oliver told Octavian that he would never be emperor.

Why it's wrong: Who's *he? Oliver* or *Octavian?*

Right: Oliver said, "You'll never be emperor, Octavian."

Also right but clunky: Oliver told Octavian that Octavian would never be emperor.

✔ Pronouns should replace nouns exactly; near misses are not acceptable:

Wrong: Because his mother studied politics, Octavian decided to become one.

Why it's wrong: Octavian didn't decide to become *politics*. He decided to become a *politician*. *Politician* is not in the sentence.

Right: Because his mother was a politician, Octavian decided to become one.

Punctuation

I really hate punctuation. Some of the rules make sense, but a lot of them are designed solely to give you a headache. Nevertheless, you have to follow punctuation rules. A quick guide:

Endmarks and quotation marks

Here are some points to remember about endmarks and quotation marks:

✔ All sentences end with an endmark — a period, question mark, or exclamation point. No sentence ends with more than one mark.

✔ To close a quotation, put the period or comma *inside* the quotation marks unless the sentence includes a source cited in parenthesis. (Chapter 18 explains parenthetical citations.) Check out these examples:

"I shall return," said Mac as he bought a round-trip ticket.

Arthur responded, "I shall not return" (Smyth 23).

✔ In quoting, use three dots to show that words have been omitted. If the omitted section of the quotation includes a period, place four dots in the gap (three to show that words are missing and one for the period).

✔ If the quotation is long, block it off from the rest of the text. A blocked quotation begins on a separate line. It is generally single-spaced and double-indented from the left and right margins. Don't place quotation marks around a block. For tips on how to insert a quotation smoothly into the text, see Chapter 16.

Semicolons

Semicolons are a useful but misunderstood punctuation mark. Consider these guidelines for proper semicolon usage:

✔ A semicolon (;) should join two complete thoughts that are closely related.

✔ Use a semicolon to join two complete thoughts connected by *however, moreover, consequently, furthermore, then,* and *also:*

Mac returned; consequently, Arthur didn't.

Commas

The comma is my nominee for the title of Most Irritating Punctuation Mark. Here's how to place commas correctly:

✔ The most important rule on comma placement: Don't sprinkle them anywhere. Before you place one, be sure it's needed.

✔ Commas separate words from the rest of the sentence. In adding descriptions to a sentence, place commas around the extra, nonessential ideas because the commas indicate that the words may be omitted without changing the main idea of the sentence. Don't place essential, identifying material between commas because essential material should be part of the main idea of the sentence, not separate from it. Two examples:

Descriptive words: who always wanted to be emperor

Extra nonessential: Octavian, who always wanted to be emperor, loves purple.

Essential, identifying: The man who always wanted to be emperor is buying purple robes.

See the difference? In the nonessential example, the word *Octavian* identifies the man; the descriptive words are an add-on. In the essential example, *man* is very general; the descriptive words identify the person you're discussing.

✔ Commas should precede a word that joins two complete sentences (a conjunction, in grammarspeak):

✔ Commas separate elements in a list: *melons, figs, grapes, and so on.* If anything on the list has a comma *in it* (in the following example, *Eleanor, Daughter of Darkness*), separate all the items on the list with semicolons:

Invited guests included Mother Goose; Father Time; Eleanor, Daughter of Darkness; and the Son of Sam.

Other grammar errors

A couple of other points will make your paper grammar-perfect:

✔ Be sure to write in complete sentences. Most grammarians allow sentences beginning with *but* or *and,* but strictly speaking, these words should join two ideas, not begin a new sentence.

✔ Don't confuse *like, as,* and *such as. Like* (not the verb, as in *I like you*) means *similar to. Like* may precede a noun or a pronoun, not a subject-verb combination. *As* may also mean *similar to* and precedes a subject-verb combo. *Such as* begins a list of examples. Check out these sentences:

Wrong: Do like I do.

Right: Do as I do.

Also right: Like you, I do what I like.

Wrong: The Yankees have great players like Joe DiMaggio, Babe Ruth, and Derek Jeter.

Why it's wrong: Those three players *are* Yankees!

Right: The Yankees have great players such as Joe DiMaggio, Babe Ruth, and Derek Jeter.

Capital letters

The first letter of every sentence and all proper nouns (names) are capitalized. If you cite according to MLA or CMS (see Chapter 18 for details), follow these rules for titles:

✔ Capitalize the first and last word of all titles and subtitles.

✔ Capitalize all nouns, verbs, and pronouns.

✔ Don't capitalize prepositions or conjunctions.

A word about spelling

Every generation or so someone starts a movement to put logic into English spelling. Sadly, none of those movements have succeeded. You probably learned a couple of jingles in school (*I before E except after C*, for example), or you may have a great spell-check program on the computer. Both will help, but neither will solve the problem of English spelling. The computer programs can't distinguish between *pain* and *pane,* for example. And no matter how many jingles you learn, you'll still come up short somewhere. Best bet: check the dictionary for any words that worry you.

If you're writing a scientific paper in APA style, the citations follow different rules on capitalization. In APA-style titles, capitalize proper nouns and the first word of the title and subtitle. Lowercase everything else.

Putting It All Together

Once your text is as perfect as you can make it, you're ready to put together a final copy for your Personal Authority Figure. Some guidelines:

- Print out the final draft or retype it one more time. If your Authority Figure allows handwritten work, write a clean copy. The text should be double-spaced, except for block quotations and the source list, which may be single-spaced.

- Use standard white paper (8½ x 11 inches) of good quality. Stay away from paper advertised as erasable because the ink tends to blur; if you're working on a typewriter and make a mistake, correct it neatly with correction fluid or an eraser.

- Use black ink and be sure that the letters are dark enough; change the ink cartridge or ribbon as needed.

- Write on one side of the paper only and leave a standard margin (about 1½ inches) around the edges. Word processing programs set the appropriate margin automatically.

- Generally, research papers need a separate title page, but some Paper Assigners ask for headings instead. (Check!) The title page should have the title of the paper, centered, presented without underlining or quotation marks unless it includes the title of another work that must be in quotations, underlined, or italicized. In the lower left-hand corner (or, if the Authority Figure prefers, in the lower center of the page) write your name, the date, the name of the instructor or supervisor, the course number (if relevant), and the name of the institution (not mental — the school or company). In a heading, those elements may be arranged at the top of page one.

- Some Authorities ask for an outline, inserted after the title page but before the text, and some prefer a table of contents. Most want only the text. In this as in everything, check with the Paper Evaluator about his or her preferred format.

- Stay away from gimmicks — cutesy fonts, word art, shading, and so on. The paper's content, not its appearance, should attract attention. Most teachers I know hate plastic covers because they make the paper hard to open and read. A simple staple in the upper left-hand corner is best, or you may use a paper clip. If the paper is very long, unbound pages may be placed in a box or in an envelope. Ask the Paper Assigner about the preferred presentation.

Presentation is especially important in business reports. Use the best-quality paper you can afford, particularly if you are asking for financing. The logic (illogic may be a better word) is that you must show that you don't need money in order to convince a bank to lend you some. If the report is long, have it bound. Illustrations should be professionally prepared or look as if they were.

✔ Number the pages in order, but don't place a number on the title page or, if you have one, on the table of contents page. If you have a lot of *front matter* — table of contents, table of illustrations, dedication page, acknowledgments, and so on — number those pages with lowercase Roman numerals (*i, ii, iii, iv, v*). The first page of text counts as page 1, though you may omit that number and begin numbering with page 2 of the text.

✔ Depending upon the instructor's preference, include illustrations in the text or group them at the end of the paper. (See Chapter 16 for information about labeling tables and figures.)

✔ Endnotes should be attached to the (surprise) end of the paper. If the paper is long, the endnotes may be grouped by chapter and numbered consecutively within each chapter — that is, the notes for each chapter begin with 1.

✔ The last element of the research paper is the bibliography or list of sources (also known as the *reference list* or *list of works cited*). These pages are numbered consecutively with the text of the paper. (In other words, if the last page of text is page 15, the first page of the source list is 16.)

✔ Resist the urge to make a bonfire of the materials you used in preparation of your research paper: notes, rough drafts, source lists, floppy disks, and so on. If the Authority Figure asks for more information or clarification, you should be able to provide what is needed. Save everything, just in case, until the paper is evaluated and even beyond that point.

Chapter 20

Solving Special Problems

....

....

*Y*ou're probably hoping that the process of writing a research paper will resemble a gold-medal ski jump — a smooth, effortless arc ending with a perfect landing. And if you follow the tips in this book, it probably will. But no matter how great your work methods, writing a research paper sometimes feels more like a trip in a small plane — always moving toward the destination but hitting a few air pockets along the way. In this chapter, I explain how to smooth out the bumps — problems of length, motivation, and research. Rest assured: Those bumps won't keep you from where you want to go — a successful final draft.

Adjusting Length: The Long and the Short of It

A few Paper Assigners don't care about the length of the finished product. If you cover the topic adequately, any number of pages will do. But you're more likely to encounter a fixed length or a range, say to five pages or to ten pages. (The resemblance to a prison term is *not* accidental.) As you're researching and outlining, it's hard to gauge how many pages you need to cover the material. Once you're actually writing, you may find that the paper is coming in under or over its page budget. Time for an adjustment.

Don't put the paper on a diet by changing to a font that can be read only through a microscope. Paper Evaluators don't like being reminded that (1) they're getting old and (2) their eyes are going. Similarly, don't lengthen a too-short paper by writing it in Movie Marquee Extra Large font. Seriously, you thought the Paper Evaluator wouldn't notice that only two words fit on each line? The next two sections provide some handy solutions to whichever length ails you — a too-short or a too-long paper.

Shortening a long paper

You're supposed to come up with ten pages on the depiction of scientists in the popular media. You've written about Einstein impersonators, Broadway plays featuring nuclear physicists, and the character of the Professor on *Gilligan's Island*. You have two cartons of notes on Frankenstein, and the paper is spilling onto the 17th page. What's a stressed-out paper writer to do? Read on:

✔ Go over the paper, pen in hand and ruthlessness in your heart. Cross out all repetition and unnecessary analysis. Also check for synonyms — what I call the *tense and nervous syndrome*. If you suffer from this syndrome, you provide pairs or triples of words where one will do, as in *she felt tense and nervous*. Cut the unneeded material and remove the extra adjective, saying simply that "she felt tense." ("Styling Your Sentences" in Chapter 19 provides some tips on cutting extra words from your prose.)

✔ Look for more-concise ways to make the same point. Instead of saying that he typed on *an outdated, 10-year-ol, desktop computer,* mention that he worked on an *Apple IIE*. Your writing will be more concise and more precise — two desirable traits.

If you've tried the two previous tactics and your paper is still long, take a look at these next three possible solutions:

✔ Consider the proof you've provided. Have you thrown in three examples when only one is needed? Is the crucial element extracted from each quotation? The right piece of evidence, presented alone, makes a better case than the right piece of evidence buried in a pile of irrelevant facts.

Trim with care. Most Paper Evaluators look for depth — a narrow focus with extensive analysis and proof. Cut anything that isn't important, but don't cut the essentials. Think narrow and deep, not wide and shallow, in evaluating your arguments.

✔ Consider dumping part of the argument. For example, in the "scientists in the media" paper I mention at the beginning of this section, you might drop the professor from Gilligan's Island or the Einstein impersonators.

✔ Refocus the thesis. (Think of this as a last resort because it's a lot of work.) Instead of "depiction of scientists in the media," concentrate on "depiction of scientists in film" or "depiction of Einstein in the media."

The same people who mistakenly claim that you can't be too rich or too thin (Wrong!) often contend that a research paper can't be too long (Wrong again!). Lots of Paper Assigners, myself included, grow quite grumpy when faced with a massive pile of typescript. We want to read your creation, but we want to have a life also. The required page range arises from the expert's view of how many pages you need to accomplish the task and from the same expert's view of how much time the expert has to devote to your master-piece. Bottom line: Follow the guidelines.

Lengthening a short paper

Professor Grouch wants ten pages on sports marketing, and you've got a grand total of 2½ — okay, 2¼ — including a full-page photo of your favorite team mascot. Now what?

The most important rule is simple: Don't pad — add. In other words, stay away from useless material. Gravitate toward stuff that deserves a place in your paper, regardless of length.

Now for the details on the best way to lengthen an overly short paper:

- ✔ Do a little more research. You may find additional valuable evidence or supporting points.

- ✔ Reconsider your argument. Have you filled in all the blanks? Have you skipped a step in the path as you lead the reader from one idea to another?

- ✔ Indulge yourself *a little*. If you're describing a battle, for example, you may add a few extra details to intrigue the reader. But — and this is a really big *but* — don't pad. One sentence about smoke and fury brings the battle alive. Ten sentences about the smoke may signal to the Paper Evaluator that you really know nothing at all about the battle's significance and are (pardon the pun) attempting to blow smoke in the reader's eyes.

- ✔ Consider broadening your thesis. If you're writing about the effects of ink on water-based solutions, you may broaden to the effects of ink on both water- and oil-based solutions.

- ✔ Talk with the Authority Figure who assigned the paper. Explain the scope of your research, your thesis, and the estimated length. Chances are the Authority Figure will point out something you haven't thought about or show you where the deficiencies lie.

A little help from your friends

One challenge of writing is distinguishing between what you've actually put on the page and what is still in your head. *You've* been thinking about the topic incessantly, but *your reader* hasn't. So as you explain that Snerdo's Theory of Relativity is false, you may forget to mention the fact that Snerdo added 2 + 2 and got 5. Snerdo's mistake is so obvious *to you* that you simply accept it as a given. Your reader, on the other hand, may *not* be aware that Snerdo's calculations included that particular link. And without that knowledge, your reader won't accept your conclusions. The solution: Ask a friend to read your paper, looking for holes. Once the holes are identified, plug them.

Now that you know what you should do to lengthen the paper, it's time to identify the poison ivy patches of the research-paper garden. *Don't* do any of the following:

✔ Don't spend five words saying what three words will accomplish, as in this example:

Padded sentence: It was here at Monster Elementary that the young Victor Frankenstein would enter his first science fair. (17 words)

Unpadded: As a student at Monster Elementary, Victor Frankenstein entered his first science fair. (13 words)

Even better version: Victor Frankenstein entered his first science fair at Monster Elementary. (ten words)

✔ Don't repeat ideas or restate the meaning of a quotation you've included in the text. You may *analyze* the quotation, but don't tell the reader what he or she has just read, as in this example:

Bad repetition: Professor Flugeldorg comments that "art, in its never-ending variety, reminds us of life's possibilities."[4] He makes the point that the many paths we may travel in life are reflected in the different types of art.

Good analysis: Professor Flugeldorg comments that "art, in its never-ending variety, reminds us of life's possibilities."[4] Flugeldorg's view was perhaps shaped by his own career path from longshoreman to senator to sculptor.

✔ Don't toss in off-topic material just to lengthen the paper. You'll spoil the logical thread of your argument and detract from the case you're making.

Overcoming Writer's Block

In the movies blocked writers yank pieces of paper out of the typewriter and throw the crumpled wads into an overflowing wastebasket. In real life blocked writers go to the movies, run to the grocery to stock up on anchovies, or drop into a chat room. Anything to avoid that blank screen or sheet of paper.

If you're stuck at any point in the writing process, a short break may be all you need to refresh your brain and get back in the groove. But if a quick trip for a latte doesn't do it for you, try one of these unblocking techniques:

✔ Write a different section. If you're blocked on section one, mosey over to section three. You've got an outline, so you know where everything goes. Who said you have to write the paper in order? Once the writing flows again, go back to the problem section.

✔ Stop aiming for perfection. Remember that a first draft is supposed to be rough. If you stop every couple of sentences to polish — or worse, if you write nothing at all while you wait for the best sentence to form itself in your head — you're doomed. Spill your ideas. Once you've got a chunk of writing out of your head and onto the paper, punch it into shape.

✔ Revise the outline. Tackle one section, making it so specific that it lists every little detail. By the time you finish, the section is almost written. All you have to do is turn it into nicer sentences.

✔ Still stuck? Here's my own remedy, but you may have to move to a major city to use it: Go for a long, boring subway or train ride. Leave your radio, newspaper, and lunch behind. Take only a pad of paper, a pen, and the outline. I find that intense boredom drives a wedge in my writer's block; after ten minutes of staring into space, I'm ready to tackle a paragraph or two. (If you live in a small town or a rural area, find your own equivalent of a subway ride. Just be sure that you choose an activity so boring that anything, even writing a research paper, is preferable.)

Once you're unblocked, carve out as much time as you can from the rest of your life and keep on writing. You never know whether the ideas will dry up again! When you do have to stop, leave off in the middle of a sentence. On returning to the project, you may be able to jump right back into the flow.

Surviving Research Disasters

Fifteen books, seven Web sites, and over a hundred articles after you started your research paper, disaster strikes. You find the perfect idea in your notes, but no source or page number. Or, you've got the perfect thesis and evidence, but you suddenly find one new fact that contradicts everything you had planned to write. Or, you've got the perfect thesis and evidence and you find one more source — with *your* thesis and evidence.

The research equivalent of fire, flood, and earthquake, these three disasters are difficult, but not impossible to overcome. The following sections show how to survive.

Disaster #1: Missing source

Careful researchers record the title, author, and publishing or broadcasting information of all sources. (For everything you need to know about keeping track of sources, check out Chapter 8.) But even careful researchers slip up sometimes — dripping cappuccino on a note card or omitting a page number in the heat of the chase for research gold. If you're missing any source information, try these tactics:

✔ If you know where the information comes from but not the page number, go back to the source and skim read until you find what you're looking for. If you have other notes above or below the problem item (or, in the case of cards, before or after), you may be able to narrow the range of inquiry. For example, if the problem item is on the same page as notes from pages 12 and 15 of the source, chances are the missing material is somewhere in there also.

✔ If you've already taken the source back to the library and can't return there easily, call. You may encounter a sympathetic librarian who will pull the book from the shelf and tell you the copyright date, publisher, or whatever else you need.

✔ In the case of material from a Web site, try to recreate the research path you originally used, re-entering the search terms and clicking on the logical connections. You may recognize the screen when it pops up.

✔ Present the problem to your Paper Evaluator, well before the paper is due. He or she may know where the material comes from.

✔ If nothing works and you can't find the source, write the paper *without* that bit of information, because *not* crediting information to a source opens you to charges of plagiarism, the research-paper equivalent to Murder One. (For more information on plagiarism, read Chapter 10.)

Disaster #2: Contradictory information

You've worked out a startlingly original thesis — that Oliver E. Oolong started the infamous Pekoe Wars because he couldn't find any other way to get a decent cup of tea during his tenure as ambassador to Greenland. You've read military dispatches, diplomatic records, and the memoirs of Oolong's five former wives. As you type page 29 of the research paper, Oolong's former butler finally agrees to an interview. Ten seconds in he mentions that Oolong loved a good cup of espresso and detested tea. Panic time! Here's what to do:

✔ First, come clean with the Paper Evaluator. Bring your notes, the pages you've written so far, and your outline. Explain what happened and ask for time to recast your thesis.

✔ Review all your notes in light of the new information. Is there a way to reinterpret the material? For example, could Oolong have started the war because of his tea phobia?

✔ Reword the thesis and reorganize the proof. Don't throw away your previous research. Simply use what is relevant for the revised thesis.

✔ Reread the draft to see what is salvageable. You may be able to recycle paragraphs or whole sections. Descriptions of the Pekoe Wars, for example, will not change.

Disaster #3: Duplicate ideas

After reading *Hamlet* 12 times and scouring the literary criticism section of your local library, you decide that something is missing. All those essays ignore Gertrude's feelings! None of the critics you've read discuss the role of women in Shakespearean times and relate that information to the play. You set to work, convinced you're filling a major gap in the world's understanding of the Bard. Then, just at the last moment, your mom e-mails you an essay on the role of women in Shakespearean times and specifically, on the character of Gertrude in *Hamlet*. Before you pour poison in your ear (the murder method of the play), try these fix-its:

✔ Read the new essay *extremely* carefully. Figure out how it resembles your paper and how it differs. For example, it may discuss the same topic but interpret the issue in another way. Or, it may have a similar thesis (which you should acknowledge in the source list and in the essay itself) but different evidence.

✔ Reread your own paper. Look for spots where your ideas and arguments diverge from those of the published essay. Can you expand on the differences? Highlight what is truly original? If so, alter the outline and rewrite as necessary. Be sure to cite the essay appropriately in the text and in the source list.

✔ If necessary, change your thesis so that it doesn't match the thesis of the published essay. For example, if the published essay concentrates on Gertrude's physical desires, write about the social and economic aspects of Gertrude's life with and without a life partner. Or, do a little more research and contrast Gertrude with Lady Macbeth, assuming of course that the published essay doesn't address *Macbeth*.

✔ Running out of time? Take all of your work — notes, outline, draft, and source list — to the Authority Figure and explain exactly what happened. Most Paper Assigners have done a lot of research themselves and know the pitfalls. Unless you're working for a truly heartless person, you can probably work something out.

The worst research disaster — loss of notes or drafts — is the easiest one to avoid. If you're working on a computer, back up early and often. If you're working with pen and paper, photocopy your work, also early and often. Remember to store the backups in a separate, safe place. (One of my students kept everything in the trunk of his car — which was stolen two days before the paper was due.) If you lose even your backup material, explain the situation to the Paper Evaluator and ask for time to re-create your work.

Part VI
The Part of Tens

The 5th Wave   By Rich Tennant

"Maybe your Keyword search, 'Astronomy, Stars, Signs, Will I be rich someday,' needs to be refined."

In this part . . .

When your favorite Authority Figure (boss, professor, ringleader) assigns you a research paper, one question, outlined in neon and flashing like a strobe light, appears in your head. (No, not How do I get out of this? You want to learn something — as well as earn a good grade or performance review.) You immediately ask, "Where do I start?" Never fear. In this part I tell you the ten best traditional and the ten best electronic "places" to begin your search for knowledge. In the appendix I also provide a lifetime's supply of "big questions" — great frameworks on which to base a research paper in every subject.

Chapter 21

The Ten Best Ways to Start Electronic Research

In This Chapter

▶ Searching the Web

▶ Reading online

▶ Locating people

*T*he Internet and the World Wide Web contain research treasure beyond your wildest dreams, but they may quickly give you nightmares as you try to navigate the immense amount of information available. Here are ten great ways to get started.

Designing a Search

What are you looking for? Brainstorm until you have the *search terms* — the headings that describe your topic. Look for the most specific terms possible (*Thailand* instead of *Asia,* for example). Look for more than one angle of approach — *dieting, media,* and *nutrition,* perhaps, when you're checking out *body image.* (Chapter 5 goes into detail on how to design a search.)

Revving Up a Search Engine

The Internet hosts dozens of *search engines,* complex mathematical structures that zoom (okay, some of them crawl) around, picking up sites that match your request, the search terms that you type in. Select a search engine and see what you turn up. My favorite search engine changes from time to time and from project to project. A little trial and error will soon show you which search engine does the job for your particular topic. Whatever you choose, be sure to design a search that minimizes irrelevant returns. (Chapter 5 lists search engines.)

Taxing Government Resources

You paid for them (assuming you spend April corresponding with the IRS) so you may as well access government documents, which, by the way, are also open to nontaxpayers. Check out www.fedworld.gov for reports written by your public servants. You won't get the Top Secrets that the Prez curls up with at night (shame on you — I'm talking about *documents*). You will get piles of data from the Drug Enforcement Agency, the Department of Defense, and other government bodies, including the Central Intelligence Agency. For many of the documents you'll have to pay a small fee, but some are free.

Hitting the Library

Not connected to the Internet at home? Hit your local public library or your school library and check out (sorry, couldn't resist the pun) their resources. Many are now wired, with Internet connections and access to other electronic databases. (See Chapter 5 for a complete description of electronic resources.) Some libraries give you a freebie, and others make you pay for computer time.

Hitting the Other Library

The Internet Public Library, that is. Click on www.ipl.org/ref to access a really neat reference library filled with reliable information. The subject area labels lead you to dozens of links to other databases. The Virtual Public Library is another top-quality online reference collection. Find it at www.virtualpubliclibrary.com.

Checking Your FAQs

FAQs — frequently asked questions — are a feature of many Web sites. Scrolling through a FAQ, you can find the basic information about each subject, usually from an expert in the field. (Usually, but *not* always. Chapter 4 explains how to evaluate the content of a Web site.) To find the FAQ that's right for you, go to www.faqs.org for a list.

Getting Down to Business

If you're writing a marketing report, an investment analysis, or anything else related to business, these sites may help: www.dnb.com (Dun & Bradstreet) and www.hoovers.com (Hoover's Online) for reports on companies and industries and www.amcity.com (American City Business Journals) for access to local business publications. **Note:** Not all of the information is free.

Reading the Paper

Check out ajr.newslink.org for links to newspapers throughout the world, though the selection is weighted towards the United States. You can read a fair amount for free, but heavy-duty research will cost you.

Opening Up a Subject Catalogue

Subject catalogues divide information into (pause for drumroll) subjects and then organize them into (guess what?) catalogues. (Chapter 5 tells you everything you need to know about subject catalogues.) A really good site for subject catalogues is Argus, located at www.clearinghouse.net. Sadly, Argus announced in 2002 that it would no longer add to its catalogues (lack of money), but it will maintain what is already there. Even so, Argus is a good spot to begin a search for scholarly articles. Click on the subject you're interested in and keep clicking until you've narrowed the focus to your specific topic.

Finding People

Sometimes a real live human is the answer to your research dilemma. Check out the electronic database version of *The Encyclopedia of Associations,* if your library subscribes to it. *The Encyclopedia of Associations,* which is also available in printed form, provides contact information for heaps of organizations devoted to every possible subject. Click on your subject, read the blurb on the group, and fire off an e-mail or snail mail (regular letter).

Chapter 22

The Ten Best Ways to Start Traditional Research

*T*he wired world makes a lot of noise, but it's not the only research source. Pieces of paper with words and pictures on them still provide tons of information for the weary researcher. Here's how to begin.

Asking the Boss

The boss, in the world of research papers, is the Authority Figure who assigned the paper — your teacher, professor, or, if you're a resident of the land of actual bosses (the business world), your supervisor. The boss can suggest a hundred tips for research sources — the best books, articles, and interview subjects on your topic. But you won't know if you don't ask!

Asking the Librarian

Powerhouses of information, the librarians at the public, school, or business library can save you tons of time by pointing you in the right direction. Trust me, these people are professionals, and they know what's on their shelves.

Opening the Catalogue

Whether in little wooden drawers or on computer screens, the library catalogue is a great resource. You'll find books, videotapes, audiotapes, CDs, DVDs, and other material neatly catalogued according to author, title, and subject. You'll also find clues to content and cross-references that point out other paths to your research destination. (For a guide to using the library catalogue, see Chapter 6.)

Referring to Reference Books

Walk through the library's reference section, zeroing in on the shelves devoted to your subject. (How will you know which shelves? Ask the librarian or check the library catalogue.) Page through encyclopedias or dictionaries dedicated to your area of interest. The chapter headings will give you some ideas for further research, and you may find a useful bibliography or list of sources. (Chapter 6 gives you pointers on getting the most out of reference books.)

Checking the Children's Section

Even if you have gray hair, you may find something useful in the children's section of your library. Flip through some juvenile nonfiction books on your topic for a quick overview. Then you can turn to adult material for in-depth studies.

Reading the Reader's Guide

Depending upon your library, the *Reader's Guide to Periodical Literature* is either a set of fat books, one per year, or an online resource. Regardless of format, you'll find articles from all sorts of magazines listed alphabetically according to subject. Once you've got a bibliography, ask the librarian which periodicals the library owns.

Noting the News

My hometown paper, *The New York Times,* likes to see itself as a historical resource. It lists all its articles in *The New York Times Index,* a paper or electronic guide to what they've published. Check the topic, make a bibliography, and ask the librarian how to locate the articles. (Chapter 6 explains further.)

Perusing the Pamphlet File

Sometimes the best sources are flimsy little piles of paper stapled at the corner. Wise librarians are aware of this fact, so they keep things that the rest of us throw out. Ask for the *pamphlet* or *vertical* file and see what the library has on your topic. (Just don't ask why it's called a vertical file; it's a librarians' secret.)

Browsing Bowker's

Bowker's is one of the best catalogues of audio and video materials. Ask the librarian, or stop in a video or music store and ask the clerk for Bowker's or a similar catalogue. You'll soon discover the audio and visual material you need.

Going Shopping

A trip to your local bookstore may whet your research appetite. Stores have the latest stuff, including books that your library may have on order or in processing but *not* on the shelves. See what's out there, and once you've reached the bottom of your wallet, bring a list to the library. If you're lucky, the library will supply what you need.

Appendix

• •

Stuck for an idea? This section provokes your creativity. Look for the subject area: Arts; History; Literature and Language; Science, Mathematics, and Technology; and Social Science and Psychology. Interdisciplinary ideas are listed in (How do I come up with these terms?) an interdisciplinary section. Each subject area includes a special list for younger writers.

Once you're in the right place, look at the big questions. *Big questions* is the term I'm using for categories that may be adapted to lots of topics. For example, a big question in literature is *What is the influence of this writer's work upon later writers?* After you've found a big question that appeals to you, check out some specific topics for that category. Naturally, the suggestions represent only a tiny fraction of the possibilities open to you. One may spark an idea!

Arts

Those who can, create art. Those who can't, write criticism and art history. If you're writing about the arts, check out what the critics and historians think and then compare their views with your own. (Chapters 5 and 6 suggest some great sources.)

Here are some big questions followed by specific topics:

✔ **How does the medium (oil, pastel, film, videotape, and so on) contribute to the overall effect of the artwork?**

- Pastel drawings of Degas

- Oldenburg's soft-vinyl sculptures

- Ancient Greek marble statues

- Medieval Spanish painted wood statues

✔ **Compare two or more works on the same subject by two different artists.**

- Mother-and-child portraits by Mary Cassatt and Rosa Bonheur

- Landscapes by Thomas Cole and Claude Monet

- Gangster movies: The Godfather, Public Enemy, Goodfellas

✔ **Compare two works by the same artist, from different stages in the artist's career.**

- Kandinsky's works before and after World War I

- Rembrandt's early and late self-portraits

✔ **Survey the reactions of critics or the general public to the artwork.**

- *Les Demoiselles d'Avignon*

- Jacob Lawrence's Migration Series

- Hokusai's views of Mount Fuji

✔ **How does the work of the artist break from previous tradition?**

- Scott Joplin's rags

- Jackson Pollack's *Blue Poles*

- Fellini's *Satyricon*

✔ **How has the work of the artist influenced other artists?**

- Caravaggio — Artemisia Gentileschi

- Cezanne — Picasso

- Ansel Adams or Georgia O'Keefe — contemporary photographers

Arts Topics for Younger Writers

Here are some big questions followed by specific topics for younger writers:

✔ **Describe the artist's life and work.**

- Painters: El Greco, Raphael, Michelangelo, O'Keefe, Aaron Douglas

- Architects: Christopher Wren, Frank Lloyd Wright

- Photographers: Ansel Adams, Diane Arbus

- Filmmakers: Spielberg, Chaplin, D.W. Griffith

- Musicians: Beethoven, Louis Armstrong, Laurie Anderson

✔ Describe the general characteristics and important works of a "school" or movement of art.

- Ashcan school

- Dada or film noir

- Abstract expressionism

- Classical Greek or Roman sculpture

History

Digging into the past? You'll want to read the works of historians and biographers, and you may find yourself unearthing primary sources as well, including letters, diaries, government records and the like. Here are some topics to get you started:

✔ **What is the effect of a specific historical event on public policy?**

- Stock market crash of 1929/regulation of stock market
- September 11, 2001, attacks/war on terrorism or racial profiling or defense spending

✔ **Compare the views of two writers on the same issue.**

- Conflict in the Mideast/Arab, Israeli writers
- Oklahoma land rush/homesteader, Native American
- Witch trials/accused witch, judge
- Civil rights/mid-19th century writer and contemporary writer

✔ **What are the immediate and background causes of a historical event?**

- World War I, World War II, Russian Revolution, other wars
- Election of Franklin Roosevelt, other presidents, leaders of other countries
- Child labor laws, women's suffrage, changes to the Constitution

✔ **What are the important social trends of a particular time and place?**

- United States in the 1950s or 1960s
- Colonial period in South America
- Tang dynasty in China
- Nineteenth century Japan

✔ **What is a revolutionary or counterculture movement protesting?**

- Communists in early twentieth-century Russia or China
- Beats in 1950s in the United States
- Transcendentalists in nineteenth-century United States
- Boxers in nineteenth-century China
- Women suffragists in early twentieth-century England and the United States

- ✔ **Why is a document historically important?**

  - Declaration of Independence

  - United Nations Charter

  - The Communist Manifesto

  - A Vindication of the Rights of Women

- ✔ **Why do people move from place to place?**

  - The "Great Migration" from the Southern United States to the North in the 1920s

  - Immigration to the United States — mid-nineteenth century, early twentieth century

  - Cherokee or other Native American group — forced relocation

  - Refugees — post–War, civil wars, during famines or epidemics

History Topics for Younger Writers

Here are some big questions followed by specific topics for younger writers:

- ✔ **Why is a particular historical figure important?**

  - World leaders: Charlemagne, Attila the Hun, Adolph Hitler, Catherine the Great, Julius Caesar, Ramses the Great, Thomas Jefferson, Kofi Annan

  - Philosophers: Confucius, Karl Marx, John Locke, Jean Jacques Rousseau

  - Reformers: Susan B. Anthony, Jacob Riis, Jane Addams, Rosa Parks, Martin Luther King, Jr., Ralph Nader

- ✔ **What is daily life like at a particular period in history in a particular society?**

  - Ancient: Egypt, Rome, China, Benin

  - Middle Ages: Europe, Middle East

  - Renaissance: England, Italy

  - Age of Exploration: South America, Africa

  - Industrial Revolution: Europe, United States

  - Postcolonial era: Africa, South America

- ✔ **What does the branch or department**
  - Congress, Supreme Court, Exec
  - Federal Reserve
  - Cabinet departments

Literature and Language

Lucky you! In my humble opinion, diving into a great book o.
words is right up there on the fun scale with hearty partying. Your
to take the text as your primary resource and then check out what critics
have to say on the subject. Here are the big questions and some topics to
choose from:

- ✔ **What is the role of a literary element in a particular literary work?**
  - Plot in the Sherlock Holmes stories of Arthur Conan Doyle
  - Setting in Emily Bronte's *Wuthering Heights*
  - Magical realism in the works of Gabriel Garcia Marquez
  - Point of view in J.D. Salinger's *The Catcher in the Rye*

- ✔ **How does the form of a literary work complement the theme or content?**
  - Interconnected short stories: Gloria Naylor's *The Women of Brewster Place*
  - Sonnet form/any Shakespearean sonnet
  - Mixture of poetry and prose in Jean Toomer's *Cane*

- ✔ **Compare two works by the same writer, from different stages in the writer's career.**
  - Early and late poems of William Wordsworth, Siegfried Sassoon, Adrienne Rich
  - Jane Austen's juvenilia and *Sense and Sensibility*

- ✔ **Compare two works written in the same form.**
  - *El Cid* and *Chanson de Roland* — two epics
  - Sonnets by Shakespeare and Spenser
  - Coleridge's *Rime of the Ancient Mariner* and a traditional ballad

✔ **Explore a theme common to several works.**

- Utopia/Dystopia: *Utopia* by Thomas More, *A Clockwork Orange* by Anthony Burgess, *The Handmaid's Tale* by Margaret Atwood

- The agony of war: poems by Walt Whitman, Wilfred Owen, Siegfried Sassoon

- Justice: mysteries by Elizabeth George, Rex Stout, Wilkie Collins

✔ **What is the critical or audience reaction to the work?**

- *Waiting for Godot* by Samuel Beckett

- *The Awakening* by Kate Chopin

- *The Adventures of Huckleberry Finn* by Mark Twain

- *Libra* by Don Delillo

✔ **How does the work of a writer break from or conform to previous tradition?**

- James Joyce's *Dubliners*

- Dashiell Hammett's mystery novels

- Claude McKay's poetry

✔ **How did a work influence later writers?**

- Zora Neale Hurston's *Their Eyes Were Watching God*/Alice Walker's *The Color Purple*

- Aeschylus's *Oresteia*/O'Neill's *Mourning Becomes Electra*

- Virginia Woolf's *Mrs. Dalloway*/Michael Cunningham's *The Hours*

- Chretien de Troyes' *Romances*/King Arthur stories

✔ **What are the goals and principles of the artistic school or movement?**

- Beats

- Romantic poets

- Bloomsbury group

✔ **What are the most important characteristics of a writer's style?**

- Emily Dickinson's poetry

- Ernest Hemingway's novels and short stories

- Basho's haiku or Sei Shonagon's lists

Literature Topics for Younger Writers

Here are some big questions followed by specific topics for younger writers:

✔ **Describe the life of the writer, his or her most important works, and the times in which the writer lived.**

- Charles Dickens — Victorian England
- Langston Hughes — the Harlem Renaissance
- Lady Murasaki — Medieval Japan
- Dante Alighieri — Italian Renaissance

✔ **What is the history of a word and how has the word's meaning changed over the years?**

- *gossip*
- *spin*
- *grammar*

✔ **Describe the characteristics of a poetic form and discuss some works written in that form.**

- Haiku
- Sestina
- Ballad
- English or Italian sonnet

Science, Mathematics, and Technology

When they're not discovering, solving, and inventing, experts in these subjects write about their discoveries, solutions, and inventions. They create great source material for your research paper. Here are some sparkplugs for your idea engine:

✔ **Describe a process and identify factors that may alter it.**

- Photosynthesis
- Erosion
- Population growth or extinction

✔ **What environmental or safety issues are raised by the development of new technology?**

- Nuclear power

- Genetic engineering

- In vitro fertilization

✔ **Describe an important concept or theory and its significance.**

- Relativity

- Chaos theory

- Heisenberg Uncertainty Principle

- Big bang

- Fractals

✔ **Describe a problem and some possible solutions.**

- Pollution (air, water, soil, food supply, and so on)

- Endangered species

- Mathematics problems

✔ **Survey the work of several scientists or mathematicians on the same issue.**

- Structure of the solar system — Copernicus and Galileo

- How traits are inherited — Mendel, Watson and Crick

- Structure of the atom — Democritus, Dalton, Bohr

Science, Mathematics, and Technology Topics for Younger Writers

Here are some big questions followed by specific topics for younger writers:

✔ **Describe the life story of a famous scientist or mathematician.**

- Galileo, Copernicus, Galen

- Marie Curie, Barbara McClintock, Albert Einstein

- Watson and Crick, Rachel Carson, Charles Darwin

✔ **Compare a fundamental life process in different organisms.**

- Locomotion: amoeba, earthworm, octopus, monkey
- Digestion: algae, fish, bird
- Reproduction: paramecium, fern, clam, human

✔ **Describe a natural habitat.**

- Polar region
- Rain forest
- Tundra

✔ **Explain how a discovery was made.**

- Gravity
- DNA structure
- Penicillin
- Calculus
- Mendelian genetics

✔ **Describe a natural phenomenon and its effects.**

- El Niño and La Niña (weather)
- Tidal waves, hurricanes, earthquakes
- Extinction of dinosaurs
- Comets, eclipses of the sun or moon, aurora borealis

✔ **What is the effect of an environmental law or regulation?**

- Clean Air Act or Clean Water Act
- Fuel efficiency standards
- Regulation of toxic waste

Social Science and Psychology

Fascinated by your fellow human creatures? If so, you'll love writing social science and psychology papers analyzing individual and group behavior. Some thoughts to start you off:

✔ **Describe how a disorder or illness develops and how it may be addressed.**

- Eating disorders

- Post-Traumatic Stress Syndrome

- Schizophrenia

- Psychosomatic illness

- Autism

✔ **Explain a school of psychology or type of therapy.**

- Freudian analysis

- Behavioral therapy

- Art, music, or pet therapy

✔ **Survey experiments on an aspect of human behavior.**

- Development of abstract or moral reasoning

- Effect of divorce on children

- Reactions to stress

- Learning styles

✔ **Describe how a society or subculture is organized.**

- Yanomani or other tribe living in a remote location

- Young urban professionals in a modern city

- Motorcycle gangs

✔ **How is status attained and symbolized in a particular society?**

- Eskimos — nineteenth century

- Feudal Japan

- United States — modern era

Social Science and Psychology Topics for Younger Writers

Here are some big questions followed by specific topics for younger writers:

✔ **Describe the life of a famous psychologist, psychiatrist, or social scientist.**

- Sigmund Freud, Karl Jung, B.F. Skinner
- Margaret Mead, Franz Boas, Bruno Bettelheim

✔ **Describe a tradition or ceremony of a particular society.**

- Navajo Blessingway ceremony
- Jewish bar or bat mitzvah
- Latino Quinceañera
- Wedding or funeral rites

Interdisciplinary Ideas

Some of the best topics don't fit neatly into one field or another. They cross party lines, or, in the language of academia, they're *interdisciplinary*. Here are some possible topics for people who think outside the box:

✔ **Does the depiction of a particular group — women, men, ethnic group, age group — reinforce or challenge the stereotypes applied to that group?**

- Female characters in Homer's *Odyssey*
- African Americans in Mark Twain's novels
- Shylock, the Jewish moneylender, in Shakespeare's *The Merchant of Venice*

✔ **How did an aspect of society or an event change because of an invention?**

- Development of aviation/military tactics
- Creation of the Internet/communication
- Development of writing/trade and government

✔ **How does the art of a period reflect the philosophy or values of the society that produced it?**

- Transcendentalism and the writing of Thoreau, Emerson, Alcott
- Existentialism and theater of the absurd
- Confucianism and Chinese painting

✔ **Describe science or technology in a historical era or trace the history of one invention.**

- Ancient Greece, Rome, China, Egypt, America

- Middle Ages, Renaissance, Nineteenth Century

- Clocks and timekeeping from sundials to atomic clocks

- Calendars of the ancient Mayans, Babylonians, and medieval Europe

- Star navigation in several ancient cultures

✔ **How accurate is an artwork that presents scientific or historical information?**

- *Beloved* by Toni Morrison — slavery and its aftermath

- *Oliver Twist* by Charles Dickens — conditions in Victorian England

- Roman history — *I, Claudius* by Robert Graves

- Physics of *Star Trek*

- Principles of physics in the paintings of Georges Seurat

- Cloning as presented in *Jurassic Park*

✔ **How did a historic event or an important scientific or philosophical idea affect art?**

- Feminism — painting, literature

- Technology — visual arts

- Theory of relativity — poetry

- Voyages of discovery — European poetry, drama

✔ **What is the role of the media in a particular context?**

- Relation between violent images in the media and children's behavior

- Media and body image

- Television and political campaigns

✔ **What are the ethical issues involved in a scientific advance or study?**

- Recombinant DNA

- Digital photography (ability to alter an image)

- Genetic testing

- Experiments with animals or human subjects

- Privacy and computer use

✔ **What role does financing play?**

- Sports teams and events

- Film

- Artworks

✔ **How does government regulation or funding affect a particular field?**

- Biomedical research

- National Endowment for the Arts

- Agriculture

Interdisciplinary Ideas for Younger Writers

Younger writers may be interested in these big questions:

✔ **How does a change of medium affect an art or literary work?**

- Shakespeare or Jane Austen on film

- Theatrical performance or film of the same story

- Internet zines and traditional print media

- Music on the Internet

✔ **How does popular music reflect the times in which it was produced?**

- Rock 'n' roll — 1960s

- Jazz — 1920s

- Grunge — 1990s

✔ **What do members of these groups owe to society?**

- Scientists

- Artists

- Journalists

✔ **How has a scientific discovery changed daily life?**

- Antibiotics

- Computers

- Cellphones

- Automobiles

Index

• *D* •

• S •

● **Y** ●

● **Z** ●

Notes